Digital Nomads

Digital Nomads

by Kristin M. Wilson

Digital Nomads For Dummies®

Published by: **John Wiley & Sons, Inc.**, 111 River Street, Hoboken, NJ 07030-5774, www.wiley.com

Copyright © 2022 by John Wiley & Sons, Inc., Hoboken, New Jersey

Published simultaneously in Canada

For general information on our other products and services, please contact our Customer Care Department within the U.S. at 877-762-2974, outside the U.S. at 317-572-3993, or fax 317-572-4002. For technical support, please visit https://hub.wiley.com/community/support/dummies.

Wiley publishes in a variety of print and electronic formats and by print-on-demand. Some material included with standard print versions of this book may not be included in e-books or in print-on-demand. If this book refers to media such as a CD or DVD that is not included in the version you purchased, you may download this material at http://booksupport.wiley.com. For more information about Wiley products, visit www.wiley.com.

Library of Congress Control Number: 2022941292

ISBN 978-1-119-86745-6 (pbk); ISBN 978-1-119-86746-3 (ebk); ISBN 978-1-119-86747-0 (ebk)

SKY10035253_071322

Contents at a Glance

Table of Contents

Introduction

Humans have traveled nomadically or lived in tribes for tens of thousands of years. It wasn't until the Industrial Revolution that people began moving to cities to work in factories. For the past 200 years, commuting to work five days per week has been the status quo. But it's also had a cost to people's health, wellness, and stress levels.

What if the 9-5 was never the way people were designed to live? What if it were a glitch in the timeline of human history?

The Internet has made it possible for anyone — regardless of age, race, citizenship, education, or job title — to earn an income. With that comes unlimited personal freedom, sovereignty, and earning potential. This book helps you return to your nomadic roots and reconnect with the creative, curious, and entrepreneurial side of your DNA.

Becoming a digital nomad is an opportunity to design every aspect of your life, from where you live to what you do for work to which country you pledge allegiance to.

Although the technology to telecommute has existed since the 1970s, corporate culture and societal attitudes took decades to warm up to the idea. It wasn't until the COVID-19 pandemic of 2020 that companies, governments, and the global workforce adopted remote work en-masse.

Fortunately, there's less resistance and fewer barriers to the digital nomad lifestyle than ever before. *You* can be one of the first people in history to live a location-independent, borderless lifestyle. That means expanding your worldview, pushing the limits of your comfort zone, forging deep connections with people of different cultures, and experiencing rapid growth in your career and personal life.

You can enjoy a freer, more meaningful, purpose-driven life. And even save money in the process. This book shows you how.

About This Book

If the idea of transitioning from a traditional to a nomadic lifestyle seems over-whelming, you're not alone. Going nomadic involves potentially changing your job, home, routine, habits, and personal life all at once. It can be confusing to know where to start. But this book clarifies the way for you, guiding you step-by-step through the process of achieving and sustaining a freedom lifestyle. It helps you with the practical, tactical, and logistical side of the process, as well as how to find your community and care for your health and safety along the way.

You can use this book as a chronological guide to becoming a digital nomad and as a resource to refer to throughout life. It's suitable for beginner and experienced nomads. Regardless of where you're starting your journey, you can read through from the beginning or skip to the section that you want help with today.

Foolish Assumptions

Call me crazy, but if you picked up this book, I assume that you feel like there's more to life than what you've been told. The world's a big place, and you want to see more of it. Whether you've had to wait until you're retired to start traveling, you don't want to wait any longer, or you're ready for a change of scenery. I also assume that:

>> You're experienced with using basic technology such as smartphones, computers, and the Internet.

>> You're curious about the benefits of living a nomadic lifestyle and how you can lower your cost of living while enhancing your quality of life.

>> You want to be able to choose how you spend your time and where you live your life from now on.

Beyond that, one of these four categories might describe you:

>> You haven't entered the workforce yet, but you know what you *don't* want to do, and that's work a standard job.

>> You already work remotely or work from home, and you figure you can do that from anywhere. You want to travel more often, but you also want to know what to expect and make sure you're checking everything off your to-do list (in the right order).

>> You work in a traditional job and you're looking for a career change that will give you more freedom, flexibility, and fulfillment. You're curious about what you can do to work online and how you can make this location-independence thing happen.

>> You're retired or retiring soon and you're ready for a change in lifestyle (potentially in a different country).

Icons Used in This Book

Throughout this book, you'll find four different icons highlighting pretty important information.

TIP

This icon highlights helpful information from experienced nomads that make your journey easier.

REMEMBER

Read this part twice for timeless takeaways and important info. Pay close attention to the concepts listed by this icon.

WARNING

This icon brings important info to your attention, some of which can protect your health, wealth, and safety. Don't skip any of these.

You'll also find sidebars throughout the book, which include stories or info related to the topics in each chapter. It's not necessary to read these, but you might learn something interesting, unique, or new.

Beyond the Book

Besides all the great info, tips, and step-by-step guides you'll find in this book, there's more waiting for you online. Check out www.travelingwithkristin.com/dummies for extra resources, including checklists, packing lists, budget templates, and a departure/arrival itinerary.

There's also a cheat sheet with additional topics. Search www.dummies.com for "Digital Nomads For Dummies cheat sheet" to find it.

Where to Go from Here

Now that you have the lay of the land, it's time to start your journey!

>> Beginner nomads can read this book cover to cover and find value in each section.

>> Remote jobseekers should pay special attention to Chapters 5 and 6.

>> If you have a remote job or source of online income and you're ready to travel, you can skip to Part 3 on traveling and living abroad.

>> If you already have experience as a nomad, Part 4 helps you sustain the lifestyle long term.

1

Getting Started as a Digital Nomad

IN THIS PART . . .

Get familiar with the digital nomad lifestyle.

Choose your path to becoming a digital nomad.

Calculate the cost of being a digital nomad.

Overcome fears and hesitations.

Decide whether to keep or quit your current job.

Chapter **1**

Getting a Taste of the Digital Nomad Lifestyle

"Man started out as nomadic, it may be the most natural state for human beings."

— CRAIG O. MCCAW, QUOTED IN THE BOOK, DIGITAL NOMAD

I n 1997, a full decade before Apple released the first-generation iPhone, *Digital Nomad* was published. In it, authors Tsugio Makimoto, a former Sony executive, and David Manners, editor at the UK's *Electronics Weekly*, prophesized the future of work with impeccable accuracy.

"Technology does not cause change but it amplifies change. Early in the next millennium it will deliver the capability to live and work on the move.

People will be able to ask themselves, 'Am I a nomad or a settler?' For the first time in 10,000 years that choice will become a mainstream life-style option. That is the message of DIGITAL NOMAD."

It was more than 20 years before the predictions in *Digital Nomad* came true. But the term has since stuck. It's a fitting way to describe someone who can roam the world with a remote office in their pocket. Portable technology, affordable travel, and lightning-fast Internet networks have transformed life as we know it — and opened limitless ways to live.

The idea of being a *digital nomad* —someone who can live and work from anywhere — resonates for a reason. It's the ultimate form of personal freedom, a way to blend what you do for work with where you want to live and the types of experiences you want to have. It's never been possible before and the world will never be the same again.

While I believe that anyone can become a digital nomad, breaking free from the status quo is hard. There's a steep learning curve as location independence is a new concept. Before "taking the leap" from a traditional lifestyle to a nomadic one, you want to know what to expect.

In this chapter, I help you get started in the digital nomad lifestyle. You get familiar with the many paths to becoming a digital nomad, as well as the pros, cons, and costs. I also introduce you to the different interpretations of location independence, debunk common misconceptions, and explain how digital nomads make money.

If the idea of becoming a digital nomad seems like a pipe dream to you, this chapter shows that digital nomads are just like everyone else. And you can be one too.

ALL HAIL THE MICROCHIP

Digital Nomad was inspired by the concept of Moore's Law. In 1965, Intel co-founder, Gordon Moore, calculated that the number of transistors on a microchip doubled about every two years as the cost of the technology dropped in half. At the time, the only commercially available computer on the market was the DDP-116. It operated on slot cards rather than microchips, weighed 500 pounds, and cost about $260,000 when adjusted for inflation today. Not very practical for a nomadic lifestyle!

But Makimoto and Manners foresaw that increasingly faster, cheaper, and smaller computers with more memory and storage would change the way humans lived and worked. Whereas the first integrated circuit was made up of a single transistor, Apple's 2022 M1 Ultra chip has 114 *billion* transistors, making it the most powerful personal computer chip in the world at the time of writing this book. It would be hard to imagine life without microchips today, as they are used in almost all forms of technology and electronic devices, from smartphones to spreadsheets, video games, cars, banking, weather forecasting, navigation, medical equipment, and more.

Defining the Digital Nomad

"Digital nomads defy a single definition."

— MBO PARTNERS

Digital nomads are hard to define because, as you find out in this book, they come in all shapes and sizes. At a basic level, a digital nomad is someone who can work from anywhere using the Internet or other technology. Not all nomads work, however. Some live on income from pensions, investments, and other recurring revenue streams they can access remotely.

Digital technology has all but erased borders for business and communication. Just as a remote company doesn't have a physical office or central headquarters, a digital nomad doesn't necessarily have a fixed place of residence. Your home can be wherever you are (or wherever you find Wi-Fi).

Digital nomads can work from anywhere with an Internet connection, and often do. In my years as a nomad, I've worked from the beaches of Bali, the rainforests of Central America, and on a cruise ship floating across the equator. The world has been my remote office for more than fifteen years, and it can be yours, too. Whether you want to work from an Airbnb or an RV, technology makes it possible. You're only limited by your imagination, and perhaps cellular data networks.

Digital nomads have all types of different jobs. They can work for themselves or someone else. They can work part time, full time, or on a contract basis. They can even *stop* working if they develop ways to live off automated or passive income streams.

Digital nomads can include:

» Home-based remote workers who can technically live anywhere but choose to remain in one city or country.

» Partially nomadic people who keep a home base and travel part time.

» Fully nomadic people who don't have a fixed address. They may have sold everything they own or keep a storage unit and travel year round or without an end date.

» Temporary nomads who are fully or partially nomadic sometimes and static sometimes. Some folks also live like nomads for a few months or years before returning to a traditional lifestyle.

Table 1-1 goes into detail about the different types of digital nomads.

TABLE 1-1   ## Types of Digital Nomads

Type of Nomad	Description
Remote Employees	People who work remotely on a salary for a company or organization.
Online Freelancers	Self-employed, independent contractors who offer services on an hourly, per-project, or other basis.
Online Business Owners	Entrepreneurs, startup founders, and anyone who runs a virtual business of any size.
Influencers and Content Creators	People who earn a living through social media, publishing online content, and leveraging their personal brand.
Passive Income Entrepreneurs & Investors	People who have achieved financial freedom through investment income or automated income streams.

A NOMAD BY MANY NAMES

The term, *digital nomad,* has become a buzzword. But, as with gender or sexual orientation, digital nomads can choose to identify with another term or kick labels to the curb altogether. Other ways to self-identify under the digital nomad umbrella include:

- Digital Freelancer
- Digital Entrepreneur
- Expat (or Techpat)
- Location-Independent Professional
- Nomadic Professional
- Online Entrepreneur or Solopreneur
- Online Professional
- Perpetual Traveler
- Professional Wanderer
- Remote Employee
- Remote Worker
- Technomad
- Wandering Professional

These are just a few examples of the many ways that people choose to describe their lifestyles.

REMEMBER

Remoteness is a sliding scale. Just as there are hybrid organizations, there are also hybrid nomads. You can combine different types of jobs and income streams to create a lifestyle that suits you. Chapters 5 and 6 give more examples.

Seeing Who's Adopting the Nomad Lifestyle

In this section, I dig deeper into digital nomad demographics. You find out where digital nomads are from, what they do for work, how old they are, and how much they earn. An overview of the U.S. digital nomad population is shown in Figure 1-1. Do you see yourself represented here?

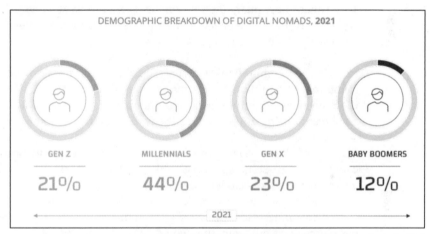

FIGURE 1-1:
The demographic breakdown of digital nomads in 2021.

Source: *MBO Partners, The Digital Nomad Search Continues, September 2021*

Generations: Z, Millennials, X, Baby Boomers

You might think that a digital nomad lifestyle is more suited to younger generations, but research shows that people of all ages dabble in digital nomadism. One Facebook groups study calculated the average age of digital nomads to be 40 years old, with the oldest nomad in the study being 72.

In 2021, Millennials made up the largest segment of digital nomads, with 44 percent, followed by Gen X, Gen Z, and Baby Boomers.

Although only 12 percent of digital nomads were Baby Boomers in 2021, according to MBO and FlexJobs, they made up a third of the population two years earlier. Researchers believe this decrease was temporarily attributed to COVID-19 concerns in high-risk groups.

People from many parts of the world

Although most of the data on digital nomad demographics comes from U.S.-based research, the digital nomad population is global. A survey of English-speaking nomads in Facebook groups recognized nomads from at least 39 countries. In a 2018 Fiverr survey of Anywhere Workers, 57 percent of respondents were from the United States, with the rest representing countries such as Kenya, Myanmar, Slovakia, Canada, Colombia, Romania, Venezuela, Indonesia, Australia, India, and the Philippines.

To estimate how many digital nomads there are worldwide, it's assumed that a certain percent of independent contractors and remote workers alike will experiment with a nomadic lifestyle at times.

In the most comprehensive report on digital nomads to date, MBO Partners found that 15.5 million Americans (or 10 percent of the U.S. workforce) described themselves as digital nomads. The number of U.S. digital nomads increased by 20 percent during 2019–2021, as the world adopted remote work on a mass scale.

The United States wasn't the only country with people working from home, of course. In 2021, China's flexible work population reached 200 million people. The government has since released a five-year "Digital Economy Development Plan," encouraging citizens to seek Internet-based employment. Currently, only 11 million Chinese identify as digital nomads. But if 10 percent of the Chinese workforce went nomadic, that would be 140 million people!

Other countries have taken similar measures to encourage remote work. In 2019, Costa Rican president, Carlos Alvarado, passed a work-from-home law regulating telecommuting for the first time. The following year, Chile's government passed a Distance Working and Teleworking law. And in 2021, Ireland passed the Right to Request Remote Work Bill in an effort to normalize flexible working in Irish society.

Governments from Angola to Belgium and beyond have passed or announced some form of remote working legislation for their citizens. That's on top of the 40 plus countries offering remote work and digital nomad visas for foreigners. The more remote work is regulated throughout the world, the more companies will adapt to such legislation, freeing millions of people from the office in the process.

Meandering men and wandering women

The reported male to female ratio of digital nomads has varied widely over the years. In the Anywhere Workers study, 63 percent of respondents were men and 37 percent were women. However, FlexJobs estimates that 70 percent of digital nomads are women. And the 2021 survey among digital nomad Facebook groups uncovered an even split of 49.81 percent females and 50.19 percent males.

Folks at every career stage

Digital nomads span all generations, industries, backgrounds, and careers. From the present day and beyond, many high school and college grads will never step foot into an office. They may be the first generation to start their careers as nomadic workers from day one.

The digital nomad lifestyle doesn't discriminate, however. Plenty of people transition to digital nomadism mid-career or in retirement.

Employees from an assortment of industries

Nomads come in an array of fields. The one thing nomads have in common is that they can do their jobs online or earn an online income. The rest is up to you! Some of the most common industries where you'll find nomads include (according to MBO Partners):

>> 19% Information Technology

>> 10% Creative Fields

>> 9% Education and Training

>> 8% Coaching and Consulting

>> 8% Research

>> 8% Sales, Marketing, and Public Relations

>> 8% Accounting and Finance

>> 30% Other Fields

The have-lots-of-money, the have-some-money, and the have-little-money sets

Because digital nomads represent a diversified mix of the global population, their income is as varied as their job titles.

Although Fiverr found that more than half of "Anywhere Workers" were freelancers in 2018, the ratio of salaried to self-employed nomads is evening out. MBO's research suggests that the number of salaried nomads tripled between 2019 and 2021, with many remote employees being "high earners." 44 percent reported earning at least $75,000.

Previously, Fiverr's Anywhere Workers study found that 57 percent of nomads earned less than $50,000 per year, with 10 percent earning $100,000 or more. That number could be on the rise, though. FlexJobs asserts that 18 percent of nomads make six figures or more, with 22 percent making between $50–100,000.

Remote working women tend to earn less than men, though, with more than one study finding that "the gender pay gap has no borders" (Fiver's Anywhere Workers study).

Either way, there's no limit on how much money you can make in the digital nomad lifestyle, especially when you combine multiple income streams. You can also save a lot, too. Many remote workers engage in geo-arbitrage, earning a high income while living in rural areas or developing countries with a low cost of living.

Fortunately, freedom doesn't have to cost a lot. 21 percent of nomads earn less than $25,000 per year, per MBO Partners. But regardless of how much money digital nomads make, 85 percent are happy at work and 79 percent are satisfied with their income. It just goes to show that money doesn't necessarily buy happiness — so long as it buys the ability to travel!

Why roam?

A better question might be, "why not?" Being a digital nomad gives you ultimate freedom and flexibility. Not only do you decide where you live and what you do for work, but you also control how you spend your time. What you do each day is up to you, without a boss looking over your shoulder and telling you what to do.

Being a digital nomad gives you options. You can change your mind at any moment about where to travel, when to settle down, and which country to pledge your citizenship to. There are few restrictions on the digital nomad lifestyle other than how you want to live and what you can afford.

Why now?

There's never been a better time to become a digital nomad because there's never been another time in history when it was possible.

In 1997, Makimoto and Manners said that digital nomadism can go mainstream "when three things change: attitudes, technology, and communications."

The previous barriers to becoming a digital nomad — clunky technology, expensive communication, and corporate resistance to telecommuting — have all but disappeared.

In 1997, it wouldn't have been so practical to travel with a desktop computer. Most businesses weren't online yet and Internet speeds hovered around 30Kpbs. But in 2022 and beyond, laptops have shrunk to the size of smartphones. Fiber optic Internet speeds and 5G networks are plentiful. And many people don't need a computer to work at all if they have a device with an Internet connection.

Attitudes toward remote work are also changing for the better. The COVID-19 pandemic forced the mainstream adoption of remote work overnight. Many companies since have announced permanent remote work or work-from home policies. As a result, the number of digital nomads tripled between 2019 and 2021, as shown in Figure 1-2.

FIGURE 1-2: Number of digital nomads in the United States.

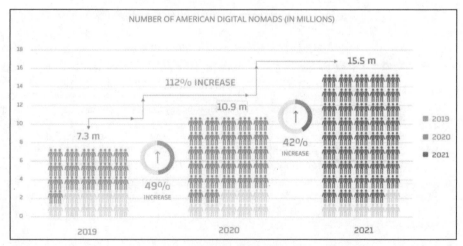

Source: MBO Partners, The Digital Nomad Search Continues, September 2021

THE HISTORY OF TELECOMMUTING AND REMOTE WORK

Humans have been working from home or in nomadic tribes since the beginning of recorded history. Over time, the workplace shifted from homes to farms to marketplaces and international trade. The Industrial Age was a turning point, however. The number of cities jumped from fewer than 1,000 in 1800 to more than 34,000 by 1950, attracting jobseekers by the masses.

Technological Age of the 1970s brought a shift from factory work to knowledge work, paving the way for the digital nomads of the future.

1760–1840: 1st Industrial Revolution (coal)

1870–1914: 2nd Industrial Revolution (gas)

1969–1999: 3rd Industrial Revolution (electronics and nuclear energy)

2000–Today: 4th Industrial Revolution (Internet and renewable energy)

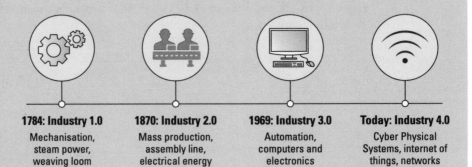

1784: Industry 1.0
Mechanisation, steam power, weaving loom

1870: Industry 2.0
Mass production, assembly line, electrical energy

1969: Industry 3.0
Automation, computers and electronics

Today: Industry 4.0
Cyber Physical Systems, internet of things, networks

In 1976, a NASA engineer named Jack Nilles released a book called *The Telecommunications-Transportation Tradeoff*, suggesting telecommuting as a new way of life. But, despite the logical arguments for remote work, employers were resistant to change. Organizations such as HP and IBM tested flexible work policies in the 1980s–90s, only to retract them in the early 2000s.

Of course, the Internet era changed everything. In 1997, *Digital Nomad* came out, predicting the return to a nomadic lifestyle. In 2007, Tim Ferriss's *The Four-Hour Work Week* became a digital nomad "bible." And In 2020, the COVID-19 pandemic finally tipped the global scales toward remote work.

The World Economic Forum attributes remote work as "one of the biggest drivers in the workplace," while IHRM thinks that it will have a bigger impact on the way we live than artificial intelligence.

Although working from anywhere has been possible since the 1970s, it's finally become the new normal. The digital nomad revolution may be a bit late to its own party. But either way, it's arrived.

If one in three independent workers becomes a digital nomad, there could be 1 billion nomads on the planet by 2035, according to the founder of Nomad List. 90 percent of remote workers say they'll never go back to an office. You can be one of them.

Flexible work is now a workplace demand rather than a perk. This reality has emboldened millions of people to quit or change their jobs between 2020-2022, a period which is known as the Great Resignation or Great Reshuffling.

Travel is also faster and more affordable than ever before. The first transatlantic flight between New York and France cost $375 in 1939 — nearly $7,500 when accounting for inflation. Today, you can fly the same route for as little as $200 one way.

The future is bright for digital nomads. Internet speeds and coverage will continue to increase. More than half the global workforce will be working independently or remotely. And the number of apps, products, services, support networks, visa programs, and tools for digital nomads will continue to increase.

So, get excited. Because there's never been a better time to make your digital nomad dream a reality. If you're reading this book, you were born at the luckiest time in history.

Busting Common Myths and Assumptions

If you've always pictured digital nomads as twenty-something-year-old tech workers, you wouldn't be alone. There are plenty of stereotypes about digital nomads, but that doesn't mean they're true. Figure 1-3 gives you a look at how everyone else perceives the digital nomad lifestyle versus the reality of the digital nomad lifestyle. The following sections bust a few of them!

BEING A DIGITAL NOMAD

FIGURE 1-3:
The myth verus the truth of being a digital nomad.

Source: Giang Cao / Very Nomad Problems

Nomading isn't a job

For most people, being a digital nomad isn't a job in itself. It's simply a way to describe the freedom to be able to work and travel on the go.

Some digital nomad bloggers and influencers make their nomadic lifestyles part of their personal brands, but they are in the minority.

You don't have to apply to become a digital nomad. The only person you need permission from is you (and maybe your boss).

Age is just a number

You're never too young or old to become a digital nomad. As long as you can earn income from anywhere, you can do it. Retirees can live as digital nomads just as much as high school grads. Want to bring your kids with you? They can be nomads, too.

There aren't many statistics on how many digital nomads there are worldwide. (After all, digital nomads are hard to track down!) The earlier section "Seeing

Who's Adopting the Nomad Lifestyle" has more on digital nomad demographics, which span across all generations.

The good news for you is that there aren't any age limits to becoming a digital nomad. You're never too early or late to start your location-independent lifestyle.

No tech skills necessary

Some folks assume that you need coding skills or a computer science degree to be a digital nomad, but that's not the case. In 2018, a FlexJobs survey found that the average digital nomad was a female Gen Xer working in education or administration.

The top ten careers reported that year were in:

>> Writing

>> Education and Training

>> Administration

>> Customer Service

>> Arts & Creative

>> Computers and IT

>> Consulting

>> Data Entry

>> Marketing

>> Project Management

Most remote jobs sites also have a category specifically for non-tech jobs, while remote employers place high value on non-technical skills such as writing and communication. You can discover where to find remote jobs in Chapter 5.

Nomads aren't backpackers

Although most nomads tote laptop bags around, they aren't backpackers. Backpackers are people who travel on a long-term holiday, funded with their savings. On the contrary, digital nomads work or earn money while they travel. (You can still be a "digital nomad backpacker" if you want, though.)

Nomads aren't travel bloggers

Many digital nomads have blogged about their travels, but chances are, travel blogging isn't how they pay the bills. Even full-time travel bloggers are known to combine multiple revenue streams to make a living. Although digital nomads may travel often, few make blogging their job. If writing is your gig, see Chapter 5 for how to find remote opportunities.

Nomads aren't tourists, either

From the looks of your Instagram feed, it may seem like nomads are always lounging on the beach or posing in front of a temple. While that's certainly the case *some* of the time, most digital nomads work more than they sightsee. MBO estimates that 71 percent of digital nomads work full time and 29 percent work part time or seasonally.

When I was a freshman in college, I told my guidance counselor that I wanted a job that would let me work from a café in Italy. "That's not a job," he said, "that sounds like a vacation." He was wrong! Digital nomads just weren't a thing yet.

Nomads aren't always traveling

If a digital nomad stops traveling, is he still a nomad?

Although digital nomads are defined by their ability to roam into perpetuity, that doesn't mean you have to *Always Be Traveling*.

As a digital nomad, you can choose when you want to travel, where, and for how long. You can also decide when to *stop*. So long as you can support yourself with a remote income, you can remain location independent forever. Eventually, digital nomads will probably just be considered regular people, because working from anywhere will be part of the status quo.

In that sense, identifying as a digital nomad is a mindset. There's no generally agreed-upon definition on how far, often, or wide digital nomads must travel each year to maintain their "status."

REMEMBER

You don't have to leave your home country (or even your home town) to become a digital nomad. According to MBO, 52 percent of digital nomads plan to stay domestic rather than travel overseas.

Traveling is more affordable than you think

At first glance, the digital nomad lifestyle might appear expensive. After all, going on vacation certainly gets pricey. But many people end up saving money when they go remote, by lowering their average cost of living, buying less stuff, and potentially decreasing their tax burdern. Find out how to calculate your digital nomad budget and cost of living in Chapter 3.

Deciding Whether the Digital Nomad Lifestyle Is Right for You

I believe that the digital nomad lifestyle can be right for everyone. After all, who *doesn't* want the ability to do what they want, when they want? A better question might be to ask yourself how nomadic you want to be and for how long.

Becoming a digital nomad doesn't need to be an extreme decision where you quit your job, sell your stuff, and book a ticket to Bali the same day. *Your* version of location independence can follow one of the examples in this book, or it can be something you design.

But, for now, here are some of the pros and cons to help you decide.

Exploring the potential benefits

Becoming a digital nomad could be the best thing since sliced bread. These are some of the benefits:

>> **Community:** Imagine if your friendship circle included thousands of people from 200 countries — that's possible when you travel the world.

>> **Cost savings:** Digital nomads can save money in many ways, such as lowering their cost of living and increasing their savings rate through geo-arbitrage, buying fewer material things, and changing their tax base.

>> **Creativity and innovation:** Immersing yourself in new cultures and places is a good way to gain inspiration in your work. Researchers have found a correlation between travel and increased innovation.

>> **Earning potential:** Many digital nomads use their newfound freedom, flexibility, and time to build multiple income streams. Many salaried digital nomads are high earners, while freelancers can earn more working for themselves than for an employer.

>> **Family:** Tim Urban, of the website Wait But Why, calculates that by the time you turn 18, you've already used up 98 percent of your time spent with family. But when you're a digital nomad, you don't have to wait until the holidays to see your loved ones. You can visit them anytime! Nomad parents can also spend more time with their children when traveling together and doing homeschool or remote learning.

>> **Freedom:** As mentioned, freedom of all shapes and sizes is the top reason people want to become digital nomads. You have micro freedoms, such as how to spend every minute of the day. And you have macro freedoms, such as changing your country of residence, taxation, or citizenship.

>> **Fulfillment:** Digital nomads are happy campers! According to MBO, 85 percent of digital nomads report being happy and satisfied in their lifestyles. Up to 90 percent say they will never go back to a traditional office job.

>> **Fun:** Being a digital nomad is really fun. Whatever you like to do, you can do more of it when you live a digital nomad lifestyle.

>> **Health and wellness:** With more time and control over your workplace, schedule, and environment, you can make healthier choices as a digital nomad. Eliminating your commute also reduces stress and increases well-being.

>> **Network:** Digital nomads have more opportunities to meet people from different cultures, backgrounds, and industries compared to when they worked in one place.

>> **Productivity and focus:** Researchers agree that remote workers suffer from fewer distractions compared to working in an office.

>> **Time:** Digital nomads can save up to 3,000 hours per year that were previously spent on commuting, meetings, office distractions, and household chores.

>> **Travel:** Undoubtedly, one of the biggest draws of the digital nomad lifestyle is being able to travel. Imagine being able to work with a view of the Eiffel Tower. That's possible when you can work from anywhere!

Recognizing the potential drawbacks

Every decision in life has pros and cons. (Even eating cupcakes.) For all the benefits of a location-independent lifestyle, there are some downsides:

» **Burnout:** Although the majority of digital nomads are happy and satisfied with their lifestyles, remote work and travel burnout is still a thing. If burnout is a concern for you, check out Chapter 12 on health and wellness.

» **Dating and relationships:** Living nomadically can complicate relationships, whether you're single and dating or living with your significant other. Friendships and partnerships at home may suffer the longer you're away. And, although you may meet more people while traveling, you might not see them again. Chapter 14 has more on dating and making friends as a digital nomad.

» **Being unsettled:** Not having a fixed home can wear on you over time. If you're planning to be a temporary nomad, this isn't much of a concern. But many long-term nomads eventually find somewhere to settle so they have more stability and community.

» **Loneliness:** Everyone experiences loneliness sometimes, whether you're a nomad or not. But traveling alone and working alone can make you feel even lonelier at times. In a Fiverr study, 30 percent of respondents said lack of community and human connection were their biggest struggles. If loneliness is a concern for you, check out Chapter 12 for tips on how to cope.

» **Productivity and motivation:** Many digital nomads are self-motivated, with only 7 percent of "anywhere workers" citing motivation as a challenge. However, it's still a factor, especially when combined with occasional loneliness and isolation from working alone.

» **Risk of failure:** Failing in business in a foreign place can be a scary prospect, especially if you don't know the culture well or have a local support system. It's important to keep a stash of emergency savings in case you end up between jobs or need to cut your adventure short and fly home.

» **Uncertainty:** Uncertainty is the flipside of the excitement and the adventure of a nomadic lifestyle. There's a fine line between living outside of your comfort zone and living in anxiety. Manage uncertainty by being as prepared and organized as possible. Chapter 11 on travel logistics helps you with that.

HOW I BECAME A DIGITAL NOMAD

I stumbled into the digital nomad lifestyle when I got the opportunity to study abroad in Costa Rica during college. I fell in love with the idea of living overseas and immersing myself in a different culture. After graduating from university, all I wanted to do was travel. So, I moved back to Costa Rica.

I planned to return to the United States eventually to resume my "real life" in Corporate America. But fortunately, technology caught up with my wanderlust.

After working in real estate in Costa Rica, I started a relocation company to help people move abroad. For the first year or so, I worked from my home office in Costa Rica's Central Valley. Eventually, I realized that I could technically work from anywhere. So in January of 2013, I sold my car, put my stuff in storage, and bid adieu (or, adios, rather) to my apartment. I set off on a one-way trip around the world with no end date.

I've worked online and lived nomadically ever since. As my perspective and worldview widened, so did my career opportunities and online income streams. After experimenting with different business models, I now earn a living through writing, content creation, consulting, affiliate marketing, digital products, and online courses, to name a few. In total, I've traveled to 60 countries in the past 20 years, many of them as a digital nomad.

Although I have many years of nomadic experience now, I started my journey like many others — without a passport or any work experience to speak of. I worked different jobs as a lifeguard, surf instructor, waitress, and real estate agent before starting my first online business. I published more than 200 videos before making a dollar on YouTube. And I took short vacations with family and friends to nearby destinations throughout the United States, Mexico, and the Caribbean before going overseas. Over the years, I gradually increased my confidence with solo travel and entrepreneurship, expanding my comfort zone and travel radius along the way.

Chapter 2

Seeing Yourself as a Digital Nomad

"This is the only way [to live], we say; but there are as many ways as there can be drawn radii from one centre." When people ask me how to become a digital nomad, I always say there are as many paths to location independence as there are people in the world. Your journey to becoming a digital nomad is uniquely yours. But taking the first step is often the hardest part.

This chapter helps you start designing your life as a digital nomad. You uncover your why, blast through any blocks that could be holding you back, and begin to see that this lifestyle can be a reality for you.

At the end, I also help you decide whether to travel solo or in a group and give suggestions for talking about your plans with others.

...ing Your Passion and Purpose:
...tablishing Your Why

A digital nomad lifestyle includes many benefits, which you can read about in Chapter 1. But *your* reasons for becoming a digital nomad are unique to you. This section helps you figure out what's motivating you. The reasons may be different than you think!

Whatever your goals are in life, your *why* informs your *how*. *Why do you want to become a digital nomad?* Do you want to work less? Have more freedom and control over your time? Meet new people? See the world? Burn your tongue on a dish of authentic pad thai?

Answering this question helps you clarify your next steps and stay on track toward your goal.

1. Why is becoming a digital nomad important to you?

   _____

2. What about [your answer for #1] is important to you?

   _____is important to me because _____.

3. What about [your answer for #2] is important to you?

   _____is important to me because _____.

4. What about [your answer for #3] is important to you?

   _____is important to me because _____.

5. What about [your answer for #4] is important to you?

   _____is important to me because _____.

6. What about [your answer for #5] is important to you?

   _____is important to me because _____.

7. What about [your answer for #6] is important to you?

   _____is important to me because _____.

Compare your seventh answer with your first answer. How are they different?

Things are not always what they seem. This exercise is designed to help you peel back the layers of why you *think* you want to become a digital nomad and reveal a deeper motivation.

When I do this exercise with my clients or in workshops, they're always pleasantly surprised with what they discover. A desire for more freedom could mean you want to spend more quality time with your kids. Wanting to learn a new language may reveal how important it is for you to connect with people from different cultures.

Your why for becoming a digital nomad may change over time. When I first started traveling, my main motivation was surfing. I only traveled or lived in places where I could surf. But eventually, my priorities changed. When I became a full-time digital nomad in 2013, I had different goals. I was newly single, growing my online business, and wanting to circle the globe as a solo traveler.

Take this exercise one step further:

What are some of the ways your life would change for the better if you had the freedom to live, work, and travel anywhere?

_____
_____
_____
_____

What will happen if you *don't* take action? What regrets will you have 20 years from now?

_____
_____
_____
_____

"Technology . . . can create the ultimate 'couch potato', someone who never leaves the living-room sofa, or the ultimate nomad, someone who is forever on the move. All that the technology will do is provide the choices. Humans will decide which they want to make."
— MAKIMOTO AND MANNERS, DIGITAL NOMAD

Envisioning Your Future as a Digital Nomad

The brain loves a plan, and few things are more enjoyable than designing a fulfilling and rewarding life for yourself.

In this section, I explain the differences between the types of nomadic lifestyles. This is your opportunity to brainstorm what *your* digital nomad life would be like. As you read through, make a note of which type of nomad resonates with you.

Full-time nomads

Full-time digital nomads are people without a permanent home base. Some are always on the move, changing locations every day, week, or month. Others are slower travelers who stay in one place for a few months at a time. What they all have in common is that their home is wherever they are. Some people become full-time nomads forever, while others want to experience a nomadic lifestyle temporarily. MBO Partners found that 54 percent of digital nomads want to stay nomadic for two to three years, while 46 percent plan to discontinue the lifestyle. However, among those who decide to take a pause from the peripatetic life, many want to go nomadic again in the future.

The benefit of being a full-time digital nomad is that it's a lot of fun. You can travel for as long as you want (or as long as your passport allows). And when you travel as a tourist, there's less paperwork. You don't have to worry about applying for long-term visas, residency permits, or changing your tax base if you're just passing through.

Being all-in as a nomad has its downsides, however. Traveling takes time, money, and energy. The more resources you invest in travel, the less you have for work, hobbies, and your personal life. And the more often you change locations, the harder it is to adapt to the local culture, stay productive at work, and form long-term relationships. Traveling full time can also get expensive and feel lonely after a while.

Part-time nomads

Being a part-time nomad is a hybrid option where you work remotely but you keep a home base. Part-time nomads may work at home for a while, take time off to travel, and repeat. While others may elect to bring their work with them wherever they go. Some part-time nomads *could* travel full time, but prefer not to. What they have in common is that they can't or don't want to be *completely* nomadic, *all* the time. Perhaps their job doesn't allow it, they have family obligations at home, or they prefer having a home base.

An upside to being a part-time nomad is stability. You don't have to sell your house, get rid of your stuff, and start living out of a backpack (or an oversized suitcase, in my case). You get many of the benefits of being a full-time nomad while having a home, routine, friendships, and your favorite bunny slippers to come back to.

The downside to being a part-time nomad is that it's expensive to pay a mortgage, lease, or monthly bills at home while you're out traveling. It's possible to offset these expenses by renting out your house or car when you're away, but there's extra overhead costs to consider.

Expats and settlers

Nomadic settlers are people who move to another city or country and stay there. Not all settlers are expats, however. And not all expats are nomads.

The exact definition of an *expat* (or *expatriate*) is subjective, but typically refers to someone who voluntarily relocates to another country. Some expats are nomads, but many are full-time employees with traditional, location-based jobs. Others may be military service members, study abroad students, retirees, and volunteers. They live abroad, but they aren't nomadic.

Some digital nomads decide to settle down or become expats when they find a place that they really like. The technical editor for this book, Erick Prince, is originally from Ohio. He traveled the world for many years before deciding to put down roots in Thailand. He still travels often, but Bangkok is where he hangs his hat.

In my case, I've been every type of nomad at one time or another. I was an expat in Costa Rica, a full-time nomad who traveled for years, and a hybrid nomad with home bases around the world. I've also been a domestic settler, when I moved back to different parts of my home country for a few years.

The benefits of being a long-term settler come from having more stability. Because when you settle in one place, it's easier to lower your cost of living and adapt to daily life in a different culture. It also frees up your time and energy for other pursuits, such as learning a language, making friends, learning new skills, or working on your side hustle. You don't have to worry about where you're sleeping tomorrow or how you'll get there. It's also easier to lead a healthy lifestyle and be productive when you have consistency and routine.

The downside of being a settler is that it's a bit less exciting and adventurous compared to globetrotting. If you move outside of your home country, you'll eventually have to apply for residency or citizenship status and potentially pay taxes there, which you can read more about in Chapter 8.

As a settler, you also stay in places long enough for the "honeymoon phase" of the cultural adaptation process to wear off, which is hard at times. (Read more about it in Chapter 15.)

Your type of nomad

Which type of nomad are you? If you're not sure, you can create your own category of nomad.

What does your ideal version of being a digital nomad look like? Would you want to travel the world on a one-way ticket, find a place to settle, or try a hybrid model where you travel a few months per year?

Would you like to be a sailing nomad or live in a van or RV?

Do you see yourself backpacking on a budget or investing in real estate abroad? Would you like to live on the beach, on a farm, or in a city skyscraper? Take a few minutes to dream up your ideal lifestyle:

_____

_____

_____

_____

_____

REMEMBER

There are no wrong answers. Your priorities may change during different phases of your life. Adjust your nomadic identity accordingly.

Evaluating Solo versus Group Travel

Once you know what type of nomad you'd like to be, who should you travel with, if anyone? Whether you're a solo traveler or globetrotting with your partner or family, there are pros and cons to joining a bigger group.

I've done plenty of solo and group travel, and you might want to give both a try, too. Both types of travel offer valuable life experiences. When traveling alone, I feel free, adventurous, and independent. I also like the agility and spontaneity of being able to do what I want, when I want. It seems I'm not alone in this sentiment, either. British Airways found in its Global Solo Travel Study that people's biggest motivation for traveling alone was the freedom and independence to do as they pleased. Relatable!

However, traveling by yourself has its downsides. Although you can still meet people this way, it gets lonely sometimes. There's also no one to watch your luggage at the airport when you go to the bathroom. In all seriousness, though, fear is a concern for many. Although solo travel isn't statistically more dangerous than group travel, that doesn't stop people from *feeling* unsafe. If safety is a concern for you, Chapter 15 offers tips for staying safe and secure when traveling.

Solo travel can be an exhilarating experience and a crash course in living outside of your comfort zone (if that's what you're after). It's not for everyone, however.

Group travel has always existed in some form or another. After all, humans are tribal creatures. There's no shortage of modern-day group travel opportunities, either. You can join a tour group for a quick vacay or go on a "workcation" with fellow remote workers.

A benefit of group travel is having a built-in community of friends from the first day you arrive in a new destination. You also have someone to turn to in case you have questions or need help. If traveling with other people is your thing, Chapter 10 has plenty of info on co-living and group travel opportunities.

Group travel has its disadvantages, though. For one, it's hard to get alone time and you have fewer opportunities to take side trips and excursions. You might feel that the itinerary is either too structured or too disorganized. And some people will feel like the group is traveling too fast while others want to speed up the pace. Group dynamics can also be tricky to navigate. Personality clashes can be an issue, or you may flat out dislike some of the folks you're with. Group travel can also be more expensive than traveling on your own or you could join a trip that doesn't meet your expectations.

Always read reviews and research group travel and co-living providers before booking.

But regardless of whether you're an introvert or an extrovert, I think it's worth trying both types of travel to figure out what you prefer. If you need some quiet time, solo travel is your bet. If you're feeling sociable, give group travel a try.

If you can't find anyone to travel with, don't let that stop you! You'll meet people in your travels either way.

Traveling with Kids

Traveling with kids takes a bit more planning than traveling alone, but it can be done! Many people wait until their kids are grown to start traveling, but you don't have to. As with solo travel, planning your travel with little ones starts *before* you leave home. Where you go and for how long depends on how old your children are and what type of experience you want to have.

If your children are young, perhaps you want them to grow up immersed in another culture or learning a second language. If they're older, maybe you'd like them to be able to study abroad or get an international education.

A few of my podcast guests have become sailing or RV nomads who homeschooled their kids while traveling the world together. Others have taken a more traditional expat route of applying for permanent residency abroad, investing in real estate, and enrolling their kids in an international school.

Think about why you want to travel as a family and talk about it together. Letting your kids get involved in the planning process could help them be more excited and invested in the experience. Jessica and Will Sueiro from World Towning have been traveling the world for more than seven years with their two children, who often pick their next destination.

REMEMBER

Your kids might not appreciate the experience of traveling or living abroad as a family until later in life. If they're old enough, allow them to voice their opinions on the idea of living a digital nomad lifestyle, but don't let their objections necessarily hold you back from something that you feel is in their best interest.

TIP

If you feel overwhelmed with the idea of traveling as a family, consider hiring a relocation consultant to help with planning and logistics, researching schools, finding housing, and aiding with the cultural integration process in different countries.

REMEMBER

Connect with other nomadic and expat families for support. Join different Facebook groups, attend local meetups, and follow bloggers and content creators for inspiration and practical tips. Resources for digital nomad families include:

>> Digital Nomad Families Facebook Group (www.facebook.com/groups/digitalnomadfamilies) has 3,000 other digital nomad families to connect with.

>> Homeschool.com has resources for getting started with homeschooling.

>> The Nomad Together podcast (https://nomadtogether.com) helps connect and enable digital nomad families.

>> OnlineSchools.org helps you find accredited online schools.

>> The Nomad Mompreneur (https://thenomadmompreneur.com) is a family travel blog and resources site for families founded by digital nomad mom and online business coach, Julia Jerg.

>> Where's Sharon (www.wheressharon.com) helps you "travel smarter, cheaper, and better with kids."

>> World Schooling Central (www.worldschoolingcentral.com) helps you get started with world schooling and connect with more than 6,000 other international families in their Facebook community.

TIP

For interviews with digital nomad and expat families, click on the "Traveling as a Family" tag on my podcast website, BadassDigitalNomads.com (https://www.badassdigitalnomads.com/category/traveling-as-a-familywith-kids/)

OTHER TYPES OF TRAVEL

The digital nomad lifestyle is for everyone! Find resources for different types of travelers below.

- **Budget travel:** For ideas on how to travel on a budget, check out my video, 65 Tips to Save Money on Travel (https://youtu.be/_pYvluN0RIg).

- **Female travel:** Meet other female digital nomads at DigitalNomadGirls.com (https://digitalnomadgirls.com/). Get female travel tips and make new friends in the Conde Nast Women Who Travel Facebook group (https://www.facebook.com/groups/womenwhotraveltheworld/) and Girls LOVE Travel (https://www.facebook.com/groups/womenwhotraveltheworld/). Join the conversation on the Nomad + Spice podcast (www.nomadandspice.com) for location-independent women, hosted by Kit Whelan and Vivienne Egan of 7in7 conference.

- **Green travel:** Calculate your carbon footprint at Epa.gov (https://terrapass.com/). Offset your travel with Terrapass (https://terrapass.com/) or "plant it forward" by planting trees with One Tree Planted (https://onetreeplanted.org/). Find more ways to go green at Sustainabletravel.org.

- **LGBTQIA travel:** Plan your trip, check out guides, get tips, and find resources and events at IGLTA.org (https://www.iglta.org/). Find a map of sexual orientation laws around the world at Ilga.org (https://ilga.org/maps-sexual-orientation-laws). For travel tips, follow gay digital nomad couple, Brent and Michael are Going Places (www.brentandmichaelaregoingplaces.com). Find friends in the LGBT Digital Nomads (www.facebook.com/LGBTDigitalNomads) and Queer Women Digital Nomads (www.facebook.com/groups/queerwomennomads) Facebook groups.

(continued)

(continued)

- **Traveling as a minority:** Gain inspiration, travel tips, and more resources at travelnoire.com and blackandabroad.com. Find community in the Black Women Digital Nomad Entrepreneurs Facebook group and the Black and Abroad Clubhouse group (www.clubhouse.com/club/blackabroad). Follow Amanda Bates, The Black Expat (https://theblackexpat.com); Erick Prince, the Minority Nomad (https://minoritynomad.com); and Jubril Agoro, Passport Heavy on YouTube (www.youtube.com/c/PassportHeavy).

- **Traveling with a disability:** Travel agencies, Wheel the World (https://wheeltheworld.com) and Travel for All (https://travel-for-all.com) help you make the world accessible. Find tips and considerations for all types of travel at CDC.gov (wwwnc.cdc.gov/travel/page/disability).

- **Traveling with a pet:** See Chapter 11 for how to bring your pet along with you on your travels.

- **Expediting your travel:** To travel easier, sign up with a Trusted Traveler program such as EasyPASS in Germany, Global Entry in the United States, NEXUS in Canada, Privium in the Netherlands, or Registered Traveller in the UK. Some airports, such as Glasgow Airport in Scotland, offer a PrioritySecurity pass for £5.99. Get access to more than 1,300 airport lounges worldwide with a Priority Pass membership (https://prioritypass.com/).

Discussing Your Vision with Family, Friends, and Colleagues

Once you've made your decision to become a digital nomad, you might feel the urge to spread the good news.

Becoming a digital nomad is an exciting prospect, but it could also give your friends and family a shock. They could have questions (lots of questions) about your plans, your safety, and what your decision means for them.

How you approach this conversation will be different depending on whether you're talking with friends, family members, or colleagues.

This section offers a few different strategies for when and how to tell people that you're making a life change.

Breaking the news that you're pursuing your wanderlust

Timing when to disclose your dreams and ideas to others is an art. Sometimes you're too early in the process and you don't feel comfortable sharing your plans just yet. That's okay. Announcing a big change like quitting your job, starting a business, or moving to another country (or all), can illicit an avalanche of "buts" from well-meaning friends and family.

At every turn, someone could try to talk you out of becoming a digital nomad, especially when overseas travel is involved. Before broaching the conversation, here are some tips to keep in mind:

>> **Don't make assumptions.** You may expect resistance to your plans, only to find that everyone supports and encourages you.

>> **Use empathy.** Think about the other person's point of view. Contemplate how you can ease any possible concerns.

>> **Listen to their side.** Even if you don't agree with their perspective, show respect by hearing them out.

>> **Be assertive.** Are you telling people what you're going to do or asking their permission? If they sense any uncertainty, they might try to change your mind.

>> **Sooner isn't always better.** If you declare your plans before following through, you might trick your brain into thinking that the hard work is done. Consider waiting until your plan is solid or in-progress before telling people.

>> **Prepare to compromise.** If your company's lack of a remote work policy is an issue, suggest a hybrid model that would work for both of you. Instead of leaving the office forever, perhaps you settle for being able to work from anywhere 1-3 months per year.

>> **Agree to disagree.** Sometimes you won't see eye to eye. It's perfectly okay to live life how you want, regardless of how anyone else feels about it. You might never get others' approval, but you don't need their permission, either.

WARNING

Think twice before moving out of the country without alerting your employer (if applicable). Some companies have restrictions on where you can work remotely.

Addressing common concerns

Your friends and family members probably want what's best for you, but they may still worry. These are some of the most common questions you'll face:

>> What if you get hurt? Explain that you have an international travel and health insurance policy. (See Chapter 12 to find one.)

>> What if you run out of money? Assure them that you've budgeted accordingly and saved money for a rainy day.

>> What if you fail? You won't know until you try. It's a risk you're willing to take because reaching this goal is important to you.

>> Isn't it dangerous? Unless you're traveling to a war zone, most countries are generally safe. Chapter 15 can help with safety and security.

>> When will we see you again? Include a trip home in your travel plans. A benefit of living a remote lifestyle is that you can visit anytime (not just on holidays).

>> What about them? At every phase of my nomad or expat journey, people have questioned my decisions, tried to talk me out of it, or gave words of warning. I followed my heart and intuition, anyway, but it was hard to go against the opinions of so many people for so many years.

WARNING

Pressure is a big reason why people don't move. It can be hard to have friends, family members, and other people you care about tell you you're making a mistake or a wrong decision. But if the digital nomadic lifestyle is truly what you want to do, go for it.

People are uncomfortable with change for a number of reasons — some selfish, and some less so. When you take action to follow your dreams, it might remind them that they crave a change, too. At the end of the day, you only live once, and you'll never know what you're capable of until you try.

The first time I moved abroad, I told people *after* I had a plane ticket. You can take it a step further by staying quiet on the topic altogether. Or waiting to share about your journey after you arrive in your destination.

On the work front, your employer, colleagues, or clients will want assurances that your plans won't adversely affect them. Prepare to answer questions about your time zone, availability, Internet security, the stability of your Wi-Fi connection, and how you'll handle deadlines and emergencies. Chapter 7 has more about remote work practices for success.

REMEMBER

You may never get the green light to travel from others. In that case, you might have to make some hard decisions that involve proceeding without their blessing or changing companies or careers to make it happen. See Chapter 4 for tips on quitting your job and Part 2 for finding a new one.

Facing the Fear of Failure as a Nomad

"Given all the technological possibilities that the next decade will bring, will people grab them as an opportunity to become nomadic, or will they see them as an opportunity to become totally static?"

— MAKIMOTO AND MANNERS,
DIGITAL NOMAD

Oftentimes, what holds people back from becoming digital nomads isn't a lack of planning or even money. It's good old-fashioned fear.

Fear is a tricky emotion, because it's there to protect you, but it's also often irrational. Fortunately, fear is usually only in your mind. It's a projection of what *could* happen, not what *will* happen.

I was *terrified* the first time I moved abroad. I remember crying as the plane landed, convinced I'd made a huge mistake. I worried that I wouldn't be able to learn the language, that I'd never fit in with the locals, and that I'd get homesick. Meanwhile, my parents were certain that I'd end up in the sequel to the movie, *Taken*. None of that happened, of course. I learned Spanish, made friends, and lived to tell the tale. The fear was temporary and the experience changed my life forever.

When you feel the fear and act anyway, you grow stronger, more confident, and more resilient. But before being able to overcome your fears, it helps to articulate them.

One strategy for overcoming fear is to face it head on through a practice of negative thinking. Stoic philosophers had a name for this — *premeditatio malorum*, or pre-meditation of evils. The idea is to imagine all the things that could possibly go wrong and examine them. Nothing is too scary or too silly to go on this list. As the philosopher, Seneca, once wrote, "if an evil has been pondered beforehand, the blow is gentle when it comes."

Give it a try:

What's holding you back from becoming a digital nomad?

_____

_____

_____

What are you afraid could happen if you become a digital nomad?

_____

_____

_____

For each fear, write down a possible solution or strategy for how you'll respond in the worst-case scenario.

Fear: All your stuff gets stolen.

Solutions: Save important work in the cloud; get travel and equipment insurance; follow safety tips in Chapter 15.

Fear: You lose your job.

Solutions: Apply for a new job; start freelancing on the side; house-sit for free rent or live with a friend or relative until you get back on your feet.

Fear: Your online business fails.

Solutions: Move to a country with an extra low cost of living so you can bootstrap easily; start your business part time while keeping a salaried job; keep an emergency savings account for a rainy day (or month); diversify your income so if one revenue stream dries up, you have another one.

Fear: You feel lonely.

Solution: Plan regular trips home to visit friends and family. Chapter 14 also has plenty of tips on meeting people and making friends while traveling.

Hopefully, you find that your fears are resolvable and most of your worries never come to pass. Some fears may also be decisions in disguise, such as cutting ties with your company or ending a relationship.

However, if your digital nomad lifestyle doesn't work out the first time around, you can always come home, regroup, and try again. You'll be older and wiser because of it.

Fear of failure is healthy (and normal)

Fear is an evolutionary, biological response to keep you safe from harm. It's necessary for survival. But in a world where you no longer have to worry about your food hunting you back, there are arguably less dangers awaiting you compared to your paleolithic ancestors.

Sometimes, fear isn't even fear — it's adrenaline or discomfort with uncertainty. According to scientists, the body perceives anxiety and excitement in the same way. Both emotions are generated by the hypothalamus in the brain. Your brain doesn't know the difference between the fear aof watching a scary movie, sky diving, or making the leap to becoming a digital nomad. But you can choose how to interpret and react to your fears.

If you're feeling apprehensive about taking the leap to location independence, try reframing it as excitement instead. Use that energy to fuel your escape plan.

You can't control or anticipate everything that will happen when you become a digital nomad; you can't if you stay home, either. "The obstacle is the way," as Ryan Holiday would say. That which you fear the most might be what you should pursue. So, if you feel afraid (or excited) about becoming a digital nomad, see it as a good sign!

When in doubt, start small

If you sense that anxiety, fear, or uncertainty are holding you back, start small. Experiment with the digital nomad lifestyle before going all in. Surround yourself with like-minded people in your community or online. Follow digital nomad content creators and absorb their knowledge. Take a short trip to a nearby destination and bring your laptop with you.

Or attend an event where nomads will be present. I once met a New York City firefighter at a digital nomad conference in Spain. He wasn't a digital nomad yet. He just wanted to learn more about the lifestyle and meet others who were doing it.

Some other ways to convince your brain that you're on your way to becoming a digital nomad include:

>> Set up a savings account or travel fund.

>> Search remote jobs boards for available opportunities.

>> Take an online course to learn a new skill.

>> Offer freelancing services to your friends.

>> Join a one- or two-week remote work retreat through a company such as Remote Year (www.remoteyear.com) or Unsettled (https://beunsettled.co).

REMEMBER

The more time you spend immersing yourself in the lifestyle, the more comfortable and confident you'll feel. (Reading this book also counts!)

Picking yourself up, dusting yourself off, and regrouping

Few things in life ever seem to go completely as planned, and nomading is no different. On the occasions that you begin to lose your way in the world (literally or figuratively), there are a few things you can do to regain your center.

>> Check in on your mental and physical health. Chapter 12 has more tips on that.

>> Connect with like-minded friends for support. Chapter 14 helps you make friends anywhere.

>> Go home. Sometimes a visit home is just what the doctor ordered. It could also remind you why you left in the first place!

>> Return to your why. As you travel and meet people in your life as a digital nomad, your priorities and goals will change with time. *You* might even change! Check in with yourself and reconnect with your why if you feel lost or aren't sure what to do next.

>> Slow down. Is it time to put away the maps and stay in one place for a while? Sometimes, a little rest and relaxation or someone to talk to can fix whatever is ailing you. Other times, you may need a more complex strategy. But one thing's for sure, problems don't solve themselves. Traveling to the next country is probably a temporary fix. Only you know what's best for you. But be wary of attempting to escape problems by changing locations.

Chapter **3**

Setting a Realistic Budget

Although going on vacation gets expensive, long-term travel doesn't have to break the bank. In fact, many digital nomads end up saving money when they go remote, compared to their average cost of living at home. Some people become digital nomads specifically to save money, retire sooner, or lower their cost of living.

In this chapter, you get an overview of the expenses that digital nomads incur. You also find out how to estimate your cost of living in a country you've never been to and calculate how much income and savings you need to become a nomad.

TIP

Navigate to www.travelingwithkristin.com/dummies for a downloadable budget template to help with your financial planning.

Considering Expenses and Income Needs When You're a Nomad

Calculating your income and expenses as a nomad isn't much different from how you'd manage your household budget.

Before I get into the details, however, these are the main categories of income and expenses to take into consideration:

>> **Monthly income:** How much you earn from your remote job, freelancing clients, or online business.

>> **Startup costs:** Initial costs related to moving, buying equipment, and other miscellaneous one-time expenses.

>> **Nest egg:** How much money you have saved for your travel lifestyle.

>> **Miscellaneous income:** One-time windfall earned from selling your car, house, or stuff.

>> **Target cost of living:** Your average monthly living budget after arriving in your destination.

>> **Travel and transportation costs:** Ongoing travel costs when moving or traveling throughout the year.

>> **Health and insurance costs:** The cost of monthly healthcare, insurance, and out-of-pocket expenses.

>> **Business expenses (if applicable):** Remote salaried employees and retired nomads may not have any monthly business expenses, but freelancers and online business owners should account for these. My business expenses are higher than my living expenses!

REMEMBER

Transportation and moving costs are involved every time you change locations — even weird things you wouldn't think of, such as buying bottles of olive oil and spices 12 times per year. The longer you stay in one place, the lower you can get your cost of living. The farther and wider you travel, the higher your annual travel-related expenses will be.

Calculating Your Cost of Living

Beyond projecting your digital nomad income and expenses, how do you figure out which destinations you can afford to live in?

Certainly some regions of the world are more affordable than others. For example, living in Copenhagen costs more than Colombia. Living in Southeast Asia is much more affordable than living in Scandinavia. You can live anywhere on a budget, but your quality of life will be different depending on the country you choose. For the price of renting a bedroom in New York or Miami, you could live for a month in Morocco.

Even if you move to an expensive country, such as Switzerland or Australia, you can maintain a low to moderate cost of living. The cost of living within a country varies by city. As a rule, towns are more affordable to live in than cities and capitals. For instance, it costs 25 percent more to live in Washington D.C. than Knoxville, Tennessee. Likewise, living in Stockholm, Sweden is up to 40 percent more expensive than the nearby town of Uppsala.

Your exact cost of living depends on your budget, location, and lifestyle. When I researched the cost of living in Costa Rica for a YouTube video, I polled more than 300 foreigners living there. The responses ranged from $175 per month from a guy living on a sustainable farm and growing and bartering his food to $10,000 per month for a family with kids in private school. My average cost of living in Costa Rica was $2,500-3,000 per month, but many people (including couples) said they lived comfortably on $1,500 per month. And, although the average monthly wage in Costa Rica is around $750, many foreigners reported spending $3,000-6,000 per month. Some people were able to cut their cost of living in half when moving to Costa Rica, yet others spent the same as when they were living in the United States.

REMEMBER

You have control over what you want your cost of living to be, regardless of where you live in the world.

The following tools help you research the cost of living in thousands of cities so you know what to expect. And remember, the more you "live like a local," the lower your expenses can be:

>> **Expatistan** (www.expatistan.com/cost-of-living): Compare the cost of living among more than 2,000 cities (crowdsourced info).

>> **Nomad List** (https://nomadlist.com): Explore the top digital nomad destinations by cost of living. There's a different estimate for living like a local, expat, nomad, or tourist. Check out Figure 3-1 for its estimates when living in Lisbon, Portugal.

>> **Numbeo** (www.numbeo.com/cost-of-living): The world's largest crowdsourced cost-of-living database with prices in 10,000+ cities.

>> **Teleport** (https://teleport.org): Compare cities by their quality of life, cost of living, and more. There's also a quiz to help you decide where to move. Figure 3-2 shows its estimated cost of living in Buenos Aires, Argentina.

Once you have an idea of the cost of living in some of the destinations you're interested in, see how they compare with your current budget. Table 3-1 can help you compare budgets.

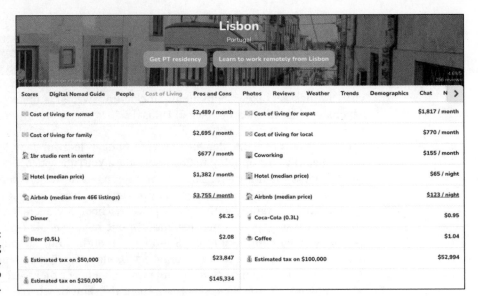

FIGURE 3-1:
The cost of living in Lisbon, according to Nomad List.

Cost of living for nomad	$2,489 / month	Cost of living for expat	$1,817 / month
Cost of living for family	$2,695 / month	Cost of living for local	$770 / month
1br studio rent in center	$677 / month	Coworking	$155 / month
Hotel (median price)	$1,382 / month	Hotel (median price)	$65 / night
Airbnb (median from 466 listings)	$3,755 / month	Airbnb (median price)	$123 / night
Dinner	$6.25	Coca-Cola (0.3L)	$0.95
Beer (0.5L)	$2.08	Coffee	$1.04
Estimated tax on $50,000	$23,847	Estimated tax on $100,000	$52,994
Estimated tax on $250,000	$145,334		

teleport
A Topia Company

COST OF LIVING

Costs of living in Buenos Aires are **in the 61st place** of all 248 Teleport cities. Average living expenses are significantly **lower** compared to other cities, especially in the housing market. Moving to Buenos Aires will very likely **decrease** your daily costs of living. Sign up for free to get access to our cost of living index and use our international cost of living calculator to do cost comparison by city.

DAILY LIVING COSTS (USD)

MONTHLY FITNESS CLUB MEMBERSHIP	$52	
MOVIE TICKET	$8	
BROADBAND INTERNET CONNECTION	$33	
MONTHLY PUBLIC TRANSPORT	$16	
LUNCH	$9	

-51%
COMPARED TO
SAN FRANCISCO

SEE MORE PRICES AND DETAILED COST OF LIVING DATA IN BUENOS AIRES

FIGURE 3-2:
The cost of living in Buenos Aires, according to Teleport.

TIP

A good way to estimate your cost of living in a new place is to follow local or expat bloggers and YouTubers who live there. Many content creators share exact breakdowns of their income and expenses.

TABLE 3-1 **Compare Costs of Living**

	Cost of Living at Home	Destination #1	Destination #2	Destination #3
Monthly Income				
Average Cost of Living				
Balance				

REMEMBER

Price isn't the *only* factor in choosing where to live. For some nomads, culture, convenience, climate, community, and quality of life are higher priorities.

Analyzing Digital Nomad Switching Costs

One thing I've learned the hard way over the years is that you incur *switching costs* every time you change locations or homes as a digital nomad. What are switching costs?

Every task has a setup cost. When you wake up in the morning, you don't roll out of bed and fall into your first virtual meeting of the day (hopefully). It takes time to get ready for work. You wake up, brush your teeth, get dressed, make coffee or tea, and eat breakfast or exercise first. (Whatever your morning routine includes.)

When you do laundry, you probably do a load or two at a time rather than washing each individual item. When you prepare a meal, there's a setup cost to prepping your ingredients, cooking your food, and cleaning up afterwards. The setup costs are higher with traveling, however.

As Chapters 8 through 11 discuss, planning each trip involves a number of logistics — including packing, booking flights, and finding accommodations. Each of these tasks requires time, money, and energy that you don't expend as much or as often in a traditional lifestyle. Each logistic represents a setup cost. And each time you change locations you incur a switching cost.

That's why traveling slowly is the most sustainable way for digital nomads to live long term. Slow travel is subjective. It's traveling at a pace that feels reasonable to *you*.

A lot of little things add up every time you change locations. But the following sections help you know what to expect and reduce some of the associated costs.

Traveling isn't as fun if you're broke and tired all the time.

Time-related costs

One type of switching cost is time. Each time you change destinations, you spend a certain amount of time deciding where to go, where to stay, and booking your travel arrangements. Most of this time is spent *before* you leave your current destination, cutting into your work or personal time.

Time-related costs include:

>> Thinking about and researching where to go

>> Planning and booking travel

>> Traveling to and from your destination

>> Checking in and out of your accommodations

>> Packing and unpacking

>> Recovering from jet lag

>> Getting acclimated with your new surroundings

>> Finding Wi-Fi and workspaces

>> Sightseeing

>> Meeting new people

>> Navigating local transportation options

>> Unforeseeable travel delays

After the planning process comes the actual traveling part, where you move by bus, plane, train, car, or boat.

Finally, you arrive in your destination. That's when the adjustment phase starts. Spoiler Alert: It takes a year or more to move through the four stages of cultural adjustment in a destination. See Chapter 15 for more on the phases of culture shock.

To mitigate and streamline some of the time-related costs of travel, you can:

>> Hire someone to plan your travel for you.

>> Enroll in a housing subscription plan for digital nomads, such as the Blueground Pass (www.theblueground.com/blueground-pass) or Landing (www.hellolanding.com).

>> Join an all-inclusive travel retreat group.

>> Travel less often.

However, as a digital nomad, switching costs can never *completely* be avoided. Group travel comes with its own hidden cost to productivity in the form of distractions, which I talk about in Chapter 13.

Money-related costs

Besides time, traveling costs *money*. At a minimum, you need funds for transportation, housing, food, travel documents, insurance, and more. Miscellaneous expenses also arise when traveling, such as excess baggage fees, overpriced taxis, or pricey airport food.

Financial switching costs include:

>> Additional security deposits for housing

>> Cost of transportation, such as airfare or a train ticket (including transportation between your home base and point of departure, such as taxis or ride shares)

>> Food and beverages (eating out)

>> Luggage fees

>> Miscellaneous unforeseen expenses

>> Short-term accommodation between home bases (hotels)

>> Supplemental expenses to furnish accommodations with extra amenities or staples such as cooking oils, spices, linens, toilet paper, and office equipment or furniture.

In addition to time- and money-related costs, "too much" travel can adversely affect your sleep and health. Chapter 12 covers ways to take care of your health as a digital nomad.

REMEMBER

Slow travel helps you save money in every aspect of the digital nomad lifestyle. The longer you stay in one place, the lower your switching costs are.

If you move four times per year instead of twelve, you'll be buying eight fewer plane tickets. Few digital nomads account for these costs in their initial planning, but they add up fast.

When in doubt, travel slowly — whatever that means to you!

Creating a Digital Nomad Budget

Budgeting is a critical step on the path to becoming a digital nomad. Organizing your finances helps you plan ahead, save money, and choose destinations that are the right fit for you.

I recommend creating two budgets — one for your pre-departure income and expenses, and one for your monthly cost of living as a digital nomad.

Pre-departure budget

Calculate these income streams and expenses *before* you leave home:

>> **Emergency fund:** A savings cushion of 3–6 months of living expenses

>> **Extra savings from reducing your normal living expenses:** Giving up your rental property or car lease, eliminating your work commute, cancelling your phone plan, closing utilities and Internet accounts, ending monthly subscriptions, changing your insurance plan, saving money on gas/parking fees/tolls

>> **Initial startup costs:** Anything related to getting to your first destination, including plane tickets, baggage fees, moving costs, monthly storage, shipping costs, passport and visa applications, new tech equipment and other gadgets, pets, vaccines, and medical tests

>> **Other miscellaneous income:** One-time windfall from selling your car/house/personal items, investments, tax refund, employee severance package, and security deposit refund (if you rent)

>> **Pre-departure income and expenses:** Your normal, pre-nomad living expenses

Monthly cost-of-living budget

Your average monthly cost-of-living budget is how much you expect to earn and spend as a digital nomad. It includes your remote salary or income less your cost of housing, food, insurance, communication, taxes, healthcare, and other living expenses.

Examples of digital nomad living expenses include:

>> ATM, bank, and foreign exchange fees

>> Back-up Internet plans and devices

- » Car and bike rental

- » Childcare

- » Data plan and SIM cards for your phone

- » Conferences and events

- » Co-working membership

- » Entertainment and eating out

- » Groceries

- » Group travel

- » Healthcare

- » Housing: rent and utilities (Find out the cost of digital nomad housing in Chapter 10.)

- » Monthly subscription services from music apps and Netflix to online business tools

- » Online courses and education

- » Personal expenses: clothing, fitness, laundry, toiletries

- » Pets and vet bills

- » Public transportation

- » Savings and investments

- » Taxes

- » Virtual office or mailbox

Some travel and relocation costs to consider are:

- » Airfare and airport transportation

- » Cultural adjustment training

- » Customs and import fees

- » Excess baggage fees

- » Foreign exchange fees

- » Furniture

- » Miscellaneous/unanticipated expenses

- » Private schooling

>> Relocation services

>> Real estate and rental commissions

>> Remote office equipment

>> Short-term housing or hotels

>> Supplemental insurance

>> Tipping

>> Transportation and tours

If you're a freelancer or online business owner, you may have monthly expenses above and beyond your personal cost of living.

Sample online business expenses include:

>> Accounting and bookkeeping expenses

>> Cloud storage and file sharing

>> Credit card processing fees

>> Invoicing software

>> Marketing and customer management software

>> Project management software

>> Remote contractors and virtual assistants

>> Web hosting and maintenance

>> Other expenses unique to your business

TIP

A travel budgeting app also helps you stay on top of your finances while on the move. Check out Trabee Pocket (https://trabeepocket.com), Trail Wallet (available only for iOS; find it in the Apple Store), TravelSpend (https://travel-spend.com), and TripCoin (https://tripcoinapp.com).

Chapter **4**

Keeping or Quitting Your Day Job

When it comes to your career, there are two barriers to becoming a digital nomad. One is if your job can't be done remotely. The other is if your company won't let you work remotely.

If your job can be done from your laptop, becoming a digital nomad could be as simple as getting permission from your employer. This chapter helps with that.

But if your job requires you to be in a physical workplace, such as a bar, restaurant, hospital, bank, or construction site, you may ultimately need to transition to a role with more freedom.

Sometimes, it's possible to convert your current job into a remote job. (Chapter 6 explains how to do that.) But in other instances, you may need to quit your job and find one that's more remote friendly.

Quitting or changing jobs is a big decision. It's not something to be done haphazardly. In this chapter, I help you weigh the pros and cons and approach your employer about getting permission to go remote, if possible.

Deciding Whether You Should Keep or Quit Your Job

When deciding whether to keep or quit your job, start by acknowledging whether you like your job and if it can be done remotely. (The next section helps you determine that.)

If it can't be done remotely but you want to become a digital nomad anyway, this is an opportunity to start learning a remote skill, giving freelancing a try, or searching for a remote job. In Chapters 5 and 6, you find out all about ways you can make money as a digital nomad.

If you love your job and would prefer to keep it, then you might want to negotiate more flexibility with your company before calling it quits.

In some cases, you may be able to negotiate a full-time remote position if your company is motivated to keep you on. But it could be easier to transfer to a company whose culture embraces remote work, rather than trying to convince yours of the contrary. Answer yes or no to the following questions:

>> Do you like your job?

>> Can your job be done remotely?

>> Would you want to keep your job if you could work remotely and travel?

If you answered, "no," to one or more of these questions, it may be time to consider a different job.

WARNING

Think twice about quitting your job before you have another one or sufficient savings to cover your living expenses during your transition. Make sure to calculate your digital nomad budget in Chapter 3 so you have a good idea of your financial picture, moving costs, and cost of living, first.

Evaluating the pros and cons of keeping your job

If you're happy in your current job role, there are plenty of benefits to keeping it. Keeping your job is typically the most familiar, predictable option.

The longer you're with the same company or working in the same industry, the stronger your network, relationships, and prospects for career advancement can be. And the more experience you have in your field, the more specialized knowledge, expertise, and career capital you accumulate.

Georgetown University professor and author, Cal Newport, describes career capital as rare and valuable skills "that can be used as leverage in defining your career."

But when you change careers or industries, you start over with generating career capital. It's a bit like climbing the corporate ladder from the bottom. For example, if you sell your restaurant to become a computer programmer or developer so you can work remotely, you'll need to learn how to code and gain experience before applying for remote IT jobs.

Keeping your job can also be better for your wallet. The Workforce Vitality Report, let by ADP Research Institute, found that workers who change companies may earn $10/hour less than those who stay put.

Of course, there are exceptions to every rule. Keeping your job can provide a false sense of security, as traditional careers aren't as stable or predictable as they once were. It's also possible to earn *more* money and benefits if you change jobs. You could decide to work for yourself as a freelancer in your area of expertise, start an online business, or make a lateral move to a competitor's firm, resulting in comparable (or higher) pay.

Among the people who quit their jobs during the Great Resignation (see the sidebar for more), many concluded that they were better off working for themselves than for someone else. Upwork found that independent contractors thoroughly enjoy the freedom, flexibility, and fulfillment that freelancing provides. 62 percent reported that they earn the same or more than they did in a traditional job and the majority prefer working for themselves instead of an employer. Figure 4-1 shows why freelancers enjoy working for themselves and the ratio of workers who prefer self-employment versus traditional employment.

REMEMBER

Despite earning a consistent paycheck, there may be downsides to keeping your job, especially if you are earning low pay, lacking benefits, or experiencing burnout and other workplace issues.

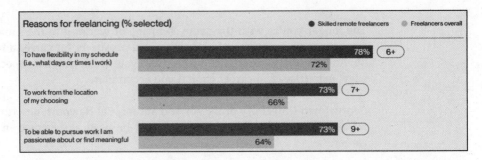

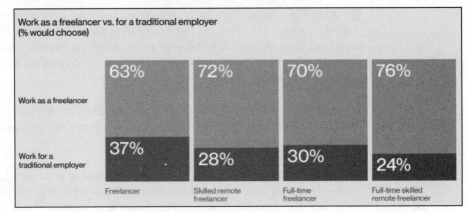

Considering the pros and cons of quitting

Quitting your job for one with more flexibility can be a freeing prospect if you're ready for a change. Research estimates that people change jobs 12-15 times in their career. It's a tough decision if you don't have a back-up plan, though. Applying for a new job can feel like a job in itself. The job search process can take months or even years to come to fruition.

If you're committed to quitting your job, try to have another job prospect lined up, first. Quitting your job is risky if you don't have a back-up plan. Build up your savings so you can support yourself until you either find a new job or can replace your income with gig work.

REMEMBER

Starting an online business or building your freelancing clientele takes time, however. That's why many aspiring nomads start a side hustle in their free time, building new income streams slowly until their earnings meet or exceed their salary and they can quit their day jobs.

THE GREAT RESIGNATION

Also known as the Great Reshuffling, Great Reset, or the Great Reimagination, the Great Resignation describes a mass transition away from the post-industrial model of working.

The term, Great Resignation, was coined by professor Anthony Klotz in April of 2021, when the U.S. Department of Labor reported that a record 4.3 million people quit their jobs. Throughout the course of the year, the U.S. resignation rate reached a 20-year high.

But the United States wasn't the only country to experience this trend. Labor shortages and reshuffling occurred on a global scale. As businesses began to call employees back to the office, workers had other ideas.

The Microsoft Work Trend Index revealed that 18 percent of respondents in 31 countries quit their jobs in 2022, while 52 percent of Gen Z and Millennial workers were considering changing jobs in the next year. Meanwhile, a 2022 PwC workforce survey estimated that 20 percent of the UK workforce was planning to quit their jobs in the next 12 months.

As for why employees quit, a Randstad study of UK workers reported that 27 percent of respondents quit their jobs in 2022 due to lack of flexibility.

Pew Research Center cited low pay, few opportunities for advancement, a lack of flexibility, and a desire to relocate.

When weighing whether to keep or quit your job, keep the end in mind. What do you see yourself doing in five or ten years? You might not be ready to quit yet, but you can begin taking steps to make it happen. Even if it takes time to reach your goal of financial or location independence, it's a journey worth starting.

Approaching Your Boss About Becoming a Digital Nomad

If your job can technically be done from anywhere, you have a good case for getting permission from your employer to work remotely and become a digital nomad. But if your company isn't yet on board with the concept of remote work, then you may have some convincing to do. Before asking your boss whether you can jet off to Thailand, however, take some time to prepare your case for why they should agree.

Gathering your research

In the research phase, your goal is to gather information that helps you make your case for working from anywhere. Approach this task with the same level of attention to detail that a job interview or salary negotiation would merit.

1. Confirm that your job can, indeed, be done remotely.

To determine this, review your job description and take stock of your tasks and responsibilities. Identify which ones, if any, require you to be physically present and if there's an alternative solution for accomplishing the same task remotely. The need to work from home during months of the COVID-19 pandemic showed that, with a little creativity and necessity, many previously in-person jobs could be done from anywhere. If you aren't sure, check a remote jobs board such as FlexJobs to see whether a variation of your job title appears in the search results. If you determine that your job can be done from anywhere using technology, go on to Step 2. If it most certainly can't, refer to the "Deciding Whether You Should Keep or Quit Your Job" section and reach Chapters 5 and 6 on finding remote jobs or working for yourself.

2. Find examples of similar roles in your company that people are already doing remotely.

Look for proof of concept that other employees in your firm are already working from home or living a digital nomad lifestyle. If you don't have access to this information, search online for competitors or other companies in your industry that have remote employees or similar remote roles available.

TIP

If you can't find examples of other people with your job working remotely, check freelancing sites to see whether the skills involved in doing your job are listed as services by independent contractors.

3. Identify the decision maker(s) at your company. Brainstorm a list of potential barriers or arguments they may have against you working remotely.

Managers could have concerns with how to know when you're working, when you'll be available, how you'll collaborate with coworkers, how you'll stay on task and meet deadlines, and how you'll contend with the distractions of full-time travel. Write down your proposed solutions to these challenges.

REMEMBER

Company policies that prohibit remote work may be outside your manager's control to change, but it's worth asking, anyway.

4. Give yourself a performance review.

Where do you shine? What value do you bring to the company? What are some areas where you could improve? Do you exhibit the traits that employers look for in remote employees, such as autonomy, proactiveness, good communication, and being a team player?

After completing this research, you should have an idea of your chances for success.

Preparing your case

In this phase, think about your request from the company's perspective. *Why should they allow you to work from anywhere? What's in it for them?*

Fortunately, remote work comes with plenty of benefits, such as better employee morale and health, lower turnover, increased productivity and creativity, and company savings of $11,000+ per year per employee.

The U.S. Office of Personnel Management found similar organizational benefits in a 2014–2015 study, including:

» Better emergency preparedness (59 percent)

» Improved employee attitudes (58 percent)

» Better retention (35 percent)

» Reduced commute miles (29 percent)

» Improved employee performance (17 percent)

» Reduced real estate costs (17 percent)

» Reduced energy usage (13 percent)

Consider the ways that your company can benefit from shifting your role to a remote position and why.

For tips on adopting best practices for remote work, such as staying in communication and adjusting for time zone differences, see Chapter 7.

Presenting your case

Before presenting your case, draft your ideal scenario and terms. When would you want to start working remotely? Do you want permanent remote status, or would you prefer a hybrid arrangement? Some companies let employees work from anywhere for a few months per year.

Compile your best- and worst-case scenarios for what you would be willing to accept. Prepare a back-up plan if your proposal isn't accepted. Perhaps you would like to stay in your job until you find another solution, transfer to a company you found in your research, or start a side hustle that can eventually replace your current salary.

When it's time to approach your boss with your proposal, consider the timing and medium.

What's your supervisor's preferred communication style? What time of day are they available? Are there any pressing issues or urgent deadlines that they may be preoccupied with? Try to identify a good time to broach the topic. If you're an accountant, the peak of tax season might not be the best time to ask whether you can move to Belize.

Finally, reach out to set a time to talk or request a meeting. Have confidence that you've done your homework but also remain flexible and open-minded to alternative suggestions.

Negotiating rebuttals

Use your prepared list of counterpoints, examples, and solutions for any protests your supervisor might have against you working remotely. Prepare to compromise. Where can you find a small win?

If your nomadic prospects aren't looking good, ask for a trial period to work from home for one to three days per week. You can always ask to increase your flexibility later if you build a solid record of work-from-home performance.

TIP

Consider asking about doing a periodic one-week or one-month "workcation" with a co-working retreat group, such as Remote Year or Unsettled. Such groups also host corporate retreats.

Knowing when to walk away

Hopefully, your boss gives you the green light to leave your cubicle behind. But sometimes, they won't see things your way. If that's the case, know when to walk away.

During the COVID-19 pandemic, many companies implemented permanent work-from-anywhere policies and began to offer perks to attract remote talent, such as travel credits, technology allowances, and relocation support. Sometimes it's easier to apply for a new job with a company that has embraced remote work than to try to change your company's culture.

FROM ARCHITECT TO WEB DESIGNER
TO DIGITAL NOMAD YouTuber

Sergio Sala grew up in Tabasco, Mexico. He chose to pursue a career in architecture, which led him to study at the University of Puebla. After his first business venture as an architect failed, however, he decided to try building websites for architecture studios, instead. After building a small client base, he realized that he could do his work from anywhere. So, in 2014, he traveled to Lima, Peru, where he could keep his cost of living low and work remotely from coffee shops.

While living abroad, he met many travelers, entrepreneurs, content creators, and digital nomads who inspired him to start a blog and eventually a YouTube channel. In 2021, he was able to quit web design to focus on YouTube full time.

In the ten years that Sergio has been self-employed, he has traveled to 115 cities and 40 countries as a digital nomad.

Regardless of the outcome, going through the process of pitching your boss on the idea of remote work is a win. You'll have researched your job scope, performance, and comparable remote roles. You'll have gained clarity on why remote working is important to you and how it's viable. You're now a few steps closer to landing a remote opportunity either way.

FlexJobs estimates that 22 percent of the U.S. workforce could be working remotely by 2025, an 87 percent increase. You could be one of them!

2

Making Money as a Digital Nomad

Get to know the different digital nomad jobs.

Find a remote job.

Start working for yourself.

Learn best practices for remote working across borders.

Find out where to hire remote contractors.

Chapter **5**

Have Laptop, Will Travel (and Work, of Course)

If you want to be a digital nomad but aren't sure what to do for work, this chapter is for you.

In this chapter, I give you an overview of the most common ways digital nomads earn a living. You find out about common freelancing and online business models for nomads and where to find remote jobs.

At the end of this chapter, I also give tips on attending job fairs, sprucing up your online presence, and using your network to find more remote work opportunities.

As you find in this chapter, there are many ways to make money online and grow your career while in a digital nomad lifestyle.

REMEMBER

The average person spends 90,000 hours of their life working. Make sure it's doing something that you like!

Previewing the Routes to Becoming a Digital Nomad

A digital nomad job is one that you can do from anywhere while traveling. Here are five examples of the main ways that digital nomads make a living:

>> **Remote employment:** Being a salaried part-time or full-time employee

>> **Freelancing:** Doing independent, contract work for other people or companies

>> **Online business:** Any type of business you can do on the Internet, from starting a small business to building a large company or founding a startup

>> **Passive income:** Living on income from investments or automated income streams

>> **Multiple income streams:** A hybrid model where you combine two or more jobs to generate multiple revenue streams

You can apply your skills in different ways to earn an online income. For example, if you work in the marketing field, you could apply for a remote job as a marketing manager, become a freelance marketing consultant, create a digital marketing or ads agency, or become an affiliate marketer.

If you work in video production, you could work remotely for a company, offer services as a freelance video editor, start your own film production business, or earn passive income from YouTube videos. You can also work in two areas as a YouTuber who freelances on the side.

In the section that follows, I present an overview of each of these models. As you read through, make a note of the types of jobs that appeal to you and think about how you can apply one or more of your skills to a new way of working.

Erin Carey, a former government employee in Australia, didn't have any online business experience when she decided to work for herself. However, she had a background in communication. So, she decided to use her writing skills to start a travel blog, which eventually led her to create a public relations agency for travel-ers. She's now able to sail the world full time with her husband and two children while working remotely from their sailboat.

Like Erin, you can transition from a traditional job to entrepreneurship. Or you can transfer skills you've developed in a past job to a remote job or freelancing option. This section helps you come up with ideas.

Becoming a remote employee

Since the COVID-19 pandemic, remote workers have surpassed online freelancers in becoming the biggest segment of the digital nomad population. Figure 5-1 shows how many digital nomads in the United States work independently versus for a company.

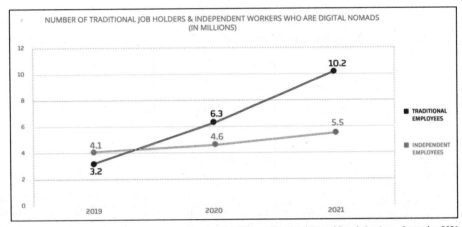

NUMBER OF TRADITIONAL JOB HOLDERS & INDEPENDENT WORKERS WHO ARE DIGITAL NOMADS (IN MILLIONS)

FIGURE 5-1:
The number of people who are in a traditional job versus an independent job.

Source: MBO Partners, The Digital Nomad Search Continues, September 2021

According to a University of Chicago study, 37 percent of U.S. jobs can be performed remotely. In the post-COVID-19 era, that number is expected to continue increasing. Commercial real estate firm, CRBE, estimates that 87 percent of large companies plan to adopt a hybrid work model in the future, up from 40 percent in 2018.

Remote jobs are available in almost every industry, including:

>> Accounting and finance

>> Administrative

>> Business development

>> Consulting

>> Creative: writing and design

>> Customer service

>> Education and training

>> Engineering

- » Human resources
- » Information technology
- » Legal
- » Managerial
- » Marketing and advertising
- » Medicine and health
- » Project management
- » Public relations
- » Sales
- » Software and programming
- » Sports
- » Web and app development

TIP

Although there's a perception that you have to be tech-savvy to get a remote job, that's not necessarily true. Most companies operate using tools you're already probably familiar with, such as email, messaging apps, and good 'ol Zoom.

FASTEST-GROWING REMOTE CAREERS

According to FlexJobs, these were the top ten fastest-growing remote career fields in 2021:

1. Virtual Administration
2. HR & Recruiting
3. Nonprofits
4. SEO & SEM
5. Bookkeeping
6. Marketing
7. Call Centers
8. Bilingual/Translation
9. Social Media Management
10. Writing

That being said, many job boards have a "non-technical jobs" category or search filter. NoDesk (https://nodesk.co/remote-jobs/non-tech) and RemoteOK (https://remoteok.io/remote-non-tech-jobs) are two examples.

REMEMBER

A remote job skill or job title can also be done in a freelancing capacity or as the basis for an online business.

Freelancing your way to freedom

If you want control over your time and income, consider freelancing. In 2021, one in three U.S. workers (nearly 53 million people), were freelancing, with freelancers making up 47 percent of remote workers. According to Pieter Levels, the founder of Nomad List, there may be as many as 1 billion digital nomad freelancers and independent workers worldwide by 2035.

Freelancing is arguably one of the fastest ways to start earning an online income because it's very versatile with low barriers to entry. You can technically become a freelancer today. All you have to do is choose a service to offer or a problem to solve and announce to the world that you're available for hire. Setting up a freelancing profile online takes a matter of minutes.

TIP

Popular websites where you can offer freelancing services include Fiverr, LinkedIn, People per Hour, Simply Hired, Toptal, Upwork, and ZipRecruiter.

Declaring yourself a freelancer doesn't mean you'll become a millionaire overnight, of course. As with anything, it takes time to grow your database of clients and build your income. However, it's one of the most common routes to becoming a digital nomad.

Freelancing offers a host of benefits, with flexibility being at the forefront. You have control over your time and schedule, how much you charge, the services you offer, and which types of clients you work with.

You could potentially earn more money freelancing than you do in an office job. According to Upwork, 44 percent of freelancers earn more working independently than they did as salaried employees.

REMEMBER

Check with your accountant or tax advisor about which type of business structure you should set up (if any). Ask them if registering a business entity or working as a sole proprietor would be better for you and get help filing your taxes, if needed. Chapter 8 discusses taxes for digital nomads.

Popular freelancing categories include:

>> Accounting and finance

>> Artificial intelligence (AI)

>> Coaching and consulting

>> Computer and information technology (IT)

>> Customer service and virtual assistance

>> Engineering

>> Graphic design and web development

>> Human resources and recruiting

>> Legal and administrative

>> Music and audio production

>> Photography and videography

>> Sales and marketing

>> Social media management

>> Software development

>> Writing and editing

There are some downsides to freelancing, however. Freelancers' incomes typically fluctuate from month to month. They don't receive the same benefits or compensation packages that many full-time employees enjoy. And they typically pay out of pocket for healthcare, fund their own retirement accounts, and pay self-employment taxes.

Then there's the hustle factor. Freelancers often need to balance their workloads with managing administrative tasks and finding new clients at the same time. Loneliness can also take a toll when you work for yourself. (See Chapter 14 for ways to overcome loneliness and meet people.)

Although freelancing has pros and cons, gig workers are generally happy campers. Upwork found that freelancers have higher job satisfaction ratings than non-freelancers, and few ever want to go back to their salaried jobs. According to Upwork, 78% of freelancers and 82% of skilled remote freelancers are satisfied with their jobs versus 74% of traditional office workers. And the gap is the same when considering a work/life balance: 73% of freelancers and 79% of skilled remote freelancers are satisfied with their work/life balance versus 65% of traditional office workers.

Should you become a freelancer? Here are a few prompts to help you decide.

>> Are you able to set and keep your own work schedule?

>> Are you comfortable with the uncertainty of earning different amounts of money each month or year?

>> Are you open to prospecting for clients? (Going to them rather than waiting for them to come to you?)

>> Do you work well with self-imposed deadlines?

>> Do you have skills or expertise that appear on freelancing sites?

If you answered, "yes," to one or more of these questions, freelancing could be for you.

REMEMBER

Successful freelancers are time management ninjas, staying organized while managing multiple projects and deadlines. See Chapter 7 for best practices on working remotely and Chapter 13 for how to stay productive as a digital nomad.

Becoming an online business owner

If you dream of building a remote company or growing a remote team, consider starting an online business.

Starting an online business involves setting up a business entity, such as a partnership or corporation. You may also have different tax responsibilities compared to individual employees and freelancers.

THE WHO'S WHO OF FREELANCERS

Who are freelancers? Upwork found that nearly half of the U.S. workforce were freelancing in 2021 (47 percent).

Freelancer demographics in 2020 according to Statista were:

- 50% Gen Z (18-22 years old)

- 44% Millennial (23-38 years old)

- 30% Gen X (39-54 years old)

- 26% Baby Boomers (55+ years old)

A benefit of starting an online business is that you can do more compared to working by yourself or exchanging your time for money. You can raise capital, bring in investors or partners, automate your income, and sell your business in the future. Starting any business or company is hard but rewarding.

For help starting an online business, reach out to your local business bureau or agency, such as the Small Business Administration. Sites such as LegalZoom offer business document templates and support.

TIP

Connect with 60,000 current and aspiring digital nomad entrepreneurs in the Digital Nomad Entrepreneurs Facebook group.

Earning passive income

Many digital nomads live on income from pensions, investments, or automated, recurring income streams. Some of the jobs described in this chapter, such as affiliate marketing, dropshipping, writing, or creating a personal brand, can all have elements of passive income. (I still earn money on videos and blogs I published four years ago.)

With passive income, you spend time, energy, and usually some money setting up an income stream once for it to pay dividends in the future.

Recurring income may come from:

>> Ad revenue

>> Affiliate marketing

>> Dropshipping and ecommerce

>> Financial trading

>> Interest income and lending

>> Investment income

>> Real estate and investment properties

>> Retirement accounts and pensions

>> Royalties from creating intellectual property

>> Self-publishing

One digital nomad I know in Thailand built a business through Airbnb arbitrage — subletting long-term rental properties for vacation rental rates. He automated the entire reservation and check-in/out processes, so he doesn't need to be in the same city or country as his guests. Other nomads live on income from long-term rental properties that they own. You could live in a country with a low cost of living on the income from a single income-earning property in a high value market such as Tokyo, Sydney, New York, or London. (Calculate your cost of living in Chapter 3.)

A few of my other nomad friends earn a monthly income through vast inventories of books and planners they sell through Amazon KDP. They spent years creating thousands of different types of products that they now monitor and manage to maintain sales momentum.

You don't need a degree to create passive income streams, but you do need patience and a willingness to learn and experiment until you find the method that works for you.

It takes time to set up passive income streams, but once you reach your target recurring income goals, you can quit your day job and experience the ultimate freedom this lifestyle provides.

REMEMBER

Although some passive income nomads eventually stop working altogether, passive income streams aren't always passive. They may require ongoing maintenance, management, and attention to prevent a decline in earnings.

Combining multiple income streams

If you don't have a salaried remote job, sometimes the key to becoming a digital nomad is to combine two or more revenue streams together. You may not be able be able to fully support a travel lifestyle by dropshipping T-shirts, but perhaps you could if you were a freelance web designer who dabbled in ecommerce on the side. This makes it interesting to answer the question, "what do you do for work?" But, in my opinion, having the freedom to work remotely and travel is more important than a job title.

When I began working online, I had two income streams: real estate commissions and relocation consulting fees. Over the next ten years, I built new income streams, one at a time, from zero to tens of thousands of dollars per month.

When I started publishing my writing online, I wrote hundreds of blog posts that didn't earn a cent. But after two years in the Medium Partner Program, I made up to $8,000 on a single article. I had similar success with YouTube and affiliate marketing, starting as a beginner with no prior experience and eventually growing my income from nothing to hundreds or thousands of dollars per month.

REMEMBER

Everyone starts with zero experience, zero subscribers, or zero income when they begin a new venture. But if you work persistently at something and don't give up, you grow your income to a level that allows you the freedom to quit your job and work from anywhere. You also gain valuable online business experience in the process.

When combining income streams, start with what you know. Focus on monetizing one skill or getting a job in your current area of expertise. Once you have a steady stream of income, add a second one and repeat. It could take a few months or years to learn a new skill and build a new revenue stream, but the extra freedom and financial stability you gain as a result is worth it.

Here are a few more examples:

>> Create a YouTube channel where you publish vlogs about your job as a mechanic. Grow and eventually monetize your channel.

>> Do online translation while driving part time for a ride-sharing company.

>> Write and sell ebooks while working as a teacher.

>> Start a cooking blog while working in a restaurant.

Considering Popular Digital Nomad Jobs

Following is an overview of the most popular ways to work remotely. Regardless of your career path, there's a digital nomad job out there with your name on it.

Accounting and finance

Accounting and finance jobs are popular for digital nomads because number crunching can be done digitally through spreadsheets, accounting and payroll software, remote collaboration tools, and websites.

You can find remote and hybrid accounting and finance jobs on remote job boards, detailed later in this chapter, and on industry-specific job boards such as Accounting Fly.

Remote job titles you can find in accounting and finance include being an accountant or bookkeeper, auditor, accounts payable/receivable specialist, CPA, financial analyst, or payroll manager, among others.

Affiliate marketing

Affiliate marketing is a form of marketing where you can earn a commission from selling third-party products and services. Affiliate marketers promote custom tracking links, which are used to track sales. Every time someone buys through your link, you earn a fixed amount or percent of the sale.

There are affiliate marketing opportunities in almost any industry, from entertainment to health and wellness. However, some industries are more lucrative than others. Financial firms, tech companies, and online gaming sites typically pay higher affiliate commissions than travel and tourism operators.

Affiliate commissions can be as low as a few cents or as high as hundreds or thousands of dollars. The amount of money you can earn per sale or referral depends on the company's terms. Some companies offer a one-time fee, while others offer a lifetime percent of recurring sales.

There are low barriers to starting out with affiliate marketing, but there is a lot of competition. Almost anyone can become an affiliate by applying directly through a company's referral program or by joining an affiliate network, such as Amazon Associates, ClickBank, or Rakuten.

Working as an affiliate is sort of like making a living through refer-a-friend programs. Except your "friends" are strangers on the Internet.

To learn more about affiliate marketing, start with an introductory course on a site such as Udemy or Skillshare and follow YouTube creators such as Santrel Media and Charlie Cheng.

Blogging and writing

Writing is one of the most oft-suggested digital nomad jobs on the web, likely because travel bloggers were some of the first people to write about the digital nomad lifestyle.

Writing is a popular digital nomad job because you can do it from anywhere. You don't need a special degree, certification, or equipment to write; you just write! Every industry needs writers, too, so there are plenty of opportunities available. However, because of the accessibility of writing, there's also a lot of competition.

When contemplating writing as your digital nomad job, consider how you would want to monetize that skill. What would you want to write about and who would you want to write for?

Here are a few ideas (besides blogging) to make money online with writing:

>> Books and self-publishing

>> Content marketing

>> Copy writing

>> Editing

>> Freelance writing

>> Ghostwriting

>> Screenwriting

>> Speech writing

>> Technical and academic writing

>> Writing for company blogs or websites

>> Writing for news and media sites

>> Writing articles and essays on Medium.com

If you choose the blogging route, prepare to commit for the long term. Making money blogging doesn't happen overnight. It could take years before you've built up a readership that you can earn a livable income from.

Former digital nomad and bestselling author, Mark Manson, estimates that "99% of blogs out there have no significant readership, and of those blogs [that do], 99% of those make little or no money." However, after "dumping ice water all over your world-conquering blogging aspirations," he says there are three compelling reasons to start a blog:

>> To promote your existing business

>> To build a platform for building a brand, testing ideas, or attracting a future book deal

>> Because you really, really like blogging

Ironically, the money you make from blogging might not come from the act of *writing*, but from the products and services you write *about*. And the community of readers you attract.

One of the top travel bloggers in the world, Nomadic Matt, started his blog in 2008. Over time, his blog has transformed into an ecommerce site where he sells books, guidebooks, and courses. He also hosts an annual travel conference in the United States and earns affiliate revenue on travel-related products.

Kiersten Rich of The Blonde Abroad has a similar business model. She sells clothing, travel products, and Lightroom presets on her website, which started out as a travel blog in 2013. She also earns income through Instagram posts, brand deals, and travel retreats.

To make a living with writing, you may want to combine strategies. For instance, John Gorman, one of the top writers on Medium, is a freelance political speech writer who also writes for tech companies.

As a writer, you have flexibility over your fee structure and the types of projects you accept. Some writers charge per word, hour, or project, while others earn a monthly salary, retainer, or portion of royalties. The options are endless!

You can browse remote writing opportunities on the remote jobs sites listed later in this chapter. There are also writing-specific jobs sites such as:

>> Contena (www.contena.co): Tools, trainings, and job opportunities to launch your remote freelance writing career.

>> Contentfly (https://contentfly.com): A place to find writing or editing jobs that pique your interest. Bonus: get paid within two days!

>> Journalism Jobs (www.journalismjobs.com): The world's largest site for finding jobs in journalism.

>> ProBlogger (https://problogger.com): A website that's been helping writers make money blogging since 2004.

>> Scripted (www.scripted.com): Job opportunities for beginning and experienced writers across 37 different industries.

>> WriterAccess (www.writeraccess.com): Connect with more than 40,000 brands looking for content writers through this site's AI-powered writer search feature.

Coaching, consulting, and teaching

Online coaching or consulting is a popular field for salaried and self-employed nomads alike. As with writing, this is another skill that you can do from anywhere with plenty of flexibility.

You can consult on any topics that you have expertise in and would like to help people with. You could teach English, consult small businesses, or be an online personal trainer. My friend, Maria Jose Flaqué, the founder of Mujer Holística, started her career as a health coach. Another friend, Freya Casey, is a former opera singer-turned online voice coach.

Coaches, consultants, and teachers are needed in all areas of expertise. Here are some ideas of ways you can make a living through coaching online:

>> Business, sales, and marketing

>> Career coaching

>> Dating, love, and relationships

>> Financial consulting

>> Health, wellness, nutrition, and weight loss

>> Life coaching and personal development

>> Personal training, sports, and fitness

You can coach people one-to-one or in groups. You can consult companies or individuals. You can work for yourself or get a salaried job teaching or consulting online. The sky's the limit!

WARNING

In some industries, such as finance, accounting, medical, and legal professions, you may need a certification or qualification to be able to provide consulting services.

TIP

Many digital nomads apply their consulting skills to an online course model, where you teach about a topic once and any number of people can buy access to your knowledge. Udemy, Skillshare, and Coursera are three online course platforms. You can teach about topics as varied as affiliate marketing, cooking, gardening, web design, and more.

Computer and information technology

Computer skills and remote work go together like peanut butter and jelly (or banana if that's more your thing).

In the field of computer science, there's a wide range of careers that are well suited to the digital nomad lifestyle, from app development to all types of programmers, software engineers, project managers, and team leaders. You can also find remote jobs in artificial intelligence, machine learning, IT security, research, and UI/UX design.

Not all computer science jobs are remote, however. Some fields, such as hardware or network engineering, may require that you work on site with special equipment.

You can find computer science jobs on all remote job boards. There are also job boards made especially for remote developers and tech workers. Here are some examples:

>> Dice (www.dice.com): Search more than 77,000 tech jobs.

>> HackerNoon (https://careers.hackernoon.com): The official HackerNoon job board is, unsurprisingly, "how hackers find work." Companies pay to post jobs, but you can search them for free!

>> Landing Jobs (https://landing.jobs): This simple and straightforward site offers tech job opportunities at Europe-based companies. You can search jobs by location, experience level, job category, or remote/in-person.

>> Ruby on Rails (https://jobs.rubynow.com): The original job board for Ruby developers has filled thousands of jobs since its inception in 2005.

Most of the world's biggest tech companies also offer remote tech job positions, including Adobe, Amazon, Coinbase, Dropbox, Facebook, Google, Quora, Shopify, Slack, Twitter, Zoom, and more.

TIP

Check company careers pages to apply for jobs directly.

REMEMBER

If you'd rather work for yourself than a company, you can become an independent remote tech worker, freelancer, or small business owner.

Interested in learning how to code? Brush up on your tech skills at Codecademy (www.codecademy.com), Envato Tuts+ (https://tutsplus.com), Free Code Camp (www.freecodecamp.org), Hackr.io (https://hackr.io), and LinkedIn Learning (www.linkedin.com/learning). You can also find online courses and bootcamps on Coursera, SkillShare,Udemy, and with your local community college or university.

Creating a personal brand as an influencer

Becoming an influencer allows you to monetize your expertise by combining different revenue streams and building a personal brand. It's a way of turning your identity, skills, and passions into a full-time job or side business.

When building your personal brand, think about how you can help people or add value. Choose a mission, idea, problem, or area of expertise that you care about. Then, choose a way to start communicating with your target audience. Some people communicate best through writing, while others prefer podcasting or video. You can also focus on building a brand on one or more social media platforms, such as Instagram, LinkedIn, or Twitter.

In 2017, YouTubers Sara and Alex James quit their jobs and gave up their house to move into their Sprinter Van. Over the course of four years, they built a brand and audience around their newfound van life. Today, they earn income through affiliate marketing, YouTube ads, brand deals, sponsored posts, and custom van builds.

Other ways to earn income through your brand include donations from your audience, received through sites such as Patreon, Twitch, and YouTube.

It takes time to create a personal brand, but the good news is that you will always be you! The more time and energy you invest into your brand over the years, the bigger you can grow your platform and impact.

Creative and design work

There are limitless ways to transfer your creative skills to the online marketplace. Graphic design and web design are two popular specialties for digital nomads. Freelance design services on Fiverr range from logo design to NFTs, book layouts, podcast cover art, landscape design, fashion, architecture, jewelry, infographics, UX/UI design, and more.

You can do design work for people or businesses or you can sell your physical or digital creations through a storefront such as Etsy or Creative Market. Photographers, videographers, and musicians can also sell their work through stock photo and video sites such as Envato, Shutterstock, Storyblocks, and Getty Images.

While many creatives become gig workers, you can also find plenty of salaried remote jobs in this arena or combine revenue streams. For example, you could do hourly client work *and* sell landing page templates or photo editing presets, too.

Some job boards and freelancing sites where you can find creative jobs are:

>> 99designs (https://99designs.com/designers): Bid for design projects anywhere in the world and get paid online.

>> Authentic Jobs (https://authenticjobs.com): The "leading job board for designers, developers, and creative pros."

- » Design Pickle (https://creatives.designpickle.com): A leading graphic design subscription service that hires global designers.

- » Dribbble (https://dribbble.com): With jobs for "the world's top designers and creatives," Dribbble is on a mission to help creatives to grow, share, and get hired. It's a social network and community as much as it is a jobs board.

- » NoDesk (https://nodesk.co/categories/creative): NoDesk has a special category just for creative jobs.

- » Robert Half Talent Solutions (www.roberthalf.com/work-with-us/our-services/creativegroup): Find freelance, contract work, and full-time jobs for the creative and marketing world.

- » Krop (www.krop.com): Find creative jobs from writing to animation to art direction and more on this site. (Primarily U.S.-based and remote jobs)

- » Media Bistro (www.mediabistro.com/jobs): Explore creative jobs in a variety of industries. There's a special section for remote jobs.

Customer service and virtual assistance

Customer service and virtual assistance are popular entry-level freelancer and digital nomad jobs.

Remote customer service representatives use technology to communicate with customers. Job activities may include customer support, problem-solving, placing orders, answering questions, and executive assistant work.

Speaking of which, virtual administration is one of the fastest-growing remote career categories, according to FlexJobs. Virtual assistants (VA) offer administrative support to companies, individuals, and teams.

VA tasks include calendar management and scheduling, customer service, data entry, social media management, and providing support in all functional areas of business from accounting to marketing, sales, and more.

You can find customer service and VA jobs on remote jobs boards, freelancing sites, Google Jobs, and through companies that specialize in matching VAs with people in need. These include Chatterboss (www.chatterboss.com), Cloudstaff (www.cloudstaff.com), iWorker (https://iworker.co), Time Etc (https://web.timeetc.com), and Zirtual (www.zirtual.com).

Digital marketing

Digital marketing is great for digital nomads because, well, it's called *digital* marketing for a reason. Digital marketing is any form of marketing that's done through the Internet.

Variations of digital marketing include:

>> Affiliate marketing

>> Content marketing

>> Email marketing

>> Marketing analytics

>> Mobile marketing

>> Online advertising

>> Pay per click (PPC)

>> Search engine optimization (SEO)

>> Social media marketing (SMM)

As with the other digital nomad jobs in this chapter, you can find a remote marketing job or apply your marketing skills to an independent contractor or consultant role. You could also start an agency or online business in the marketing field.

TIP

Find digital marketing courses, bootcamps, and certifications on Digital Marketer.com.

Dropshipping and ecommerce

Dropshipping is an ecommerce model and method of supply chain management where you act as an intermediary between the buyer and seller or manufacturer. A career in dropshipping lends itself well to a location-independent lifestyle, as you don't need to be physically present during any part of the process. With dropshipping, products are shipped directly to customers from a manufacturer, wholesaler, or fulfillment center.

A benefit of dropshipping is that there are low startup costs and risk compared to traditional retail. Dropshippers don't typically hold large amounts of inventory or assume manufacturing costs. Instead, they source products to sell and add a markup to the wholesale price.

When you buy a product on Amazon, you could be purchasing from a dropshipper. There's even an Amazon-specific type of dropshipping, called Fulfilled-by-Amazon, or Amazon FBA.

With Amazon FBA, Amazon packs, ships, and provides customer service for the products that intermediaries sell on its site. Dropshippers source products to sell from manufacturers or wholesalers, such as Alibaba, create a brand or storefront online, and then buy ads on Amazon or external traffic to drive sales.

Almost any product can be dropshipped, from jewelry to photo prints, clothing, nutritional supplements, and more. Although dropshipping can be a lucrative business, there's a lot of competition for your product to rank on the first page of search results. To succeed, dropshippers must be knowledgeable in skills such as supply chain management, digital marketing, SEO, and web development.

To learn the ropes of dropshipping and ecommerce, check out Alibaba, Amazon FBA, Dropified, Oberlo, and Shopify. Hubspot also has a library of free ecommerce resources.

For more online business and ecommerce inspiration, look up Anton Kraly of Dropshiplifestyle.com, Andrew Youderian of eCommerceFuel, Neil Patel, Noah Kagan of Appsumo, Greta van Riel, and Foundr Magazine on YouTube.

Medical and health

Healthcare is one of the biggest industries to find remote jobs in a range of career fields. You could work remotely with patients as a doctor or nurse, or behind the scenes in administration, compliance, security, staffing, and more.

Remote job titles you may come across in the medical field include being a Clinical Research Coordinator, Healthcare Data Analyst, Medical Scribe or Coding Auditor, or a Remote Recruiter, Interpreter, Physician, or Pharmacist. Teletherapy is also a growing field.

Project management

Businesses of every size and industry need project managers, and with more work being done remotely, demand for project managers is on the rise. Anderson Economic Group predicts that project management job openings will increase by 33 percent through 2027.

You can find a remote job in the project management field or be a freelance project manager. You can be a generalist or specialize in one platform or methodology such as Agile, Gantt, Scrum, Kanban, and Six Sigma.

Check out the Project Management Institute (www.pmi.org) for more about acquiring skills and certifications to work in this field.

Sales

Sales is another popular field for remote workers because all you need to sell something is an Internet connection or a phone. Sales roles are also among the highest-paying remote jobs, with many paying over $100,000 per year.

You can find a remote sales role as an account executive or manager or sales director, representative, or trainer. There are also many remote roles in business development and managements.

You can find sales jobs using the search strategies at the end of this chapter or work for yourself as an independent contractor.

TIP

Consider searching for remote sales jobs by industry, such as insurance sales, medical sales, or real estate sales.

Social media management

It seems like everyone is on social media these days, which means there's high demand for social media managers.

The three different types of social media management include:

>> Community management, moderation, and customer service
>> Content and post creation
>> Social media account growth

Some social media management jobs are specialized to one platform, such as Instagram, while others are more general in nature.

You can find social media management jobs on remote job boards, freelancing sites, or through social media itself. That's right, you can use your social media profiles to announce that you're offering social media management services. Or use the platforms to seek and reach out to your ideal clients.

Using Online Platforms to Find Work

At the beginning of this chapter, I cover the main categories of digital nomad jobs. But how do you go about finding one for yourself?

The widest range of remote jobs available is found online. But with 1.9 billion search results for "remote jobs," where do you start? This section helps you make sense of the different corners of the Internet where you can find remote work.

Navigating the top remote jobs boards

Searching remote jobs boards is a great way to kick off your remote job search and get ideas. There are thousands of different sites, so you have plenty of options. Jobs boards verify job listings before they're posted, to filter out work-from-home scams. So, you can be confident in finding legitimate jobs.

Remote jobs boards are either generalized or specialized in nature. On the larger jobs boards, you can find listings in every category. However, there are also niche jobs boards for different industries.

The most popular remote jobs boards include:

>> AngelList (https://angel.co): "Where the world meets startups." On this site, you can browse more than 100,000 jobs at 25,000+ companies.

>> Google: If you search "remote jobs" on Google, a special jobs search portal comes up where you can select different job categories. You can also search for remote jobs from companies based in a certain city or country, as shown in Figure 5-2. Or, you can search directly on Google for specific remote jobs titles.

Other keywords for searching remote jobs on Google include:

- Flexible Work
- Fully Distributed
- Hybrid Jobs
- Telecommuting
- Temporary Jobs

>> FlexJobs (www.flexjobs.com): FlexJobs has more than 30,000 hand-screened full-time, part-time, and hybrid jobs in 50+ categories. It's free to search job listings, but for access to FlexJobs' full suite of site resources, membership starts at $24.95 per month.

>> Indeed: Ten new jobs are added every second on Indeed, one of the biggest jobs portals in the world. You can create a profile, post your resume, and get career resources.

>> Pangian (https://pangian.com): Pangian considers itself the "fastest-growing remote community worldwide," with more than 85,000 members and 16,000+ job listings shared. New jobs are posted daily. It's free to create an account, but Pangian Pro starts at $8.25 per month. It also has a Facebook group called Remote & Travel Jobs & Life.

>> Remote.co: Founded by the former CEO of FlexJobs, Remote offers a large selection of verified remote job listings, as well as remote work resources and career coaching.

>> RemoteOK (https://remoteok.com): Built by the founder of Nomad List, RemoteOK has nearly 50,000 job opportunities in tech and non-technical fields. It's free to create an account.

>> The Muse (www.themuse.com): The Muse is on a mission to unite talented companies and people, offering a range of search filters to help you find the remote job you're looking for. The site is also full of blog content and resources, with an option for career coaching.

>> Virtual Vocations (www.virtualvocations.com): Virtual Vocations is a paid service featuring hand-screened telecommuting jobs. Each week, its researchers scan hundreds of specialty job boards, websites, and blogs for new job leads, bringing the best ones back to the site. You can create a free account or register for paid access with monthly, three-month, and six-month subscription options.

>> We Work Remotely (https://weworkremotely.com): More than 1,000 new jobs are posted each month on WWR, the world's "largest community of remote workers." This site is user-friendly and straightforward without any fluff. As with most remote jobs sites, you can search jobs by company, category, keyword, or job title. You can also register to receive daily job listings by email.

>> ZipRecruiter: In addition to being a place to source full-time remote jobs, ZipRecruiter is a good place to find freelance or part-time work and research salary data.

There are also job boards for different types of career niches or industries. Here are some examples:

>> Elpha (https://elpha.com): A private community for women in tech, backed by Y Combinator.

>> Europe Remotely (https://europeremotely.com): For finding remote jobs with European companies.

>> HigherEd Remote Education Jobs (www.higheredjobs.com): Remote jobs in education.

>> Idealist (www.idealist.org): Looking for more meaning in your work? Idealist offers jobs to help you change the world. You can also find internships and volunteer opportunities here.

>> Jobrack (https://jobrack.eu): Job opportunities for Eastern European workers.

>> PowertoFly (https://powertofly.com): Specializing in remote jobs for women.

>> Remoteml (https://remoteml.com): Remote machine learning jobs.

>> Travel Massive Marketplace (https://travelmassive.com/marketplace): Find remote travel industry jobs.

Exploring remote jobs forums and Slack communities

Besides job boards, plenty of work-from-anywhere opportunities can be found on forums and membership communities.

This is also a way to get tips and advice from fellow members, search members-only job listings, or even find a remote business partner or clients.

Popular remote forums and communities include:

>> #Freelance (https://slofile.com/slack/hashtagfreelance): The top Slack community for freelancers, brimming with advice and job opportunities.

>> HubSpot Remote Work Community (https://community.hubspot.com/t5/Remote-Work/bd-p/remote-work): Find news, resources, advice, and job opportunities here. Or just indulge in some remote water cooler chat.

>> Nomad List (https://nomadlist.com): A paid community of more than 50,000 remote workers around the world.

>> Nomads Talk (https://nomadstalk.com): Slack community with a remote jobs hiring channel.

>> Reddit: r/DigitalNomad (www.reddit.com/r/digitalnomad) and r/RemoteJobs (www.reddit.com/r/RemoteJobs): Places to talk all things digital nomad and find remote job opportunities.

>> Remote Clan (https://remoteclan.com): Weekly updates on remote jobs.

>> Ruby on Rails (www.rubyonrails.link): Community of nearly 20,000 developers from around the world with 28 different Slack channels.

>> Remote jobs site online communities: Many remote jobs boards also have Slack channels or Facebook groups you can join. Pangian, Remotive, and We Work Remotely and are a few examples.

>> TechRecruiter (http://techrecruiter.herokuapp.com): Find remote tech jobs through Slack.

Checking out Facebook groups

Many people enjoy searching for jobs in Facebook groups. You can find groups specific to remote jobs, the digital nomad lifestyle, or organized around specific industries or topics. The upside to searching in Facebook groups is that you might find some unique opportunities not found on job boards. There may also be less competition compared to larger sites.

A downside, however, is that it can be time consuming and difficult to stay organized regarding threads that you commented on or people you messaged.

Nomadbase is one of the largest digital nomad Facebook communities in the world, with more than 50,000 members. Safety Wing hosts the biggest group for remote work and digital nomad jobs with over 130,000 members.

If you have a specific travel destination in mind, you can also find Facebook groups with jobs for foreigners in different countries, such as the group, Jobs in Thailand for Farang with nearly 40,000 members.

Attending virtual job fairs

Virtual career fairs are becoming popular, and rightfully so. Career fairs have long been a way for employers and employees to come together. The only difference now is many have moved from college campuses and convention centers to the Internet. So you can chat with company reps without leaving the comfort of your living room.

Remote jobs boards, such as FlexJobs and We Work Remotely, host annual career fairs. You can find career fairs specific to an industry by searching online.

Check events websites, such as Eventbrite, to find more career fairs in your region. Universities also host career fairs, some of which may be open to alumni.

When preparing for a virtual career fair, keep these tips in mind:

>> Research companies and job descriptions in advance.

>> Update your resume or CV and online profiles, such as LinkedIn.

>> Adjust your cover letter and resume to every remote job you apply for.

>> Ask colleagues or mentors to review your resume and LinkedIn profile or hire a career coach for professional feedback.

>> Run your resume through a website such as Jobscan (`www.jobscan.co`) to estimate its ATS Score compared to the job description you're applying for. Many companies use Applicant Tracking Systems to sort, filter, and rank job applicants.

>> Research salary data for the companies, job roles, and industries you're interested in and set your salary terms. Remotive.io maintains a crowd-sourced list of thousands of remote job salaries at `https://docs.google.com/spreadsheets/d/1VOehQv0bOs2pY7RkKJ8RmlUbuu8UmSgzfvjR0m5hyxQ/edit#gid=1145296357`.

>> Find out how interviews will be conducted. Will you receive a list of written questions or sit for a video conference call? If you'll be on camera, make sure you have a professional background or use a virtual background or green screen. Dress professionally as you would for any interview in your industry.

>> Double-check your technology and Internet connection in advance to help prevent mishaps.

>> Look up common interview questions of the companies you're interested in. Company blogs are also a good place to start.

>> Search for podcast or media interviews with top company executives to get more insight into their hiring practices, business goals, and company culture.

>> Practice answering possible interview questions in front of a mirror or record yourself with your phone.

>> Practice making eye contact with the camera or webcam lens versus the computer screen.

Reaching Out to Real People

If the idea of applying to jobs through job boards or human resources departments overwhelms you, reaching out to people the old-fashioned way also works. This section offers four ways to find jobs through your network.

Going old school with cold outreach

Frequently, your best pool of potential employers already exists in your professional or personal network. Brainstorm a list of people you can reach out to and let them know that you're looking for a remote job or offering services as a freelancer or independent contractor.

You can also reach out to companies that aren't actively hiring but that you would want to work for and inquire about remote opportunities.

Another way to find leads is to join membership sites or trade groups in your industry. LinkedIn reported that 85 percent of jobs are filled through networking. By building relationships in your industry and contacting people proactively, you can be among the first to hear of such opportunities.

Find email addresses with tools such as Clearbit Connect (`https://connect.clearbit.com`) or RocketReach (`https://rocketreach.co`).

Leveraging LinkedIn

At the time of writing this book, there are more than 332,000 remote jobs listed on LinkedIn. There are many ways to find jobs on this platform. Give the following methods a try:

>> Search for remote jobs by selecting the Remote filter on the LinkedIn Jobs feature.

>> Reach out to your existing network of LinkedIn connections to see whether they know of any opportunities that fit your skillset.

>> Follow and engage with remote companies and key decision makers.

>> Network with people in your industry who you admire but don't know yet.

>> Update and optimize your profile. Recruiters are always using LinkedIn to find qualified candidates. If your profile shows that you're actively seeking a remote job and you're qualified for the positions you're looking for, they could find you before you find them.

Posting and engaging actively on LinkedIn, asking for endorsements, and growing your number of connections also aid in building a robust LinkedIn presence.

If you identify gaps in your skillset for the jobs you want, check out LinkedIn Learning for a suite of online courses to help advance your career.

Attracting employers through social media and content

Sometimes, your online reputation speaks for itself (in a good way, hopefully!). If you share your expertise online and position yourself as an expert in your field with your personal brand, you may be able to attract employers to you. This is a long-term strategy, but it can pay off with interesting opportunities.

Choose the platform that resonates with you the most and where potential employers will take notice, such as a blog, podcast, YouTube channel, LinkedIn, or Twitter. Post content consistently about topics in your industry.

Refer to the earlier section in this chapter "Creating a personal brand as an influencer" for tips on creating a personal brand attracting job opportunities through content creation.

Networking at conferences and events

Conferences and events are always good places to expand your network, brush up on new trends, and uncover potential employment opportunities.

You can go the traditional route and attend events in your industry or branch into something new. You can meet people in person or focus your efforts at virtual events.

TIP

Running Remote (https://runningremote.com) is the world's largest in-person remote work conference, where you can network with reps from remote companies. Search online to uncover events in your industry or find out about digital nomad conferences and events in Chapter 14.

TRADITIONAL WORK AND TRAVEL JOBS

Besides remote jobs, you can look for in-person jobs to travel or work abroad. Examples include:

- Cruise Ship Staff
- DJ or Musician
- Flight Attendant
- Foreign Service
- Hotel and Hospitality Jobs
- Language Teacher
- Musician
- Nanny or Au Pair
- Personal Trainer

- Pilot
- Private Chef
- Sailing Jobs
- Scuba Diving Instructor
- Seasonal Jobs: Ski resort staff, fishing, tree planters, festival and events staff
- Surf Instructor
- Tour Guide
- Traveling Nurse or Physician
- Volunteer
- Waiter or Bartender
- Working Holiday Visas
- Working on Farms
- Yoga Teacher

IN THIS CHAPTER

» **Getting ideas for how you could work remotely**

» **Identifying what you're good at**

» **Choosing what you want to do**

» **Articulating how you solve a problem and help people**

» **Reaching out to prospective clients**

Chapter **6**

Creating Your Own Remote Job

aving a remote job or source of income that already allows you to work from anywhere is the shortest path to becoming a digital nomad. But how do you become one if you aren't sure what to do for work? Perhaps you don't feel qualified to work remotely, you aren't sure what skills you have that would carry over to a remote career, or you've never worked for yourself before.

Fortunately, we live in a time where almost anything is possible. If you don't have a remote job yet, you can create your own. One thing's for sure, though — to become a digital nomad, you need money. If the job you have now can't be done remotely (or if you don't want to do it anymore), then it's time to find another solution.

If you've always dreamt of working for yourself or you've never found a job that suited you, this chapter is for you. Read on to find out how to monetize your skills and passions, build a new skillset, and channel your expertise into a new or existing remote career. In this chapter, I provide exercises, tips, and examples to help you decide whether you want to apply for a remote job, do your own thing, or go in an entirely new direction.

REMEMBER

There are no constraints on the type of job you can create. If you feel called to do something in the world, follow your curiosity. With enough patience, persistence, and time, you can make a living doing anything you dream up. This chapter shows you how.

Turning a Traditional Job into a Remote Job

There are a few different ways to transition from traditional work to remote work while staying in the same field, as shown in Figure 6-1. You can:

>> Apply for a remote version of your job

>> Offer consulting or freelancing services in your current area of expertise

>> Start an online business based on skills or interests you have or problems you can solve for prospective customers

>> Combine multiple jobs, business models, or remote income streams together

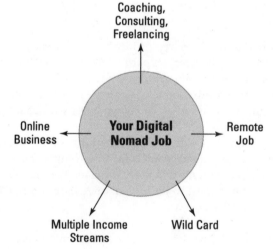

FIGURE 6-1:
Your options for different career paths as a digital nomad.

Take a look at a few examples:

>> A teacher who normally works in a classroom can teach remote-learning classes online, offer freelance tutoring, or start an eLearning company. They can also generate extra income selling books or study guides online.

>> A wedding photographer can apply for a salaried job as a remote photo editor, become a freelance product photographer on Fiverr, or start a business selling prints and presets online. They can also earn extra income selling digital photos on stock websites or shooting lifestyle photos for fellow travelers.

>> A lawyer who works in a law office can get a remote salaried job as a Compliance Officer or Remote In-House Legal Counsel. They can offer freelance services reviewing contracts, build a website offering legal consulting services, or start an entirely new online business using their legal skills.

My friend, Erika Kullberg, quit her corporate law job to build a legal startup called Plug and Law. Her company helps online businesses and entrepreneurs with their LLCs, trademarks, and contracts. She also taught herself how to become a content creator and is now one of the most followed lawyers on Instagram, TikTok, and YouTube, with an array of different income streams.

Another friend, Ashley Laux, used to make a living selling her handmade jewelry at trunk shows in the United States. Now, she's a part-time nomad with an online jewelry store, belivinglight.com. She also earns an online income giving virtual astrology readings over Zoom.

Finding examples in your field

Before designing a new career from scratch, see whether your current job already exists in a remote context. Many jobs (especially knowledge work jobs) can be done from anywhere.

So, before jumping ahead, search for your job title (or any job you want) on one or two of the following job boards. This helps you get an idea of the types of remote jobs and service providers in your field.

>> **Fiverr:** Search for a skill, service, or job title that interests you. Sort by "bestselling" to see the most popular freelance service providers. (The people who come up in the search results are proof that you can earn an online income offering similar services.)

>> **FlexJobs:** Search for your job title or a related keyword. A list of companies hiring full-time and part-time remote jobs in your field will appear.

>> **UpWork:** Search by Talent, Projects, or Jobs. See what comes up in your area of expertise.

>> **We Work Remotely:** Click "Job Seekers" and enter your job title in the search bar or select a Job Category from the search filters.

Other places to get ideas for remote careers include LinkedIn and the Careers pages of remote company websites. You can also browse online learning platforms, such as Skillshare, for ideas of skills you can offer as a service, teach, or consult about online.

Make a note of salary ranges or how people price their services as you research. Doing this gives you an idea of how much you could earn or how to set your rates as a freelancer.

What did you find out? Can you transform your job into a remote job?

The goal of this exercise is to get the wheels in your head turning about creative ways that you could work remotely with the skills you already have.

You might not have to quit what you do for work, just where you do it and for whom.

Podcast host, Palle Bo, also known as The Radio Vagabond, used to work at a radio station in his home country Denmark. When he quit his job to travel, he didn't abandon his career. He just found a different way to get paid. He funds his nomadic lifestyle by selling radio advertising and editing audio for companies while traveling the globe.

In the next section, you look closer at your skills and expertise to see how they can become the basis for a job of your creation.

Mapping your job

If you have a location-based job that you *can't* do remotely, don't fear. Your next step is to dissect your job and identify skills that you *can* do from anywhere.

Say you're a bartender who works at a bar or restaurant. Skills needed in bartending include making drinks, processing sales transactions, providing change, and talking to customers. Many of these skills can be transferred into a remote job.

If you're passionate about making drinks, you could start a YouTube channel about how to make cocktails, self-publish books of drink recipes, or create an online course that trains beginning bartenders.

If working with people is more your thing, you could become a remote customer service rep, work as a virtual assistant, or work at a remote call center.

If your favorite part about bartending is making sales or processing transactions, a remote sales role or freelance bookkeeping job could be a good fit.

Now, it's your turn.

1. **Write down a few of the skills in your current job.**

   _____   _____

   _____   _____

   _____   _____

   _____   _____

   _____   _____

2. **Circle the ones you like to do. Cross out the ones you don't.**

3. **Brainstorm possible remote jobs that require similar skills.**

   _____   _____

   _____   _____

   _____   _____

4. **Search for them online.**

   Using the bartending example, I found remote job titles including Mixology Instructor, Bartender Trainer, and Customer Happiness Agent.

You could also go in a new direction. YouTuber Futcrunch used to work at a restaurant in Venezuela, but he hated waiting tables. After searching ways to make money online, he decided to become a professional Instagram and TikTok influencer. That didn't work out well, but he eventually discovered YouTube, where he now earns a full-time income making videos for his two channels.

Analyzing Your Skills and Expertise

What if you don't think you have enough skills to work remotely? Chances are, you have some work experience under your belt. But even if you haven't yet entered the work force, you've learned valuable skills in school. The next section helps you come up with a long list of skills and strengths that can be converted into a remote job.

What you think you're good at

In this first step of this process, brainstorm a list of everything you think you're good at. It should include things you like (including hobbies) and don't like to do.

Don't judge or edit yourself during this exercise. Just compile a list of everything you can think of.

_____

_____

_____

_____

_____

TIP

If you get stuck, consider things that come easily to you, things you used to like when you were younger, and things you would do without being paid for them.

Look at your most recent resume or LinkedIn profile to pull specific skills, certifications, and qualifications you might have forgotten.

Also consider an online career aptitude or skills test that could help you uncover even more hidden talents and opportunities. Options include:

» 123 Career Test (www.123test.com/career-test): Find a career that best fits your personality.

» 16Personalities (www.16personalities.com): "Freakishly accurate" personality test that can give you insight into your work style and strengths.

» CareerExplorer (www.careerexplorer.com): Platform that has helped millions of people uncover their ideal careers.

» CliftonStrengths Assessment (www.gallup.com/cliftonstrengths/en/254033/strengthsfinder.aspx): Find out how to live your best life at work (and everywhere else).

» RedBull Wingfinder (www.redbull.com/int-en/wingfinder): Figure out what you're naturally good at and give your career some wings.

» Truity (www.truity.com): Free personality test that helps you "understand who you truly are."

What other people think you're good at

Next up, it's time to hear from other people. Ask three to five people what they think your strengths are. You can ask family members, friends, colleagues, mentors, teachers, or a supervisor.

It can be uncomfortable to ask people's opinion of you, but don't overthink it. You might be surprised at what they say!

Doing this exercise gave me the confidence to start a YouTube travel channel, which now has more than 125,000 subscribers.

TIP

If you get stuck, think about what people ask you for help with. It might be a "hard" skill, such as solving a computer issue, or it could be a "soft" skill, such as providing relationship advice.

What people pay you for

If you've ever earned a dollar, you have skills. What jobs have you had in the past? What does your current role entail? Pull up your past job titles and responsibilities and note anything that piques your interest.

Before becoming a consultant and content creator, I worked as a lifeguard, waitress, and real estate agent. Each job required different skills:

>> To be a lifeguard, you have to be physically fit, pass a First Responder or CPR test, and have a strong attention to detail.

>> Servers must be able to multitask, manage their time well, and be attentive to customers.

>> Real estate agents are responsible for sourcing and marketing property listings, negotiating contracts, and closing deals.

>> Content creators understand digital marking, SEO, writing, video editing, podcasting, sales funnels, and more.

These are just a few examples, but you can see how each skill within each job you've ever had could be a clue to a different remote career path.

Bridging a skills gap

Sometimes you want a job you aren't yet qualified for. If that's the case, start slow. Begin by learning the basics of the career you're interested in. The Internet is full of information. There are online courses (and *For Dummies* books) on almost every topic under the sun.

You can become a digital nomad in a new field by learning a new skill and gaining some work experience before looking for a remote job or giving freelancing a try. It's not the fastest way to become a digital nomad, but it's a viable one. When I started my YouTube channel, I didn't know anything about video production. But after taking a few online courses, watching tutorials, and publishing videos for two years, I was able to monetize my channel and begin producing content for freelance clients.

Matt Bowles, host of The Maverick Show podcast, used to work at a non-profit (until he was fired). The day he lost his job, he drove to a bookstore and started reading books about how to make money in real estate. Over time, he gained enough skills and experience to create a location-independent real estate investment firm, called Maverick Investor Group.

TIP

To bridge a skills gap, check out online courses on Coursera (www.coursera.org), LinkedIn Learning (www.linkedin.com/learning), Skillshare (www.skillshare.com), and Udemy (www.udemy.com).

Evaluating Your Passions

If you're going to quit or change jobs to become a digital nomad, you might as well do something you like! The ideal digital nomad job is found where your skills and passions intersect, as shown in Figure 6-2. This section helps you decide whether to work in something you're good at, passionate about, or both.

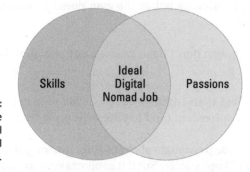

FIGURE 6-2:
How to combine passion and skill for a digital nomad job.

Leveraging what you love to do

"The core of life [is] living an existence you're proud of with people you love doing the things you like."

— PIETER LEVELS

If you think back to childhood, there were probably many things you liked to do but you didn't think you could do them for work. Working remotely, however, is a chance to re-integrate your passions into your career.

Some people say that the quickest way to lose your passion is to work in it, but I disagree. Working in something you like to do isn't always easy, but it can be very fulfilling.

Whatever you're interested in, you can turn it into a business. I once met a guy at a co-working space in Amsterdam who loved running. So, he started a blog about it. He began buying and reviewing running shoes that readers could purchase through his affiliate links. The idea was a hit. His blog took off and companies took notice, sending him products to review for free. As a result, he's now a full-time, location-independent blogger and digital nomad who can live, travel, work, (and run!) anywhere.

REMEMBER

You have the freedom and technology to work in ways your ancestors couldn't conceive of.

Finding the limits of your passion's potential

Although you *can* work in something you're passionate about, that doesn't mean you should turn *every* passion into a job. Loving travel doesn't mean you should become a travel blogger. Working out at the gym doesn't mean you should be a personal trainer.

On the flip side, though, you don't have to *love* what you do to become a digital nomad.

One nomad I know is less than enthusiastic about his remote job as a corporate travel agent. He loves the freedom (and paycheck) it provides, however.

Likewise, you might not be passionate about coding, learning affiliate marketing, or selling furniture on a Shopify store. But if it supports your location-independent lifestyle, that might be all the motivation you need.

REMEMBER

According to the Bureau of Labor Statistics, the average person has 12 jobs in their lifetime. You don't have to find the "perfect" remote job to become a digital nomad; you just need *a* job. Start with one. Gain some experience. You can always build skills, diversify your income streams, and pivot along the way.

Designing a New Job

Now that you've brushed up on your skills, researched remote jobs, and brainstormed the possibilities of working for yourself, you can use these insights to invent a new job.

Suffice to say, my previous job as a "Poker Player Relocation Consultant" has never appeared in a jobs database. But that's just one of the many weird, wild, and unique jobs that you can create for yourself as a digital nomad.

Here are more examples of real jobs that can be done remotely:

» Amazon Kitchen Gadget Dropshipper

» Certified Ethical Hacker

» Chief Listening Officer for Social Media

» Corporate Happiness Engineer

» Digital Painter

» Document Translator/Transcriber

» Ecommerce Mogul

» Medical Scribe

» Music Research Specialist

» Nail Polish Namer

» Netflix Tagger

» Online Dating Coach

» Professional Live Streamer

» Recipe Developer

» Scrum Master

» Video Game Avatar Designer

» Virtual Librarian

» Voice-Over Actor

A good way to create your own job is to start with skills you already have or combine multiple strengths or areas of expertise together. Over time, you can build multiple revenue streams this way. Here are a few examples:

>> Freya Casey was an opera singer (and single mom) in Germany who wanted to spend more time with her daughter. She took what she is best at — singing — and turned it into an online business. She's now a YouTuber who gives voice coaching lessons and sells courses.

>> Marysia Do used to teach yoga classes in person at a studio in Singapore. Over time, she transitioned to a location-independent business model leading virtual classes online and hosting retreats around the world. She also has a subscription-based yoga app.

>> Pieter Levels, the founder of Nomad List and RemoteOK, could have gotten a job as a developer at a tech company. Instead, he decided to use his coding skills to build websites and become a serial entrepreneur. He also self-published a book called The Indie Maker Handbook, which has earned him over $300,000 in sales.

Giving This Remote Thing a Try and Telling the World What You Do

Once you're ready to jump into the remote economy, it's time to put yourself out there and spread the word. This section explains how to articulate your offer, clean up your online footprint, and find your first clients.

Communicating your core offer

"The core of building companies [is] about creating a great product that gets customers that pay for it."

— PIETER LEVELS

Monetizing your skills is about more than being good at what you do. It's about who you work for and how you help them. Before looking for clients, you should first get clear on who your ideal client is and how you solve their problems.

There's a lot to say on identifying your target market and crafting a signature offer, but it all boils down to how clearly you communicate how you serve people (why they should pay you).

A short and sweet way to do this is with an "I Help Statement."

I help [target customer] do [the thing you're good at].

What do you help people do? The more specific or niched you get, the better. Saying, "I make music" is too broad. "I create podcast jingles" is better. Also consider how you can differentiate yourself from your competitors. Will you compete on price, quality, or something else? If you create podcast jingles, perhaps you offer a 48-hour turnaround time or other guarantee.

Here are some more variations:

>> Health coach: I help busy, single moms lose weight.

>> Web developer: I build websites for fintech companies.

>> Designer: I provide UX/UI design to retail brands.

>> Editor: I edit academic and scientific research papers.

>> Writer: I write sales copy for small business consultants.

>> Executive assistant: I provide virtual assistant services to accountants.

>> Digital marketer: I manage Facebook Ad campaigns for real estate agents.

TIP

If you get stuck on this part, hit the digital pavement. Do as much market research as you can by talking to people one on one and asking what they need help with. Refine your offer over time based on customer feedback.

REMEMBER

It's possible that you won't know exactly who you help and what you do when you first start out with freelancing or online business. You'll learn through doing, however. Don't sweat it.

Updating social media profiles

Before reaching out to potential clients, make sure your online presence is in tip-top shape. (That means deleting those photos of you funneling beer in college.) Potential employers and clients alike will look you up online, so you want to know what they'll find and put your best foot forward.

Review each of your social media profiles. Update your profile picture with a professional headshot. Update your About info or headline. Remove any content that conflicts with the image you want to present. Consider making your accounts private and deleting inactive accounts. On public-facing accounts, change what you share (for example, hold the cat videos). Instead, begin sharing content that would attract your ideal customer or present your professional side to the world.

Delete old tweets with TweetDelete.

Finding Your First Clients

You can find clients in two ways: going to them or attracting them to you. Both ways work, but proactively contacting people is much more effective than hoping and praying they will find you.

You don't need a fancy website or profiles on every freelancing site to start working for yourself. You just need to find where your clients hang out online and contact them. The following sections are ways to reach out to clients or bring them to you.

Your personal network

Your best source of clients is probably people you already know. Start spreading the word about the services you're offering by reaching out to your inner circle, first. These could be personal friends, acquaintances on social media, or people in your professional network. If they aren't interested or it's not a good fit, ask if they can refer you to someone else who might benefit from your help.

After contacting everyone you know who fits your target customer profile, you should have some leads to start working with. Once you get some experience under your belt, begin expanding your reach by cold-contacting other people and businesses in your target market.

When it comes to pitching your services, focus on how you add value or help people. Practice makes perfect. It's natural to feel awkward at first. But the more you do it, the more comfortable you'll feel.

You can engage potential clients through social media (but don't spam people).

Posting on online platforms

When offering services online, the biggest platforms, such as Fiverr and Upwork, are good places to start. However, they can also be the most competitive.

Consider creating a freelancing profile on more niche sites for independent workers. For example, Dribbble (https://dribbble.com), 99designs (https://99designs.com), and designhill (www.designhill.com) are online marketplaces for creatives.

If you're a highly skilled expert in your field, there are also premium platforms to find work, such as LinkedIn and Toptal, an exclusive network of the top 3 percent of talent in the world across industries. There are also sites for vetted talent within different fields, such as Gun.io for world-class developers.

TIP

For inspiration on how to structure your freelancing profile, look up the highest-rated or bestselling service providers in your field on Fiverr and Upwork.

Gathering Proof of Concept

As you begin working for yourself, keep track of the results you get for your clients. This section gives you ideas for how to market your services through presenting case studies, collecting testimonials, and getting referrals from past clients.

Collecting case studies

Plenty of companies use case studies in their marketing as proof that they can deliver results. You can do that, too! The elements of a case study include:

>> The problem your client had (why they hired you).

>> What you did to solve their problem (methods used or services provided).

>> Examples of work samples you created in the process (if applicable).

>> The results or solutions you achieved for your client.

You can share case studies privately or publicly on LinkedIn, social media, or your website.

REMEMBER

People don't necessarily care how many years of experience you have. They just want assurance that you can get them the result they want.

Getting testimonials and referrals

Word-of-mouth is *powerful*. According to the American Marketing Association, 64 percent of marketing executives say that word-of-mouth is the most effective form of marketing. It gets better, though. A Nielsen survey found that 83 percent of people trust referrals from friends and family over traditional advertising. That's great news for independent contractors and small business owners.

Before dropping a fortune on ad spend and paid traffic, ask people for referrals. It's an effective and reliable way to begin building and growing your clientele. Collect testimonials easily using a tool such as Testimonial.to.

TIP

If you're new to the idea of working for yourself, offer to provide your services for free in exchange for a case study or testimonial.

> » Communicating and collaborating remotely
>
> » Finding a comfortable work environment
>
> » Hiring remote contractors
>
> » Getting to know the best remote work tools

Chapter **7**

Adopting Best Practices for Success

Although telecommuting has been possible since the 1970s, remote work is still a new concept in practice. When the COVID-19 pandemic sent millions of people to work from home in 2020, few companies were prepared for the transition. Adapting your work style from a physical workplace to a virtual one is a challenge, to say the least.

In this chapter, I share some of the best practices I've learned for working from anywhere. You find out how to communicate on remote teams, cultivate a remote culture, find co-working spaces, hire remote help, and use remote work tools to your advantage. I also share alternatives for getting things done without adding more meetings to your to-do list.

Creating Your Work-From-Home Plan

When you eliminate daily commutes and office distractions, working remotely can be a boon for your productivity. All else held constant, that is.

Alas, working from home is challenging in other ways, with different types of interruptions than you would find in a traditional workplace. You could have kiddos running around, the TV and fridge calling your name at all hours of the day, and that pesky neighbor who decides to mow the lawn at the most inopportune times.

Remote working challenges multiply when you change accommodation often or work while traveling. Sluggish Wi-Fi speeds, noisy cafes, and sweltering humidity are a few of the conditions you might experience in your journey. That's why it helps to have a plan when you work from anywhere and everywhere.

In addition to having a daily work-from-home routine and schedule, which Chapter 13 explains, I use two strategies to create a framework for my day. One is assigning work to my most and least productive hours of the day. The other is linking different tasks with an ever-changing environment.

Maximizing your peak hours of the day

Although many businesses operate from 9am to 5pm, that doesn't mean it's *your* best time to work.

The origin of the eight-hour workday can be traced back to Spain's 6th Law of Organized Labor of 1593, when King Felipe II decided that, "all workers will work eight hours each day — four in the morning and four in the afternoon." He wanted to protect factory and "fortification" workers from the harshest hours of the day (how nice of him!). However, the eight-hour workday has stuck since then.

If it doesn't make sense to you to organize your workday around concepts conceived in the 16th century, you're not alone. Most international labor legislation was developed with *physical* labor in mind, in contrast to the *knowledge* work that most digital nomads engage in today.

Rather than working from 9am to 5pm, you can customize your workday to your needs, working during the hours that make sense for you. You don't have to sit behind your laptop for eight hours per day or five days per week. Shift your mindset from filling your time with work, to estimating how long your work will take and scheduling it accordingly.

Parkinson's Law suggests that "work (especially paperwork) is elastic in its demands on time." A task expands to fill the time given for its completion. If you don't corral your work into a schedule with deadlines, it will control you.

To figure out your best hours of the day, track your time for three days.

1. **Make a list of tasks or goals you want to complete during this period.**

2. **Before and after each task, rate your energy on a scale of 1 to 5.**

3. **At the end of each day, write down any reflections and insights.**

   How did you feel during each work block? When were you most focused or in a flow state? When did you feel tired or distracted? At what times did your energy and motivation peak or dip?

4. **After the three days, look for patterns and arrange your schedule accordingly.**

Try scheduling your most difficult tasks during your peak hours. This may include "deep" or difficult work that challenges you, such as writing, strategizing, coding, problem solving, or creative work.

Likewise, leave less cognitively demanding work ("shallow" work) to your least focused hours of the day. (Answering email and sitting in virtual meetings might come to mind.)

As a self-employed digital nomad, I've tinkered with my work-from-home schedule *a lot* over the years (and I'm constantly adjusting). I discovered that I do my best creative work before 2pm. So, I leave other tasks for later or take the afternoons off altogether. My friend, Christa Romano, a digital nomad based in Bali, is the opposite, however. Her best hours of the day are from 3-5pm (when I would rather be taking a nap!).

You can vary your schedule. I tend to get a "second wind" after dinner and sometimes work until dawn. (I often ponder the irony of being a night owl who loves mornings.) Blogger, vlogger, and digital nomad entrepreneur, Tom Kuegler, also likes to work late. He has written about why he chooses to work at night and sleep until 11am.

What about you? Are you an early bird or a night owl? Are your most productive hours of the day in the morning, afternoon, or evening?

Reflect on which time of day best fits your work style and job responsibilities.

CIRCADIAN RHYTHMS

All living things have a circadian rhythm or internal biological clock (bacteria and bugs included!).

Researchers say that being in sync with your internal and external environments is "critical" for "well-being and survival." Jet lag, working late, sleep deprivation, and blue light from screens can disrupt your circadian cycle, negatively affecting cognitive function and work quality. When choosing where to travel and when to remote work, keep your circadian cycle in mind.

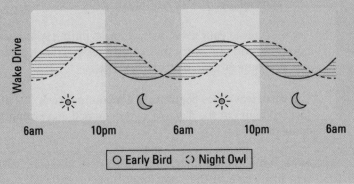

Example Circadian Rhythms

Early Birds and Night Owls Are Naturally Driven
to Be Awake or Asleep at Different Times

REMEMBER

When *not* to work is equally important. Chapter 13 has more tips on productivity and finding work–life balance as a digital nomad.

If you're in a job that doesn't fit your ideal schedule, speak with your supervisor about making changes or moving to a different time zone. If it's not possible, see Chapters 4, 5, and 6 if you're interested in quitting your job, finding a new one, or creating one that fits you better.

Mixing up your work environment

"You are responsible for shaping and choosing the environments that will ultimately shape the person you become and the destiny you have."

— BENJAMIN P. HARDY

Where you work is just as important as *when* you work. Your environment is full of cues that trigger your daily habits and influence your behavior. As author James Clear says, "the environment you surround yourself with determines the default actions that you take on a day-to-day basis."

Many studies have explored the link between workers' environments and productivity levels. As a digital nomad, you get to design your ideal work environment. Take advantage of seeking out a workspace that fits your mood and needs. If you like a bustling environment with people, you can work from a co-living or co-working space, restaurant, or café. If you need quiet time to focus, consider working in a library, private office, or from your current home base. With a Wi-Fi hotspot or a SIM card, which you can find out about in Chapter 10, you can turn anywhere into a remote office. I enjoy working from parks, museums, and hotels, but a sailboat or cottage would also do.

Working in different places (and with cool people!) can help you stay motivated and inspired. But sometimes, changing workspaces becomes a distraction. If you start to feel like deciding where to work is taking too much time and energy away from your *actual work*, experiment with adding more consistency to your workday. Having a dedicated workspace in your home or rental property can help you get into a flow state faster, as you begin to associate that space with work. You don't necessarily have to have a cushy home office, either. The corner of a studio apartment or a makeshift desk in the back of your RV will do just fine.

The moral of the story is, you're in charge. When you work from anywhere, you can get creative with where and when you work. You can even assign a project to a city or country! I once relocated to Estonia to work without distractions in a quiet place surrounded by nature. And when I lived in Iceland, I met a group of remote workers from Berlin who had traveled there to launch a new startup.

TIP

Before booking a rental property, review the property listing photos closely to ensure there's a comfortable workspace. Some apartments don't have a desk or dining room table to work from — only bar stools or a coffee table. Get more tips on finding housing in Chapter 10.

Some environments aren't suitable for work. Contrary to popular belief, few digital nomads work from pools, hammocks, or beach chairs. A best practice for remote working is to separate leisure activities from your workspace. But — no judgment — do what works best for you!

Exploring Co-Working Spaces and Alternate Workspaces

Working from a co-working space is a great way to add variety to your workday, meet new people, and get involved in your local community. Working in a shared office is also a way to combat the loneliness of working from home.

There are plenty of co-working spaces to choose from around the world. For instance, Coworker.com has more than 18,500 spaces listed worldwide, with an additional 300 new spaces joining per month.

In this section, I help you find the right co-working space for you.

REMEMBER

You can always find privacy in a co-working space by renting a private office or conference room.

Choosing a co-working space (what to look for)

With thousands of co-working spaces to choose from, you can find more than one that fits your needs, budget, and work style.

When choosing a workspace, consider the location, amenities, cost, and community.

>> **Access:** Will you have a private office, shared office, or work in a common area? Will you have access outside of business hours?

>> **Amenities:** What amenities are offered? Some spaces offer free coffee, tea, and printing, plus discounts on food.

>> **Community:** Are there any community events going on, such as meetups, happy hours, speakers, or networking opportunities?

>> **Connectivity:** What is the Internet speed? (Very important!)

>> **Location:** How far is the space from your home base? How will you get there? Can you walk, bike, or take public transportation?

>> **Platform:** Can you book the space directly or through an intermediary such as Coworker or Regus?

>> **Price:** What is the cost per day/week/month? Are there any long-term packages available?

Booking shared and remote offices abroad

Once you've decided what you want in a co-working space, it's time to give co-working a try. You can book one today, whether you're traveling or in your hometown.

On sites such as Coworker or Regus, you can book a space per day, week, or month. You can also sign up for a monthly or annual membership with access to multiple spaces for one flat rate.

>> Coworker.com (www.coworker.com) is one of the biggest platforms to find co-working memberships and day passes around the world. Coworker also offers an international Global Pass membership, as shown in Figure 7-1.

FIGURE 7-1: Coworker Global Pass.

>> Copass (https://copass.org/network) is similar to Coworker, with nearly 1,000 co-working spaces listed worldwide.

>> Croissant (www.getcroissant.com) is another booking platform where you can book workspaces worldwide with short notice.

>> Deskpass (www.deskpass.com) boasts an on-demand network of co-working spaces in more than eight countries, with individual pay-as-you-go and team options.

>> Regus (www.regus.com) is a global network with tens of thousands of locations in 120 countries.

>> WeWork (www.wework.com) offers a pay-as-you-go flex desk membership among 320+ locations in 70+ cities.

REMEMBER

Co-living operators, such as the digital nomad–friendly hotel chain Selina, also offer shared workspaces. To find more co-living operators, check with your local startup association or tourism board. iAmsterdam does a good job of collecting co-working opportunities in one place.

You can also find plenty of local co-working spaces with an online search or searching for "co-working spaces nearby" in your favorite maps app. That's how I found Common Grounds, a co-working membership in Europe.

GETTING CREATIVE WITH CO-WORKING

The best remote office for you might not be an office at all. Co-working at bars, restaurants, and hotels is a new alternative to traditional co-working spaces, whether you're looking for a private or shared space. It can also be more affordable!

- Hotels such as Marriott and Hilton offer daytime passes to use hotel rooms and lobbies as workspaces.

- NeueHouse (www.neuehouse.com) is a members-only work and social space with locations in New York for "creators, innovators, and thought leaders."

- Kettle (www.kettleos.com) is a remote teams app that offers hotel and desk booking options.

- Public libraries make fantastic workspaces. One of my favorite places to work in the world is the Amsterdam OBA Oosterdok Public Library.

- Soho House (https://www.sohohouse.com) is a global members club with access to hotels, social spaces, communities, and workspaces around the world.

- Workchew (https://workchew.com) turns hotels and restaurants into co-working spaces. Memberships start from $75/month and you can cancel anytime.

- Workspott (https://workspott.com) is a company with drop-in workspaces across London, UK, that "move with you." Memberships range from £39-139 per month.

Ensuring Smooth Cross-Border Communication

According to the Society for Human Resources Management, communication is one of the top skills employers look for in a remote employee. Thus, it's an important skill to master as a digital nomad. In this section, I help you hone your personal communication style, navigate time zones like a pro, and stay connected anywhere.

Finding your communication style

"Wherever possible I try to communicate asynchronously"

— ELON MUSK

One benefit of remote work is the ability to work *asynchronously* at different times and in different places. *Asynchronous*, or *async*, is a fancy way of explaining how you probably already communicate. Rather than calling someone on the phone or popping your head into their office to ask a question, you communicate in a way that they can respond later. If you've ever sent an email, text message, or voice memo to someone, that's async.

Inefficiencies occur, however, when remote communication happens too often in real time (conference calls) or through casual mediums, such as email and instant messages.

As a digital nomad, you can define your communication style before it defaults to what author Cal Newport describes as the "hyperactive hive mind," in *A World Without Email*. "Put bluntly," writes Cal, "the hyperactive hive mind is not compatible with remote work."

The hyperactive hive mind lives on Slack, Zoom, and email. But a working paper from researchers at the University of Chicago found that operating this way decreased productivity among IT professionals by 20 percent and increased total work hours by 30 percent.

See Figure 7-2 for a look at how remote meetings can go.

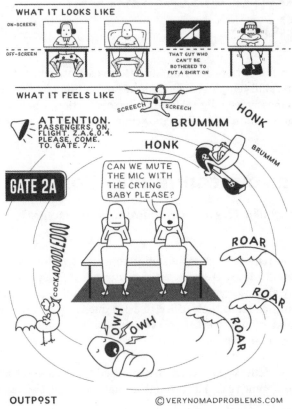

FIGURE 7-2: What remote meetings can look like.

Source: Giang Cao / Very Nomad Problems

When choosing a communication style, avoid hive mind mentality as much as possible. Opt for policies and platforms that keep email, messaging, and meetings to a minimum. Use automation tools, such as Zapier, and project management software, such as Notion or Monday, to help you stay organized and minimize chatter back-and-forth. If you have a website, rather than having an email address, consider linking a contact form with a customer service system, such as HelpScout.

Once you find a communication style you like, build your business practices around it and advise your colleagues, clients, and personal contacts on the best ways to reach you. For example, perhaps you use FaceTime to talk to family members, WhatsApp for emergencies, and a project management system for daily remote collaboration.

Use technology to guide how people can reach you. Close social media accounts and platforms where you aren't active or hire a virtual assistant to answer for you. Cancel subscriptions to apps you don't use (or want to be available on).

For some nomads, such as Pieter Levels, their preferred communication style is zero communication. Read his blog post on `https://levels.io/contact` to find out why he's "unreachable and maybe you should be, too."

Becoming an expert in converting times across time zones

Scheduling calls and meetings across different times zones can make your head spin, especially with seasonal time changes such as Daylight Saving Time. Fortunately, technology can help. Here are a few tools and apps that calculate time zone differences for you, helping you stay organized (even while crossing borders):

» **Appointment schedulers:** Companies such as Appointlet (`www.appointlet.com`), Calendly (`https://calendly.com`), and Zoho (`www.zoho.com/bookings`) automatically adjust for time zone differences.

» **Browser extensions:** Many time zone converter websites, such as Time.is (`https://time.is`), offer a desktop app or extension you can add to your web browser.

» **Dateful** (`https://dateful.com/time-zone-converter`): Convert the time between two destinations with this simple, easy-to-use website.

» **Google Calendar:** If you save Google Calendar meetings in your host's time zone, they update automatically when you change locations.

» **Remote teams collaboration software:** Software platforms for remote teams, such as Hubspot (`www.hubspot.com`), frequently have built-in time zone management tools.

» **World Clock:** Add the time zones you work in the most often to your smartphone's clock app. It's easy to tap back and forth between the current time, your phone's alarm settings, and the world clock.

» **World Time Buddy** (`www.worldtimebuddy.com`): The free version of this visual world clock, time zone converter, and meeting scheduler allows you to see the times across four destinations at once. If you upgrade to the paid version, you can see 20+ locations at the same time. World Time Buddy also has a mobile app.

Be mindful of your clients' and colleagues' designated work hours, especially if you're traveling and they aren't.

Collaborating on Remote Teams

Remote or *distributed* teams are people who work together from different physical locations using technology. They're spread out geographically but connected to a central network or virtual "headquarters." Teams can be semi-remote, fully-remote, and everything in between.

Figure 7-3 is a humorous way to illustrate how it feels to work with people on the other side of the world.

REMOTELY WELL DONE

FIGURE 7-3:
How you work
with virtual
coworkers.

Source: Giang Cao / Very Nomad Problems

Your team members will vary depending on whether you're a remote employee, freelancer, or online business owner. Your team may consist of coworkers, partners, suppliers, contractors, or customers, among others.

In this section, I share tips on how to collaborate remotely or lead a remote team.

Clarifying communication expectations

As mentioned in the previous section, issues arise where there is too much or too little communication.

Too much communication leaves people in a reactive pattern of responding to messages or sitting in meetings all day, which is counterproductive.

Insufficient communication has other implications, however, such as poor customer service, missed opportunities, delayed projects, mistakes, or lost productivity and profitability.

Remote team leaders and team members share the responsibility of clear communication. If you're a team leader, you may oversee designing communication guidelines and expectations at your company. As a remote employee, your job is to abide by policies or suggest areas of improvement.

Either way, setting clear expectations about how team members should communicate is key. Choose the communication style that works best for your company culture and helps you achieve your business goals.

TIP

Scrum and Kanban are two frameworks that help teams communicate and collaborate on projects remotely.

Here are a few tips for remote communication:

TIP

>> Be clear on your role's responsibilities, objectives, and deliverables.

>> Create standard operating procedures for team communication and update them when necessary.

>> Encourage teammates to contribute to your company's shared knowledge-base on a regular basis. Use a tool such as Loom or Yac to record your screen to answer frequently asked questions or for hiring and training purposes.

>> Provide extra context when using email to reduce the overall volume of messages sent and received.

>> Never make assumptions. If something is unclear, ask for clarification.

>> Record your thoughts and questions on a daily list and batch them once or twice per day so you don't disrupt your attention span.

>> Reply to pending messages at the end of each workday day.

>> Set defined business hours and response times.

>> Set reminders for important dates and deadlines.

When it comes to communicating on remote teams, go above and beyond. If something isn't working for you, speak with your supervisor to find a solution. Or consider if it's time for a career or company culture change.

Remaining accessible (or not)

In today's 24/7 world, it's easy to stay connected all day and digital nomads are no exception. To stay in communication, all you need is a device and an Internet connection. But studies show that remote workers are more likely to remain online rather than off.

Although you want to be accessible during work hours, be just as clear about when you *won't* be reachable. For mental health and productivity reasons, experts recommend setting a cut-off time for electronics each day.

Regardless of what time of day you choose to work, choose a daily cut-off time from technology to prevent your work from seeping into your personal life. Chapter 13 helps you strike a balance between work and play.

TIP

Consider a "No Meetings Fridays" policy. Twitter created "Perch Time" — a recurring time blocked off in companywide calendars for employees to go offline and focus without meetings or distractions.

Staying visible and bonding with your remote team members

How do you stay visible at work when your boss and colleagues can't see you? In a 2018 study on Anywhere Workers, 24 percent of respondents reported concern about opportunities for recognition and advancement in their careers.

Kevin Eikenberry, the co-founder of the Remote Leadership Institute, recommends changing your mindset from seeing yourself as someone working from home to being a "remote teammate." Harvard Business Review echoes this advice, suggesting that you get to know your remote team members and come into the office on occasion (if you have one).

Join in on an after work "happy hour" via a Slack channel or Google Hangout. Meet offline and in real life when possible, such as at an annual company retreat. Figure 7-4 shows how you might need to make more of an effort to get to know your colleagues.

FIGURE 7-4:
Office coworkers versus remote coworkers.

Source: Giang Cao / Very Nomad Problems

TIP

Offsiter and Surf Office specialize in planning retreats for remote teams.

Also ensure you're fulfilling the responsibilities of your role and producing high-quality work on time. Follow the tips in this chapter to design a schedule, work environment, and communication style that supports your success.

Being proactive and helpful never hurts, either. Turn in work early, engage your boss for feedback, volunteer to participate in special projects and events, celebrate others in your organization, and be a team player.

I also encourage you to share your knowledge online. Regardless of your area of expertise, you have skills that can help other people. By building a personal brand, you can become a recognized expert in your field, expand your network, attract opportunities, and contribute to your company's image.

THE REMOTE WATER COOLER

Do you miss office water cooler chat? Check out tools such as Sococo (www.sococo.com) and Remo (https://remo.co), virtual workplaces for remote teams. You can create custom floorplans for your remote "office" and see which team members are on a phone call or hanging out in the break room. Sococo wants to help you build relationships with people you've never met in real life, while Remo aims to "humanize the online experience."

REMEMBER Visibility isn't just about being visible within your remote organization. Use your nomadic lifestyle to meet people across industries and make connections wherever you're traveling.

See Chapter 14 for more tips on networking and making friends as a digital nomad.

Sourcing Contractors and Virtual Assistants

Hiring an independent contractor can help you grow your business or reduce the number of tasks on your to-do list. In this section, I help you determine which tasks to outsource and where to find remote help.

Deciding whether you need support

If hiring help or building a remote team appeals to you, make a list of tasks that you'd like to outsource. It may consist of tasks you don't like to do, tasks that are difficult for you, or tasks that aren't worth your time.

Consider:

>> Which tasks, if outsourced, would free up the most time for you? Social media posting, data entry, research, and administrative tasks could be options.

>> Which tasks do you like doing the least? For me, it's accounting and bookkeeping.

>> What are your weaknesses or skill gaps?

>> What tasks can only you do?

If you need a new website but aren't skilled in web design, is it worth your time to learn or hire one of millions of WordPress experts online? That's for you to decide.

The 80/20 rule can help you figure out which tasks to delegate. Try starting with the 20 percent of tasks that take up 80 percent of your time (but don't account for much of your income).

Knowing where to find contractors and administrative help

Depending on your staffing needs, you may want to hire part-time or full-time help. To find someone full time, consider posting a job opening on a remote jobs site. You can find a list of examples in Chapter 5.

Before drafting a job posting or browsing freelance sites looking for your next hire, calculate your budget and outline a list of job responsibilities.

When you're ready to hire hourly or contract help, freelancing sites such as Fiverr, Upwork, and Zip Recruiter are good places to find candidates.

There are also staffing agencies specifically for sourcing virtual assistants: Bottleneck (https://bottleneck.online), Fancy Hands (www.fancyhands.com), Virtual Staff (www.virtualstaff.ph), and Zip Recruiter are a few (www.ziprecruiter.com).

Facebook groups, forums, or your personal network are also ways to find virtual help.

Consult with your accountant or tax advisor before hiring anyone. It's important to review tax implications and reporting requirements and to know which forms or info to request from contractors. Companies such as Payoneer (www.payoneer.com) and Oyster (www.oysterhr.com) help you pay contractors and stay compliant with international hiring.

Be wary of growing your remote team too fast, too soon, especially if you're on a tight budget. Payroll expenses can increase quickly. Start small and add more people as needed.

Choosing Between Remote Work Tools

When it comes to remote tools, less is more. Every tool has a cost or subscription fee associated with it. The more remote work tools you use, the higher your potential overhead costs. There's also a learning curve for every remote work tool you add to your arsenal.

The most common virtual remote work tools I use include:

» A notes, organization, and to-do app, such as Apple Notes, Evernote, Notion, Doist, or Things for Mac

» A money transfer app, such as Wise or Revolut.

» A time zone tool, such as World Time Buddy

» A Calendar scheduler, such as Calendly or Google Calendar

» An email account and server

» Cloud storage, such as Dropbox or Google Drive

» Communication tools, such as Slack

» Customer relationship management or customer service software, such as SalesForce, PipeDrive, HelpScout, and HubSpot

» Document signing software such as Adobe Sign or DocuSign

» Email marketing software, such as ActiveCampaign or MailChimp

» Invoicing and bookkeeping software such as Freshbooks or QuickBooks

» Mind mapping software such as Miro or MURAL

» Project management software and remote collaboration tools, such as Airtable, Asana, Monday, Trello

» Sales funnel and online course hosting software such as Kajabi, Kartra, or Podia

» Screen recording software, such as Loom or Vidyard

» Time tracking software, such as Harvest or Toggl

» Web hosting software such as Dreamhost, Squarespace, or WordPress

The most common physical remote work tools I use include:

- » A comfortable chair
- » A laptop and sleeve or case
- » A laptop stand
- » A power strip and electricity adaptors or a converter
- » A wireless mouse
- » An external hard drive
- » An external monitor
- » A planner
- » An unlocked smartphone
- » An unlocked Wi-Fi hotspot
- » Blue light-blocking glasses
- » Cable organizers
- » Noise cancelling headphones and Bluetooth headphones

REMEMBER

This is not an exhaustive list. Your remote tool and app needs are unique to you and vary by industry. You may rely on developer tools, such as GitHub or InVision, or a creative suite such as Adobe Creative Cloud.

TIP

Go to `travelingwithkristin.com/dummies` for a downloadable list of remote work, online business, and freelancing tools, services, and apps, as well as travel gear.

3

Traveling and Living Abroad as a Digital Nomad

IN THIS PART . . .

Create a plan for your relocation.

Compare and contrast destinations and decide where to move.

Move with kids or pets.

Find housing anywhere or travel with co-living tribes.

Organize your stuff and tie up loose ends.

Know what to pack and bring with you.

Sort your banking, flight, phone, Wi-Fi, and other logistics.

Plan your arrival and settle into your new location.

Manage your money and taxes.

Chapter **8**

Choosing a Destination

When preparing to become a digital nomad, one question you might have in mind is, "where should I go first?"

And with so many amazing places to visit in the world, how do you decide where to go, first?

In this chapter, I guide you in choosing your first (or next) destination and deciding when to travel there. You discover the different regions of the world and some of the most popular digital nomad hotspots. I also teach you how to plan your travel around the seasons of the year and present some travel and living abroad resources. Bon voyage!

Dreaming of the Ideal Destination

Before researching where to go first, know that there are no "wrong" answers when it comes to where you decide to travel or move and why. Perhaps you've always pictured yourself in Paris. Or eating homemade pasta in Italy. Or getting lost in translation in Tokyo. Maybe your dream is to buy a house in Portugal, sail the islands of the South Pacific, or see the northern lights.

Whatever your motivation for traveling as a nomad is, there's no such thing as a "bad" destination (although some places have faster Wi-Fi than others). People crossed borders, immigrated to different countries, and traveled, lived, or worked overseas long before there were any digital nomad hotspots. Every country has pros and cons, as you find out in this chapter. If you end up somewhere that doesn't resonate with you, that's okay. Wherever you decide to go, you'll have a memorable and life-changing experience either way. Plus, you'll gain valuable insights to help you choose your next destination.

An ideal digital nomad destination is one that:

>> You want to go to

>> Fits your lifestyle

>> You can afford

>> You can travel to with a passport, visa, or other entry permit

>> Has attributes you're looking for, such as a certain community, climate, Internet speed, or things to do

To answer the question of *where* to go, consider *why* you want to travel, first. (See Chapter 2 for how to define your passion, purpose, and reason for pursuing the digital nomad lifestyle.) What are you looking for in a digital nomad destination?

_____

_____

_____

Next, write down a list of up to ten cities or countries you'd like to visit or that you see yourself living in someday (in your home country or abroad):

1. _____

2. _____

3. _____

4. _____

5. _____

6. _____

7. _____

8. _____

9. _____

10. _____

Circle or highlight the top three that appeal to you the most. Keep them in mind while reading this chapter, to help you narrow down where to go, first.

Considering Key Factors

You should consider eight elements when choosing a digital nomad destination. Each one represents a *fixed* factor (something out of your control) or a *flexible* factor (something you can control):

The four fixed factors in choosing a destination are:

>> **Border control:** How long you can stay in the country and the requirements you need to get in.

>> **Climate:** The type of weather or temperature you would like to experience.

>> **Cost of living:** If your monthly budget aligns with the average cost of living in a destination.

>> **Safety and security:** Always good to consider for your peace of mind, especially if traveling alone.

The four flexible factors in choosing a destination include:

>> **Bucket list:** Things you want to see, do, or experience.

>> **Community:** Opportunities to meet people (or lack thereof) or proximity to friends and family members.

>> **Lifestyle:** What you'd like your daily life to be like.

>> **Work environment:** Time zones, Internet speeds, infrastructure, and the like.

As a digital nomad, you have the freedom to choose the lifestyle and experiences you want to have, as well as the type of environment you want to be in. However, you may be limited by your budget, visa options, or travel restrictions.

After comparing the places you want to go to with the following criteria, you should have a good idea of which destinations will best fit your budget and needs at the moment. Consult Figure 8-1 and the following sections to help make your decision.

CONSTRAINT	FREEDOM
COST OF LIVING	LIFESTYLE
BORDER CONTROL	BUCKET LIST
SAFETY AND SECURITY	COMMUNITY
CLIMATE	WORK ENVIRONMENT

FIGURE 8-1:
The make-up of your dream destination diagram.

Border control

Before deciding which country to travel to, it helps to know if you'll need more than just a passport. To determine whether you need a visa for travel and how long you can stay, check with the immigration department in your destination or with your home country's embassy, consulate, or travel authority. You can also use a tool such as VisaHQ (https://www.visahq.com/) or WhereCanILive (https://www.wherecani.live). Chapter 9 explains more about visas and long-stay permits. Chapter 20 lists ten countries with digital nomad visas.

TIP

If you're curious about current travel restrictions and health entry requirements, look up destinations you're interested in on the SafetyWing Borderless website (https://borderless.safetywing.com/) or IATA Travel Map (https://www.iatatravelcentre.com/world.php).

Climate and seasonality

When you go to a country is almost as important as *where* you go. Use seasonality to your advantage. Planning your move based on seasonal differences can save you money, stress, and enhance your overall experience.

Seasonality refers to the actual season in a year, such as spring, summer, fall, and winter. It also relates to the ebb and flow of tourism throughout the year. Some destinations have very distinct high and low seasons for tourism. For example, summer is peak season in Ibiza, Spain, or on Italy's Amalfi Coast, while winter is low season. On the flip side, winter is high season in Whistler, Canada, while summer is the low season.

REMEMBER

Keep in mind that seasons are reversed in the northern and southern hemispheres. Ski season in the United States and Canada is from November through April, whereas in Chile and Argentina, it runs from July to September. Traveling to a destination is more expensive in the high season, which may be summer or winter, depending on where you go.

TIP

If you can't decide, travel during the *shoulder season* (between the high and low seasons). You can find better deals on flights and accommodation and fewer tourists during this time. Shoulder season in Europe is April through June and September through October, for example.

Seasonality is important for digital nomads to think about because the time of year that you arrive in a new place could reduce your housing options and increase your cost of living. A villa in Mexico that rents for $1,500/month in low season could cost $1,500/week in high season or $1,000/night during holidays such as Christmas and Easter.

Likewise, you might want to avoid traveling to the Caribbean during hurricane season (June–November) or to the Philippines during typhoon season (August–October). I once made the mistake of going to Chiang Mai, Thailand during the annual crop burning season, which takes place from January to March each year. Little did I know, many foreigners leave during that time to avoid the smoke and poor air quality. I was one of the only digital nomads in town and ended up being stuck inside all day due to the heavy smog. Lesson learned!

The time of year that you travel can also dictate which activities you can do. If you love hiking and want to check out Norway, summer would be a great time to go, when the days are long, and the weather is mild.

WARNING

Don't underestimate the effect of weather on your life and mood. Moving to a place that's cold and dark can result in Seasonal Affective Disorder, a type of seasonal depression associated with a lack of sunlight. A winter night in Tallinn, Estonia can last up to 18 hours, whereas the longest day in summer is nearly 19 hours!

Cost of living

Cost of living is a big concern for budget-conscious digital nomads looking to save money by traveling or relocating to a new place. See Chapter 3 for how to calculate your budget. But you can use tools such as Expatistan (`https://www.expatistan.com/cost-of-living`), Nomad List (`https://nomadlist.com/`), or `Teleport.org` as a quick reference.

If the average cost of living is higher than you anticipated, don't despair. It's possible to live in an expensive city or country on a budget. You can save money by living in suburbs or small towns, renting long-term or shared housing, and by eating meals at home more than going out.

For instance, if you want to move to Canada but keep your expenses low, consider a border town such as Sarnia, Windsor, or Niagara rather than Toronto, Vancouver, or Montreal. You could also move to a rural area in Alberta or Nova Scotia. According to the website, Numbeo, rent prices in Windsor are 63 percent lower than Vancouver. Grocery prices are 25 percent lower.

Likewise, if you're from Spain and work remotely from Madrid, you could move to nearby Valencia or Seville, potentially shaving about $1,000 per month off your cost of living.

Safety and security

Safety is always a concern while traveling, but safety can also be subjective. Some countries that have reputations for being "dangerous" are actually quite safe. To find out, search online for the crime rate of the city you want to go to. Also check the Global Peace Index (`https://www.visionofhumanity.org/maps/#/`), which lists the most and least peaceful countries in the world. See Chapter 15 for protecting your safety and security as a digital nomad.

Bucket list

A fun way to choose a destination is based on the experiences you want to have. What's on your bucket list? Do you want to tour Patagonia, swim in Iceland's Blue Lagoon, or experience life on the Las Vegas strip?

I moved to Costa Rica initially so I could enjoy a relaxed pace of life, surf, and practice my Spanish. I moved to Miami in 2020 to learn to DJ in one of the world's biggest music hubs. And I've spent many winters snowboarding (and remote working!) in Canada, Colorado, Japan, and Bulgaria. But you could decide to avoid winter completely and live an endless summer. Or, your goal could be to live at home year-round and spend summers in Ibiza or winters in Southeast Asia.

List three things at the top of your bucket list:

_____

_____

_____

Try to check at least one item off in the first place you go.

Community

Part of choosing a destination is considering the activities and opportunities you'll have to meet people there. You could choose a destination based on the size of its population or the presence of a digital nomad community. Chances are, there are already people remote working in the places you want to visit. Find out by searching for digital nomad or expat Facebook groups in your favorite destinations. (For more tips on meeting people and making friends in new places, see Chapter 14.)

Likewise, you might want to move somewhere with a strong business network in your industry. When I worked in affiliate marketing in the online gaming industry, I considered spending part of the year in Tel Aviv, Israel, where many of my colleagues lived.

TIP

One way to find a place to live and community at the same time is to join a digital nomad retreat group or workcation. Check out the travel calendars of Hacker Paradise (www.hackerparadise.org), Wifi Tribe (https://wifitribe.co), and Remote Year (www.remoteyear.com) to see upcoming destinations.

The term, digital nomad, wasn't coined until 1997 and digital nomad communities didn't pop up until decades later. Going off the beaten path can be a good thing. Don't feel limited to choosing a destination based on the number of nomads that are there. You might have other goals and interests or be just feeling introverted at the moment. Regardless, the world is your oyster!

Lifestyle

Quality of life is another factor to consider in choosing a destination. Which aspects of daily life are most important to you? Examples include restaurants and amenities, air quality, Internet speeds, weather, climate, healthcare, LBGTQIA-friendly, public transportation, nature, art galleries, museums, and more. Your dream may be to live in the countryside or at the beach, while someone else craves city living. Your idea of quality of life can be as simple as being walking distance from the grocery store and a good coffee shop. Or having access to public transportation and not needing a car to get around.

List three quality-of-life aspects that are important to you:

_____

_____

_____

Then, look up a city or country you want to go to on NomadList.com (`https://nomadlist.com`) to see how they rank on the quality-of-life metrics that you value the most.

TIP

Take the "where to move" quiz on Teleport.org (`https://teleport.org`) for more ideas of places that might be compatible with your needs.

Work environment

When considering where to move, make sure that the location is compatible with your job role. For example, it might become an issue if you can't make conference calls with your colleagues because you're trekking the Himalayas without Internet service! Consider these questions:

» What time zone is your ideal destination located in? Will that work for your schedule? Compare time zones on `TimeZoneConverter.com`.

» How fast is the Internet? Check global Internet speeds on `Speedtest.net`.

» Where will you work? Are there any co-working spaces in the area or does your company have an office or headquarters nearby? Look up co-working space locations on `Coworker.com`.

Scoping Out Regions of the World

Whether you're exploring far and wide or sticking closer to home, anything goes in the digital nomad lifestyle. In this section, I give you an overview of the different regions and top digital nomad destinations around the world.

After reading about where you can go, continue your research online to explore more about specific destinations that interest you. Nomad List is a good place to start, where you can find an overview of cities and countries at a glance. Figure 8-2 shows the top ten most popular destinations for digital nomads in 2022.

FIGURE 8-2:
The top ten
destinations on
Nomad List in
May 2022.

Compare what you find with your notes from the previous sections to decide where to go first. Also, check out Chapters 19 and 20, which list more places to go.

REMEMBER

Choosing a destination is partly about considering practicalities and partly about following your heart. Where do you feel called to go? Where is your curiosity leading you?

Africa

Africa is an attractive destination for nomads looking for nature, adventure, friendly people, fun nightlife, a growing startup scene, and a low to moderate cost of living. Besides the many nature reserves, national parks, and UNESCO World Heritage Sites to explore, there's also plenty of diversity in places to visit or live, from the bustling cities of Cairo and Lagos to the beaches of Cape Town and Tagazhout. Depending on where you go, you could experience a range of outdoor activities. Safaris, surfing, hiking, and mountain climbing are just a few examples.

Nomad List boasts 84 "best places" to live in Africa, with average Internet speeds of 20 Mbps and an average cost of living of $1,600 per month. Countries where you'll find nomad communities in Africa include Egypt, Morocco, Kenya, Uganda, and South Africa. Also consider Cape Verde, Mauritius, and the Seychelles for their remote work visa programs.

Some drawbacks to living in Africa (depending on the country) include safety and security risks in some areas, slow Internet with download speeds in the single digits, a lack of infrastructure, hot weather, and political instability. Some countries have a poor record on equality and human rights or have laws prohibiting homosexuality. Flight times can also be long. Travel times from Johannesburg to London range from 11 hours nonstop to 24 hours with a layover.

Asia

Southeast Asia gets a lot of attention in the digital nomad realm due to the warm climate and low cost of living found in hotspots such as Bali, Bangkok, and Vietnam.

But Southeast Asia is just the tip of the iceberg when it comes to exploring this part of the world. There are upwards of 50 countries and six different subregions in Asia, a continent which spans from Japan in the east to Cyprus in the west.

The most popular countries for Asia-bound digital nomads include Thailand, Vietnam, Cambodia, Malaysia, Indonesia and the Philippines. Japan, Taiwan, India, Sri Lanka, and South Korea are top picks as well. More adventurous nomads enjoy the "Stans:" Uzbekistan, Pakistan, and Krygyzstan.

The cost of living in Asia varies widely — from $600 per month in Nha Trang, Vietnam to more than $4,000 in Singapore.

In Southeast Asian countries, you can live like a king or queen on as little as $1,000 per month, but your expenses could double in cities such as Tokyo, Hong Kong, and Shanghai.

Besides the generally affordable cost of living, benefits to living in Asia include amazing food, a diverse culture, and fast mobile and cable Internet speeds. There are plenty of islands, beaches, and temples to explore as well. You can find significant digital nomad communities in Bali, Bangkok, Chiang Mai, Ko Pha Ngan, and beyond. It's also easy to get around by bus, train, or ferry, or to country-hop on one of Asia's low-cost airlines, such as Jet Star or AirAsia.

Drawbacks to living in Asia include often hot, humid, and muggy weather, strict health entry requirements, language barriers, cultural differences, restricted Internet in China, and a challenging time zone for certain jobs.

There aren't many digital nomad visas in Asia, yet, but some nomads apply for a study permit in Thailand or the Thailand Elite Retirement Visa, the Taiwan Gold Card work permit, or a business visa in Cambodia. Although developed areas have fast Wi-Fi networks, islands throughout Indonesia and the Philippines can be very remote with slow (or no) Internet and limited things to do.

Since the COVID-19 pandemic, many Asian countries have remained closed to tourism. Make sure to check travel restrictions before you go.

REMEMBER

Caribbean and North Atlantic

There are more than 700 islands and 30 sovereign states, territories, or overseas dependencies in the Caribbean and North Atlantic region.

One nation, Barbados, was the first country in the world to announce a digital nomad visa program in 2020 (the Barbados Welcome Stamp). Neighboring islands quickly followed, with Anguilla, Antigua, Aruba, the Bahamas, Bermuda, Curaçao, Dominica, Montserrat, and more announcing remote work programs soon after. See Chapter 9 for more about digital nomad and remote work visas.

If a laidback, tropical lifestyle full of sun, sand, sailing, and watersports appeals to you, this region of the world could be a good match. Many Caribbean nations have tourism-based economies with a friendly population that's welcoming to foreigners. English is widely spoken, and the time zones are close to the Americas and Europe. Most of the digital nomad visa programs offered are family-friendly and provide integration support on arrival.

There are some downsides, though. While the Caribbean provides a beautiful backdrop for your Instagram photos and a relaxing lifestyle, the Internet speeds are slower than the rest of the world on average (especially in Cuba). Island life can also be expensive. The cost of living on Grand Cayman for a nomad or foreigner is more than $5,000 per month. Flights in and out of the region are pricey, too, and routes aren't exactly ideal. Airfare from St. Kitts and Nevis to California starts at $1,000. Due to the high cost of living and spread-out geography, there's a smaller digital nomad community here compared to other corners of the world.

After a few months of island living, you also might crave a bit more variety in food, culture, and things to do. That is, if you ever get bored with relaxing on the beach or swimming through clear, blue water.

Central and South America

Destinations throughout Central and South America appeal to nomads for having a low to moderate cost of living, diverse climate and terrain, and plenty of opportunities for adventure. And did I mention the food, music, culture, and friendly people?

Popular countries to find nomads in this region include Costa Rica, Columbia, Peru, Ecuador, Brazil, Argentina, Bolivia, and Chile. Costa Rica is one of the top eco-tourism and retirement destinations in the world while Brazil is known for its beaches, rainforest, and dynamic cities of São Paulo and Rio de Janeiro. Nomads also flock to Buenos Aires, Argentina and Medellín, Colombia.

The cost of living ranges from $500 to $5,000 per month, depending on your location and lifestyle. You can rent a studio in La Paz, Bolivia for $150 per month. Or you can live large in a Panama City penthouse for $3,000 per month.

The infrastructure in Latin America has improved over the years. When I first moved to Costa Rica in 2002, Internet speeds at cafes hovered around 128 Kbps. In 2022, fiber optic Internet is widely available and pre-paid SIM cards with 4G and 5G Internet are plentiful. However, you'll still come across areas without Wi-Fi or a cell phone signal, especially on islands or in mountainous regions of Central and South America.

Whether you prefer a cosmopolitan city, a coastal lifestyle, or a home base in the rainforest, you can find what you're looking for in Latin America. However, theft, security, and political instability are a few of the drawbacks. Some cities have high crime rates, and many Latin countries rank in the middle or bottom of the Global Peace Index. High heat, humidity, and language barriers can also be a challenge.

Middle East

Many up-and-coming digital nomad destinations are throughout the Middle East. Amman, Jordan, Beirut, Lebanon, Tel Aviv, Israel, and Abu Dhabi and Dubai in the United Arab Emirates are a few options. Dubai, a popular beach and business destination for nomads, has a "Work Remotely from Dubai" program, launched in 2020.

Throughout the region you can find amazing food, beaches, historical and cultural sites, shopping, and a mild climate in the winter. Many countries have low to no income tax and a diverse international business community.

Drawbacks include slow Internet speeds in the single digits in some areas, language barriers, religious and cultural differences, political instability, equality and human rights concerns, and the risk of armed conflict. The U.S. State Department encourages travelers to exercise caution with regard to terrorism, drone strikes, and limited consular services in Saudi Arabia, Yemen, and Syria, among other countries. A tourist or other entry visa is required to visit most countries in the region, even for durations of 30 days. As with any international travel, do your research before traveling.

North America

North America is a popular place for digital nomads to live because, whether you're north or south of the U.S. border, the time zones align with business hubs between New York and Los Angeles. There's also typically good infrastructure throughout the continent and a diverse selection of places to live. Whether you want to be in the mountains of British Colombia, the sprawling Midwest, the beaches of Naples, Florida, or cosmopolitan Mexico City, you have options.

Destinations that rank highly for digital nomads and remote workers in the United States include Austin, Texas; Miami, Florida; Atlanta, Georgia; Hawaii; and New York. In Canada, Toronto, Vancouver, and Montreal top the list.

Mexico is one of the top digital nomad destinations in the world, and for good reason. For a cost of living between $1,000–3,000 per month, you can live in diverse locations such as Cabo San Lucas, Guadalajara, Oaxaca, or the Mayan Riviera. There's widespread fiber optic Internet and co-working spaces galore throughout Mexico. A 1 Gigabyte plan through Telmex costs MXN $1,499 or USD $76 per month. Many people also travel to Mexico to receive affordable healthcare.

A downside of living in North America is that major cities in the United States and Canada are among the most expensive in the world. (Although, living in rural areas can be a fraction of the price.) The risk of crime and gun violence is also a concern. In 2018, the United States had the second-highest volume of firearm-related deaths in the world after Brazil.

Getting permission to visit the United States and Mexico as a tourist can be tricky. Mexican authorities cracked down on digital nomads entering on tourist visas in 2022, with some nomads buzzing online about receiving a passport stamp for a one-week or one-month stay upon arrival, versus the 180-day maximum. If you would like to travel for tourism to the United States from abroad, see whether your country is part of the Visa Waiver Program at Esta.cbp.dhs.gov. Canada offers a tourist visa for stays of up to 180 days for citizens of many countries.

Another downside to living in North America is the pace of life. For some nomads, the "rat race" in the United States leads to burnout. For other nomads, the lifestyle in Mexico can feel too laidback (or, just right!). It depends on your perspective and what you're looking for. Also, the sheer quantity of foreigners living in Mexico has driven up the cost of living in areas such as Tulum, Playa del Carmen, and Puerto Vallarta.

TIP

Compare the cost of living in different cities worldwide on Numbeo.com (www.numbeo.com/cost-of-living).

Europe

Europe is one of the biggest regional hubs for digital nomads for its safety, amenities, food, culture, history, and high quality of life. Europe also has a highly developed infrastructure and transportation system. You can zip from one country to another on one of the high-speed trains and work from your laptop as the countryside whizzes by. Or hop a domestic flight on a budget airline such as Flybe, easyJet, or Wizz Air for as little as €20–50 one-way (without baggage).

Popular destinations for nomads in Western Europe include Lisbon and Porto in Portugal and Barcelona, Valencia, and the Canary Islands in Spain. Budapest, Hungary, Berlin, Germany, Krakow, Poland, Athens, Greece, and London, UK are other hotspots, among *many* others.

Countries in Eastern Europe and the Balkans such as Albania, Bulgaria, Croatia, Romania, Serbia, and Slovenia offer a lower cost of living than Western and Northern Europe while still offering a high quality of life. Romania has one of the fastest average Internet speeds in the world. And digital nomads particularly enjoy the sunny, warm climates of Albania and Croatia.

REMEMBER

Istanbul, Turkey, at the intersection of Europe and Asia, is one of the top ten digital nomad destinations on Nomad List. Antalya, Izmir, and Ankara, Turkey aren't far behind.

Also consider the Baltic States of Estonia, Latvia, and Lithuania, which are peaceful countries with nice beaches, nature, and people. Estonia is considered one of the most digital societies in the world, where Internet access is a human right. (Although half of Estonia is forested, there's Wi-Fi or mobile Internet coverage everywhere.) However, temperatures in the Baltic region often drop below freezing in the winter.

As a solo female traveler, I've enjoyed visiting Finland, Norway, and Sweden in Northern Europe. Finland was ranked the Happiest Country in the World by the United Nations five years in a row. (France is also one of my favorite countries.)

Many European countries offer digital nomad visas that allow you to work remotely for up to one year or more, such as Croatia, Cyprus, Estonia, Georgia, Greece, Hungary, Iceland, and Romania. (Get more details about digital nomad visas in Chapter 20.)

Europe is generally good for safety, fast Internet, public transportation, digital nomad community, remote work visa programs, lovers of food, history, architecture, and culture.

It's not so good for warm weather in the winter, finding air conditioning or avoiding crowds in the summer, low taxes, or budget travelers. Cities such as Geneva, Vienna, Copenhagen, and Helsinki rank among the most expensive in the world. (However, the cost of living varies widely throughout the continent.)

If you're from Europe, a benefit to living in your homeland is that you can live and work throughout the EU. You may be able to keep your healthcare plan or qualify for a European Health Insurance Card.

If you're from abroad, citizens of many countries can travel to most European nations on a tourist visa from 90 to 180 days at a time (or 180 days per 365 days in the UK). Depending on your passport, you may also be able to travel for tourism for up to 90 days per 180 days within the Schengen Zone, an area of 26 member nations. Find out if your destination is part of the Schengen at Europa.eu.

REMEMBER

Make sure to check health and entry requirements before you travel. Many European countries require proof of full vaccination status for COVID-19.

Oceania

If you're looking for adventure, consider crossing into the Southern Hemisphere. Australia and New Zealand have an English-speaking population and a blend of cosmopolitan city or coastal living mixed with rugged nature and action sports.

In Australia, nomads enjoy living in walkable, safe, developed cities such as Sydney, Melbourne, Perth, and Brisbane. The beaches of the Gold Coast and Byron Bay are also attractive.

However, Sydney, Melbourne, and Auckland rank in the Top 100 most expensive places to live according to the Mercer 2021 Cost of Living City Ranking. Wi-Fi coverage could also by spotty to non-existent in the Australian outback and rural New Zealand.

TIP

If you're between the ages of 18 and 30, you can apply for a Working Holiday Visa in Australia or New Zealand and stay for up to one year. Otherwise, register for travel authorization with Australia's Electronic Travel Authority for unlimited stays of up to three months each in a 12-month period.

Meanwhile, an island in Polynesia or Micronesia could be your next remote working home. Tahiti, Fiji, and Vanuatu are options, although they don't have much of a digital nomad community due to their remote locations, slow Internet (4 Mbps in Suva, Fiji), and hot climates.

Another downside to working on this side of the world could be the time zone for working in the United States or Europe. When it's 9am in London, it's 10pm in Samoa.

Make sure to double-check travel restrictions and requirements before heading to this region, as many countries have been closed to tourism during the COVID-19 pandemic.

Deciding Where to Go and When

Once you've evaluated different destinations against your criteria, lifestyle, and budget, choose where you'd like to go first and what time of year you would arrive.

My ideal first digital nomad destination is:

_____

Other places I would like to visit soon include:

_____

_____

_____

REMEMBER

This is just a starting point. You can always change your mind later.

GETTING PAID TO RELOCATE WITHIN YOUR HOME COUNTRY

If you're a remote worker who wants to stay within your country's borders, consider moving to a nearby city that offers a remote work incentive program. Typically found in rural areas, such programs offer cash payments, grants, tax credits, reduced rent, moving expenses reimbursement, or a combination of perks to attract remote workers.

Check with your country's national and local government agencies to see whether any remote work incentive programs are available. Ireland plans to provide grants and tax credits to residents who relocate through its Rural Future Development Policy. Portugal has a similar "Work in the Interior" program that offers up to €4,827 in financial support. Villages such as Albinen, Switzerland, Ponga, Spain, and Candela, Italy also have programs that pay people to settle there. If you can work from anywhere, it's an option for you.

And U.S. workers can now take advantage of the $100 billion in economic incentives that state and local governments generate each year to attract companies and create jobs.

The following programs could be for you if you can work in the United States and want to stay domestic, or if you want to create a home base with a low cost of living to travel from.

Make sure to read the fine print and weigh the pros and cons before applying, however. Some programs pay out incentives over months or years. Others require you to stay for a certain amount of time to qualify or open to a limited number of applicants each year. Moving to a different state may increase your tax burden.

- Ascend West Virginia (https://ascendwv.com) offers $12,000 in cash, an outdoor recreation pass worth $2,500, free co-working, and community support to people who move to West Virginia.

- Choose Topeka, Kanasa (https://choosetopeka.com) offers select professionals $15,000 in cash if you move there for a full-time position and purchase or rent a home within one year of your move.

- Hawaii Movers & Shakas (www.moversandshakas.org) is a "cultural orientation program" aimed at attracting remote workers who want to live in Hawaii for one month to one year. The first program offered 50 applicants a free round-trip flight, discounts on hotel rentals, and assistance with finding a co-working space.

- Tulsa Remote, Oklahoma (https://tulsaremote.com) offers self-employed and remote workers $10,000 in cash, free desk space at a local co-working space, and community perks and events. To be eligible, you must be at least 18 years old and move to Tulsa within the next 12 months.

- Remote Tucson, Arizona (www.startuptucson.com/remotetucson) offers approved applicants a compensation package valued at over $9,000. Incentives include $1,000 cash, Airbnb credits, a year of free Internet, and more.

- Remote Shoals, Alabama (https://remoteshoals.com) will pay you $10,000 within your first year of moving there. You must earn at least $52,000 per year as a remote employee or independent contractor from outside the local area to qualify, and relocate within six months.

- Savannah, Georgia Creative Technologies Incentive (https://seda.org/resources-and-data/incentives-database/creative-incentive) reimburses up to $2,000 in moving expenses of qualified tech professionals. Whether you are self-employed or work remotely for a technology company, you must have three years of experience, live in Chatham County for 30 days before applying, and sign a minimum one-year lease or purchase a property to qualify.

Chapter **9**

Creating Your Digital Nomad Relocation Plan

In this chapter, I help you create a plan for your relocation and get your affairs in order before you leave home. This chapter introduces the idea of slow travel and includes handy info you need to know about arranging essential services, such as banking and credit cards, and how you can access your money from different countries. You also find out about updating your identity documents, address and phone plan, organizing and shedding your stuff, and thinking ahead about tax considerations.

At the end of this chapter, I tell you about the options for visas and permits for short-term and long-term travel and how to know where you can travel with your passport.

Finding Your Travel Flow

Ever since I experienced living abroad for the first time in 2002, I've thought that if everyone in the world could spend at least *one month* of their lives in a different country, the world would be a more compassionate, empathetic, and creative place. But even if you stay close to home, being able to travel more often is a life-changing experience for the better.

One of the biggest adjustments for new digital nomads is reframing how you think about travel. For most of human history, travel for leisure was a luxury. But today, it's more accessible than ever. And as a digital nomad, you don't have to wait for your annual vacation to hit the road.

How often you should travel depends on your goals. If you're feeling energetic, you might want to see the world as fast as possible. If you're focused on building a business, you may want to take it slower. Your digital nomad goals could also have less to do with full-time travel and more to do with relocating to a new place or achieving a different lifestyle.

When creating your digital nomad relocation plan, consider how often you will change destinations and why. This section introduces the concept of batching your travel and how far to plan in advance.

Batching your travel

As mentioned in Chapter 3, you incur unavoidable setup and switching costs every time you travel to a new place. The only way to minimize or avoid such costs is through slow travel or batching your travel.

Slow travel is traveling at a pace that feels sustainable for you — see Figure 9-1. Batching your travel is a way of tying your work or personal goals to a particular location. It's also a way to travel more efficiently.

Working a full-time schedule while traveling at a fast pace can lead to burnout. But assigning a project to a location and rewarding yourself with time off when you finish can help motivate you.

For example, if you're writing a book or coding a complex project, you can choose to spend a few months in a place where there won't be many distractions. (Iceland is a good option.) Then, you can reward yourself with a month of relaxation on the beach in Mexico.

FIGURE 9-1: Find a travel pace that works for you, whatever that may be.

Source: Giang Cao / Very Nomad Problems

If you're retired, living on passive income, or working part time, you might have different priorities. Rather than isolating yourself in the Swiss Alps to work, you might have more free time for socializing and leisure activities. In that case, your travel plan could involve settling or hanging out in places with a vibrant international community and plenty of things to do.

Likewise, if you have a lot on your travel to-do list, you can arrange your itinerary in a way that saves you time and money. For example, if you have multiple conferences and events to attend, you can schedule them back to back in your calendar. Take a few weeks off for networking, learning, and fun, and then get back to your regular work schedule.

Another way to batch your travel is to plan time to visit family members. When my niece was born, I moved to California for a month to spend time with her and help her parents out. I also used to go on a "Tour de Family" where I would visit multiple family members in a row, traveling from Austin to Florida to New York and London.

REMEMBER

How much and how often you travel is a personal choice. Just remember that batching your travel can help you conserve time, energy, money, and resources without compromising your work or well-being.

Planning your travel in advance

There are trade-offs to how far in advance to plan your travel. If you plan very far out, you'll have peace of mind over where you'll be and when. But if you plan *too* far, your plans could be too rigid and it becomes difficult and expensive to make changes.

If you prefer spontaneity over structure, you could book your travel on a whim. You'll have more flexibility, but you'll likely end up paying more for last-minute transportation and accommodation.

THREE TRAVEL STRATEGIES: 6/6, 6/3/3, AND 3/3/3/3

Experienced digital nomads have become fond of three different slow travel strategies. You can employ these strategies in different countries or in different cities within your home country.

The 6/6 strategy implies that you spend six months per year in one place and six months in another. You might spend half the year in Florida and half the year in New York. Or six months in Mexico and six months in Europe. Or six months in Sydney, Australia, and six months in Perth.

With the 6/3/3 strategy, you spend six months in one place and three months each in two other destinations of your choice. This strategy works with just a passport and tourist visa if you choose one destination where you can stay for up to 180 days and two destinations where you can stay for 90 days each.

With the 3/3/3/3 strategy, you change destinations every three months. This strategy works well if you want to visit four destinations where you can stay for 90 days at a time with a passport. It's also great if you want to experience the four seasons in four different places (or avoid winter and travel to four summer destinations in a row).

The ability to spend three, six, or nine months in a destination allows you to adapt better to each place, form a daily routine, and stay productive without affecting your work-life balance too much.

Some digital nomads prefer to move every week or month, but I've found that's too fast for me to stay happy and productive. How fast and far you travel is up to you!

Plan as far in advance as feels comfortable for you. If you *know* you want to be in Prague for the Christmas Markets or celebrate your birthday in Bangkok, book it! But if you aren't sure which hemisphere you'll want to be in, let alone which country, wait until you have more clarity.

TIP

You can outsource your travel planning to a travel agent, virtual assistant, or remote work and travel group to save time. See Chapter 10 for more about travel retreats and co-living operators.

Getting Your Finances in Order

Finances can be an intimidating topic when you're thinking of cutting ties to your home country or hometown. But it's not as complicated as you may think! In the sections that follow, I explain the basics of how to access your money anywhere in the world and where to get help with international tax planning.

Updating your banking services

It's always a good idea to keep a bank account in your home country. However, it's possible that your current bank won't serve your needs if you move abroad. Small, private banks and local credit unions can sometimes be complicated to deal with from overseas. To find out, contact your bank's customer service department. Share your travel plans with them and try to anticipate any challenges before they occur. Ask if they recommend changing your account type, filling out any paperwork, or authorizing another user on your account. Many banks have adjusted during the pandemic to offer remote access to services.

The same goes for investment accounts. Check with your financial advisor to ensure that you will be able to access and manage your investments from abroad.

If you need additional banking features and services, consider opening a second account with a larger bank. The best banks for international use are typically the biggest banks.

If you are a U.S. citizen, some banks that function well abroad include Bank of America, Charles Schwab, JP Morgan Chase, Citigroup, and Wells Fargo.

If you're from outside the United States, banks that may work well for you include your home country's largest banking entities or international franchises such as BBVA Bancomer, HSBC, ING, Scotiabank, UBS, or Unicredit.

Regardless of where you're from, also see whether there are any "remote" online banks in your country (banks without physical branches). Ally, Capital One, and Discover are popular in the United States, but you can find online banks in almost every country, such as Monzo in the U.K., N26 in Germany, or Nubank in Brazil.

Before you move, ensure that:

>> You can use your debit card abroad.

>> Your card has low ATM withdrawal fees and no foreign transaction fees.

>> Your card can be easily replaced if lost or stolen.

>> Your security token can be easily replaced if lost or stolen.

>> You can change the phone number associated with receiving text messages (and that you can receive text messages to an international number, if applicable).

>> You can access a robust online banking system from anywhere.

>> You can send and receive international transfers from your online bank.

>> Your bank has accessible and helpful customer service.

TIP

Renew your debit and credit cards early in case they expire while you're out of town, to avoid shipping costs, delays, or disruptions to service. Also consider ordering a duplicate card to leave with a trusted party or in a safe deposit box.

Accessing your money with money transfer apps

One of the most revolutionary developments that has made digital nomad life easier is the invention of international money transfer apps and services, such as OFX, PayPal/Xoom, Revolut, Venmo, Wise, and Zelle.

A benefit to using money transfer apps is that it can be cheaper and faster to send, receive, and withdraw money internationally compared to a traditional bank. For example, with a traditional bank, a wire transfer could cost $20–50 and take multiple days to credit to an account, whereas with money transfer apps, you can send peer-to-peer almost instantly. Charles Schwab offers a brokerage account that digital nomads love for its competitive wire transfer fees and no ATM fees anywhere!

Money transfer apps typically have lower ATM fees compared to traditional banks, and low or no international transaction or monthly account management fees. For instance, Bank of America charges $5 per withdrawal to use an out-of-network ATM, plus a 3 percent international transaction fee for withdrawals in a foreign currency. Comparatively, Wise allows two free withdrawals per month (depending on which country your debit card was issued in) and $1.50 plus a 2 percent fee for additional transactions over $100 per month. PayPal charges an international ATM fee of $2.50 per withdrawal (with or without a currency conversion).

You can link your regular debit card or bank account with a money transfer app to fund your account, withdraw money, or send funds to other people in multiple currencies. In that sense, money transfer services act as an intermediary between your traditional bank account and an ATM or a recipient.

REMEMBER

It's a good idea to open an account with one or more banks or money transfer platforms before you leave home, so you have time to receive your debit card in the mail.

Getting paid remotely

How you receive your paycheck when you become a digital nomad depends on how you get paid now. If you work for an employer who pays you online through a bank transfer, you can probably continue receiving money to that account while traveling. Once it's in your account, you can spend it with a debit or credit card, or transfer it to an online account such as Wise.

If you work for yourself, you may receive money through a credit card processer such as Stripe or by invoicing your clients. As long as you can access the accounts or apps where you receive those funds, whether it's through PayPal, crypto, or a regular bank account, you can keep using those accounts anywhere in the world.

Say you have an online store on Amazon or Etsy, which is linked to your PayPal account. Whether you live in Manila or Mozambique, you can still use your PayPal account and link a local or online bank account to it. So, nomad or not, you wouldn't need to change anything about your payment methods.

If you're a freelancer who gets paid through a site such as Upwork or Fiverr, you should still be able to use the same bank account you have linked with the site.

If you're retired, you should be able to continue receiving your Social Security or other pension payments to your domestic bank account and use your debit or credit card abroad.

You could also transfer pension funds from your traditional bank to your Wise Revolut, or PayPal account. Then, you can withdraw it at international ATMs, spend it using your debit card, or transfer it somewhere else.

Applying for travel rewards cards

Once your banking is sorted, consider applying for some type of travel credit card. A travel credit card is a credit card that offers points or perks for travel. Many hotels, airlines, and travel providers offer a branded credit card. Large banks such as Bank of America, Chase, and Capital One also offer their own travel rewards cards.

One benefit of having a travel credit card is that you can earn points or cash back on money you would be spending anyway. If you do all your spending on a debit card, you won't earn much (or anything) in return. Meanwhile, travel credit card points can be worth three times more than cash when redeemed for travel.

Travel credit cards can also provide extra travel or car rental insurance and be a source of emergency funds through a cash advance. Credit cards can also be cancelled and replaced easily. Most credit card companies will send you a replacement card anywhere in the world via FedEx or UPS, but call your card provider to verify.

The best travel credit card for *you* is the one that meets your needs the most and that aligns with your spending habits:

>> **Airline:** Best for frequent fliers. (Almost all global airlines offer a branded credit card.)

>> **General travel:** Good if you travel often and use different travel providers. Points are worth more when exchanged for travel compared to other purchases. Examples include the Capital One Venture Card and the Bank of America Travel Rewards Card.

>> **Hotel:** Best for business travelers or if you stay in hotels often. Examples include IHG, Starwood, and Marriott Bonvoy.

>> **Platinum:** Best for luxury travelers and jetsetters. Almost all credit card companies offer a platinum or VIP card but be warned that they come with high annual fees of $500 or more. Examples include the Visa Black Card and American Express Platinum Card.

TIP

If you're traveling on a tight budget, get a fee-free or low-fee card that you can earn points on through living expenses such as groceries, gas, business, and miscellaneous purchase.

REMEMBER

Travel credit cards won't save you money if you rack up debt. Spend within your means and pay off your credit card balance every month to avoid accruing interest.

CRYPTOCURRENCY CREDIT CARDS

Crypto credit cards have become more popular and widely available in recent years. `Crypto.com` offers a Visa card with no annual fees and 8 percent back on spending (more than most traditional credit cards). It can be topped up with fiat or cryptocurrency. Crypto.com's card offers travel perks such as 10 percent back on Airbnb and Expedia bookings and unlimited airport lounge access.

Accounting for Taxes at Home and Abroad

Taxes! A complex but important topic.

The two biggest questions people typically have about taxes are:

» Do you have to pay taxes in your home country if you move abroad?

» Do you have to pay taxes in new countries that you travel through or move to?

The answers to those questions are complicated and depend on many factors, from where you're from to where you live to your type of employment or business structure. I am not a tax or financial advisor. However, the general rule is:

» The United States has citizenship-based taxation. That means citizens are subject to taxes on worldwide income and must file an annual tax return (unless you renounce your citizenship).

» If you're from outside the United States, you may be from a country with a residence-based tax system that allows you to change your tax domicile if you stop living there. A typical requirement for changing your tax base is to spend more than 180-183 days out of your home country or in another country. However, the specifics depend on your country's tax laws and the tax categories in your destination. Your business classification and earning structure may also affect tax rates and filing/reporting requirements. Hire an accountant to advise you.

The tax situation gets quite murky and complex for digital nomads, especially if you're traveling the world on a tourist visa versus applying for a work permit, residency, or other official status. Most tax systems weren't designed with remote workers in mind. But some authorities are cracking down on digital nomads who don't pay taxes anywhere, who pay taxes in one country but live in another, or who work on a tourist visa.

The good news is, becoming location independent could help you save on taxes. I've met digital nomads from countries with high taxes, such as the Netherlands, Denmark, and Sweden, who have established residency in a country such as Bulgaria, which has a 10 percent income tax rate. If you're from a U.S. state with high state income tax, such as New York or California, you could move to a state with no income tax, such as Nevada or Florida.

U.S. citizens who are physically present in foreign countries for at least 330 days per year could qualify for tax credits and deductions under the Foreign Earned Income Exclusion. Read more about it at IRS.gov.

Before traveling internationally or moving abroad, research the tax laws and tax treaties in your home and destination countries. Contact your tax advisor or the tax authorities if you have any questions.

It's best to hire an accountant or tax professional that specializes in working with digital nomads. Greenback Tax Services (www.greenbacktaxservices.com), Gracefully Expat (www.gracefullyexpat.com), Nomad Tax (www.nomadtax.io) and Taxes for Expats (www.taxesforexpats.com) are a few examples.

Deciding What to Do with Your Stuff

Throughout life, everyone accumulates stuff, which can quickly turn into junk or extra baggage that's weighing you down. It's totally normal and happens to the best of us. The longer you've lived in one house, the more stuff you probably have.

Luckily, we live in the Marie Kondo era! There's no need to keep anything that no longer brings you joy. Transitioning to a lifestyle of location independence is the perfect opportunity to clean house — literally and figuratively.

This process is easier said than done, though. You may find out that you have *a lot of stuff*. But don't worry; it's completely normal!

It might take you a few weeks or months to organize and downsize your belongings. Plan accordingly.

If you plan to be a part-time or temporary nomad, storing your stuff in your house or a storage unit could be a better option than getting rid of it.

How will you decide what to do with your stuff?

For each item, big or small, you can do one of four things with it: trash it, sell it, donate it, or keep it. (Figure 9-2 shows the four quadrants.)

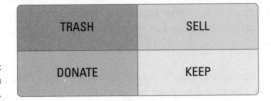

FIGURE 9-2:
What to do with
your stuff.

When trying to decide what to do with an item, ask yourself:

» Have I used this in the last year?

» Will I need this where I'm going?

» Does this item spark joy?

If the answer to one or more of those questions is, "no," it's probably time to part with that item.

Repeat the process and do as many rounds as needed until you're happy with what you have left.

What can you trash?

You can throw away anything that doesn't have sentimental or monetary value. Examples include old papers and files you no longer need, expired food products, old clothing and worn-out shoes, bath products, clutter, and knickknacks. Contact your local waste management for how to properly dispose of items.

REMEMBER

Throwing things away is the easiest thing to do, but it's also wasteful. Keep the planet in mind. Try to donate, recycle, or "upcycle" what you don't need before adding it to a landfill.

What can you sell?

You can sell anything that has value but that you don't currently need or use, or if it's something you can easily replace abroad. For example, you can sell designer vintage clothing, art supplies, furniture, appliances, cars, electronics, and other big-ticket items. You can also typically sell anything that hasn't been opened or used.

What to do with your house

Selling your home is a big decision. You can also keep, rent, or sublet your house if you plan on coming back and don't need the money. Another option is to downsize to a small apartment or studio (that can double as a storage unit for your valuables and keepsakes). You can also list your house on a home swap or house-sitting website. See Chapter 10 for more details.

TIP

Renting your home on Airbnb can be an extra source of monthly income to fund your travels if there's demand in your neighborhood. Airbnb has a step-by-step guide for how to prepare your property to rent and become a host.

What to do with your car

Depending on if you lease or own a car and what the value is, there are many options for what to do with it. The most common solution is to sell it to a private party, car dealership, or online.

If you lease a car, you can get out of your lease by listing it on sites such as LeaseTrader or Swapalease.

You can also rent your car to a private party or with apps such as Turo or HyreCar. Or donate it!

WARNING

Storing your car long term can cause it to deteriorate and lose value quickly.

What can you donate?

You can donate anything that can be used by other people. Churches, homeless shelters, and women's shelters accept donations such as food, clothing, hygiene products, and electronics. Find more examples of what you can donate on the Goodwill website.

What should you keep?

Consider keeping family heirlooms or anything with sentimental value, such as photographs, books, and other keepsakes. You may also want to keep items that you expect to use regularly in the future when not traveling, such as winter clothing if you are moving to a summer destination temporarily.

You can store valuables with trusted friends or family members or in a local storage unit. Find a local storage unit near you and choose one that is the appropriate size for your needs (with or without climate control).

Whatever you have left, you can store in a storage unit or pack it and bring it with you. See Chapter 11 for what to pack.

Getting Your Affairs in Order

When preparing to go nomadic, there are many details to think about. In this section, I share a few of the miscellaneous but important things you should do before leaving your home base.

Checking your health

Schedule a checkup with your doctor at least one to two months before you leave home to discuss your personal healthcare needs and stock up on prescription medications. Search online or check with healthcare providers overseas to see whether any medicines you need are available over the counter. Also verify with the customs or health authorities in your destination to see whether the medications you can bring into the country have any restrictions.

Make sure you're up to date with any routine and recommended vaccinations. I was once denied from boarding a flight from Colombia to Costa Rica because I didn't know I needed a yellow fever vaccine.

To find information about vaccinations at home and abroad, check with the health department or Department of Foreign Affairs in your home and destination countries. The Center for Disease Control (CDC) and the Department of Health and Human Services provide resources for U.S. travelers. You can also inquire with your doctor. The World Health Organization also provides guidelines on international travel, disease outbreaks, and vaccines (www.who.int/health-topics/travel-and-health#tab=tab_1). If you're traveling to more than one destination, the International Society of Travel Medicine provides a list of travel clinics around the world (www.istm.org/AF_CstmClinicDirectory.asp).

REMEMBER

Depending on where you're going, being fully vaccinated against COVID-19 may also be an entry requirement.

Getting insured

Every digital nomad should have an emergency travel/medical insurance plan and general health insurance that covers you at home or internationally. See Chapter 12 for details about prices, coverage, and choosing international travel/medical and health insurance plans.

The most popular international travel/medical insurance providers for nomads include:

>> SafetyWing Nomad Insurance (https://safetywing.com)

>> World Nomads (www.worldnomads.com)

>> Insured Nomads Travel Insurance (www.insurednomads.com/travel-insurance)

You can also book trip insurance with your airline (just read the policy first) and find providers on www.insuremytrip.com.

TIP

Check with your coverage provider to see whether electronics and other valuables are covered under your plan. The Professional Photographers Association of America provides insurance for technology equipment and data loss.

Travel-branded credit cards and platinum cards also may have provisions that cover travel-related incidents, rental cars, or trip cancellation, but each card is different. Check with your card's terms and conditions or call the number on the back of your card to inquire about extra coverage.

WARNING

Although many credit card companies offer trip insurance, I never rely on it as a primary insurance source. Coverage is limited and there can be a lot of exclusions in the fine print. Also, it's not accepted everywhere.

Changing your mailing address

For physical mail that can't be received electronically, enroll in a mail-scanning service or virtual mailbox. Such services provide a real street address to retain in your home country and let you open and manage your mail anytime, anywhere.

Anytime Mailbox (www.anytimemailbox.com), Earth Class Mail (www.earthclassmail.com), Sasquatch Mail (www.sasquatchmail.com), and Traveling Mailbox (https://travelingmailbox.com) are popular options among digital nomads. Prices start at $5–25 per month. However, prices may vary by how much mail you receive and if you forward any physical mail to an international address.

Many virtual mail scanning companies can also provide a physical address for you to retain in your home country.

For more robust virtual office services, Alliance Virtual Offices (`www.alliancevirtualoffices.com`) and iPostal (`https://ipostal1.com`) offer receptionist services and virtual phone numbers in addition to a physical business address. Prices start at $39–49 per month.

TIP

If you plan to be a short-term nomad, you may be able to hold or forward your mail temporarily with your local postal service.

Choosing an international phone plan

When it comes to what to do with your domestic phone plan, you have a few options:

>> Keep your current number and provider, paying for it monthly.

>> Upgrade to an international plan or switch providers to ensure you have good coverage abroad.

>> Put your plan on pause or hold, paying a nominal fee per month until you come back (if you plan on returning and want to keep the same number).

>> Cancel your phone plan and domestic number altogether.

Contact your phone provider to see which plans they offer for travel abroad. Change providers and/or plans before leaving home (if necessary). Also ensure your phone is unlocked so you can use SIM cards from anywhere in the world. (More on that in Chapter 11 on travel logistics.)

For U.S.-based digital nomads, short-term solutions such as Verizon's $10/day Travel Pass get expensive. You need something that you can afford monthly or year round.

T-Mobile offers a Magenta plan with unlimited data and texting, plus calling at $0.25 per minute in 200+ destinations. However, Internet speeds are capped at 128–256kbps.

For Android users, Google Fi is faster and cheaper comparatively. You can get 15GB of high-speed data in 200+ destinations starting at $20/month plus $10 per GB of data consumption.

Other possible international phone solutions include a OneSimCard plan or Mint Mobile's $15/month plan.

Regardless of where you live in the world, contact your home provider before departure to inquire about international roaming and data plans they offer.

TIP

I like to travel with two phones. One with my home country SIM card and a T-Mobile international plan and another unlocked phone that I can use with SIM cards in different countries. Many Android phones have dual-SIMs, however.

You can also use Internet calling plans to stay in touch almost anywhere. However, if you ditch your long-term phone number, you may need a way for people to reach you without updating your number every week or month.

In that case, I recommend getting a Skype-In number or Google Voice number that runs via Internet anywhere in the world. These services offer call forwarding, international text messaging, and email notifications. Other options include iPlum and NumberBarn.

Bringing your Internet with you

In addition to your unlocked phone, you should also travel with a Wi-Fi hotspot device. You can buy an unlocked device on Amazon that works with local pre-paid SIM cards and some international SIMs.

A second option is to sign up for an international data plan with a company such as Solis (`https://soliswifi.co`). Solis is a portable Wi-Fi hotspot that works in over 130 countries. No SIM card is needed! Instead, you enroll in its service plan and activate a pass when you need it. You can choose between monthly plans, pay-per-GB data plans, or 24-hour day passes. It's not as fast as a local 5G SIM card, but it's a reliable and portable connection you can carry with you.

TIP

The fastest and most reliable international WiFi device I have found is a Netgear Explore hotspot with EZ Mobile Data service.

Tying up loose ends

Before officially hitting the road, make sure to set up a will and/or a trust. Add beneficiaries to all your accounts, assets, and life insurance policy. Store important documents and copies of your ID and passport with your accountant, attorney, or in a safe deposit box. Scan and save or make copies of any important documents to bring with you. Also consider leaving a power of attorney for someone to act in your absence. Cancel all services you no longer need, such as utilities and subscriptions. Renew your driver's license, debit cards, and passport (if less than one year from expiration).

In addition to researching travel visas, which I talk about in the next section, applying for an International Driver's Permit is also a good idea. In some countries, small rental car agencies require it. If you live in the United States, you can get an International Driver's Permit through AAA at a cost of $30. The permit is valid for one year.

Applying for Travel Documents, Visas, and Permits

Knowing where you can travel and work as a digital nomad and for how long is an important part of the relocation planning process.

This section explains how to find out where you can travel on a passport and the different types of travel and long-term visas you can apply for.

Obtaining your passport

A passport is a document with your name, birthday, gender, and photo that verifies your identity and country of citizenship. To travel internationally as a digital nomad, you'll either need a passport or a passport *plus* some type of entry visa. Whether you need a visa depends on where you're from, where you're going, and how long you want to stay. (More on that in the next sections about visas.)

Regardless of where you're traveling, your passport should have at least six to twelve months left before the expiration date — for *each country* you're traveling to. If you plan to be gone for more than a year, you might want to have some extra runway (pun intended) on your passport's expiration date. If you don't, you may need to renew your passport from a foreign country, which involves visiting your consulate abroad.

To apply for or renew a passport, visit your country's State Department or Department of Foreign Affairs website. In the United States, it's `Travel.State.Gov`.

REMEMBER

Although many travel authorizations are electronic, it's a good idea to have extra blank pages for passport stamps and paper visas.

When you're looking to apply for a passport or renew your existing passport, follow these tips:

>> Look closely to select the correct form to apply for a new passport or renew an existing one. You may also have to fill out a different form if you're applying from overseas.

>> Start the process long before you need your passport. It can take weeks or months to receive a new passport. Give yourself sufficient time for the office to process your application and ship your travel document. If your arrival date is close, you can pay extra to have it expedited.

>> If you expect to travel overseas often, order a passport with extra pages. It costs a little bit more, but it's a small investment when you consider that your passport is valid for ten years. Every country is different, but in the United States you have the option of ordering a passport with 28 or 52 pages.

WARNING

Make sure to keep your passport in tip-top condition. Avoid getting it wet and be mindful of the expiration date. Some of my digital nomad friends have been barred from boarding a flight or deported because their passports were too close to expiring or in a compromised condition. Renew your passport within one year of its expiration date to be safe.

TIP

A passport cover helps you protect your passport and keep it dry. It also makes a nice souvenir or gift!

Knowing if you need a visa for travel

A visa gives you permission to travel to (or through) a foreign country. There's an array of different visa categories you could apply for, but some of the most common short-stay visas are for business, tourism, family, or leisure purposes.

For many years digital nomads have worked remotely while traveling primarily on tourist visas. It's a controversial practice, however, because working on a tourist visa is illegal.

The problem is, there weren't any visas created specifically for remote workers until 2020. Most visas were designed with tourists or other short-term visitors in mind. But with the digital nomad movement gaining in popularity over the years, authorities have been taking more notice and cracking down on the practice of working remotely while traveling on a tourist visa and deporting people on occasion.

This is a bit of a grey area because most digital nomads travel for leisure and tourism to begin with — they just happen to be funding their travels with income earned online or accessed remotely. However, that doesn't mean it's allowed.

REMEMBER

Just know that a tourist visa does *not* give you permission to work in-person or remotely in a foreign country.

In the next section, I describe a few categories under which you can legally reside or work in a different country long term. But this section focuses on ways to get authorization to enter a country as a visitor or travel there short term on a tourist visa.

Most tourist visas grant permission to stay in a country for 30–180 days at a time. The following are a few examples of how long you can stay in different countries for tourism with a U.S. passport:

>> 30 days: Egypt (visa required), Jordan (visa required), Thailand, Qatar

>> 90 days: Colombia, Costa Rica, Malaysia, Morocco, South Korea, EU Schengen Zone

>> 180 days: Armenia, Belize, Canada, India, Mexico, Panama, United Kingdom

>> 365 days: Albania, Georgia, Palau

Some visas are single-entry, where you can enter once per visa application. Some are multiple entry, allowing you to travel in and out without applying for a new visa (Australia ETA visitor visa). Some visas renew each time you re-enter (Costa Rica, Panama, and Mexico tourist visa), while others have limits such as 90 days per 180 days (Schengen visa).

Whether you need to apply for a visa for travel and tourism depends on the strength of your country's passport, your desired length of stay, your purpose for travel, and the entry requirements of the country you're going to.

If you're from a country with a *strong passport* (one that allows you to travel visa-free or with a visa on-arrival to many countries), you may not need to apply for a visa to enter a country for tourism purposes.

The Henley Passport Index ranks 199 countries by their mobility score, or ease of travel. Singapore, Japan, and South Korea are tied at the top of the list as the three strongest passports of 2022. The United States, Canada, Australia, New Zealand, Mexico, and most countries in Europe also rank highly. Citizens of Japan and Singapore can travel to 192 countries visa-free, while South African citizens can travel to 104 countries, Armenian citizens can travel to 65 countries, and Iraqi citizens can visit 28 countries without applying for a visa.

In countries where you can travel visa-free or with a visa on-arrival, you can receive a stamp in your passport at border control instead of applying for a visa in advance. In some cases, you may need to fill out an immigration form on the plane or at the airport, but you can also do that sometimes when you check in for your flight online or through your airline's app.

Some countries require a travel permit or electronic authorization for entry. The United States has an online application called ESTA for citizens and nationals of countries in its Visa Waiver Program. Australia has a similar ETA visitor visa that you can apply for through the Australian ETA app.

REMEMBER

You are responsible for knowing whether you need a visa and collecting the correct documents for travel. Your airline will ask you to show your travel documents at check-in (online or in person) and again before boarding.

You may also come across *transit* visas, which give you permission to pass through a country on a layover or stopover en-route to your final destination. And some countries have *exit visas*, which grant permission to leave a country. An exit visa usually comes in the form of a fee or departure tax you pay at the airport or the border. In the Dominican Republic, it's $20.

You can find out about entry, exit, and visa requirements for your destination through one of following resources:

>> Your home country's government website or Department of Foreign Affairs: In the United States, it's the State Department. In the UK, it's the Foreign, Commonwealth & Development Office.

>> Your home country's consulate or embassy in your destination: For example, if you're a Finnish citizen traveling abroad, look up the Embassy of Finland in the country you're going to.

>> Your destination country's immigration website or its embassy/consulate in your home country.

>> Third-party services that provide visa information and application support, such as Visa Hq (www.visahq.com/visas.php), CIBTvisas (https://cibtvisas.com), or the Passport Index (www.passportindex.org/visa.php).

TIP

To find the right resource online, you can also search for "travel advice *your country* citizens."

WARNING

Never overstay your visa. You could be liable for fines or deported and banned from re-entering (in some cases, for years). Tread with caution!

Applying for visas

Typical visa requirements include filling out an application online, submitting a recent passport photo (and sometimes your passport itself), and paying processing and shipping fees.

Authorities may also ask for a copy of your itinerary, health data, and proof of income (such as bank statements) to ensure that you can afford to support yourself when you're there. In some cases, you may also need to present a letter or invitation from a local company, resident, or sponsor and appear in person at a consulate for an interview.

The processing time for a visa may be weeks or months.

Some visas and permits can be obtained while you are already abroad, but many require that you apply *before* you travel. Travel authorization can be emitted electronically. Often, it's in the form of a physical stamp or card glued into your passport.

Again, you can apply for a visa on your own through your destination country's government portal, embassy, or consulate. Or you can hire a service to help you.

Some countries allow a one-time tourist visa extension, such as Thailand. You can extend a Thai tourist visa for 30 days with a 1,900 Baht (USD $55) fee. Other countries require you to exit the country for a period of time before you can re-enter as a tourist. Non-EU citizens visiting countries in the European Schengen Area for business or tourism can get a short-stay visa (permission to stay for up to 90 days in a 180-day period). Tourists from approved countries traveling to the UK can stay for up to 180 days in a one-year period.

WARNING

As you're planning your itinerary, keep in mind:

>> Even if you have a valid passport and visa, entry to a country is not *guaranteed*. The immigration or border control agent who stamps your passport can deny you from entering for any reason (or no reason) at all.

>> A travel or tourist visa is *not* permission to work or live in a country. You need a work permit, residency permit, or digital nomad visa for that.

>> Always check the entry and exit requirements *before* booking travel to any country.

Extending your stay

Figure 9-3 shows a humorous look at the housing cycle a digital nomad goes through.

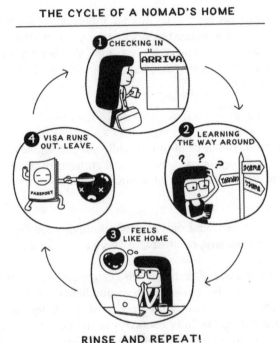

THE CYCLE OF A NOMAD'S HOME

1 CHECKING IN
ARRIVAL

2 LEARNING THE WAY AROUND

3 FEELS LIKE HOME

4 VISA RUNS OUT. LEAVE.

RINSE AND REPEAT!

© VERYNOMADPROBLEMS.COM

Source: Giang Cao / Very Nomad Problems

FIGURE 9-3:
The cycle of a
nomad's home.

If you want to stay in a country for longer than your short-stay or tourist visa allows, you need to apply for a for a long-stay visa, immigrant visa, or other permit such as work or study. Although many countries now offer visas specifically for digital nomads (which you can read about in the last section), you may qualify for other types of visas as well.

The specifics between the application requirements, costs, and details of different visa types vary by country. But the following is a list of long-term visas, work permit, and residency categories you can choose from:

>> **Business:** For people starting a small business in another country. Citizens from countries that are part of the Dutch American Friendship Treaty can apply for the 2-year DAFT permit in the Netherlands with a minimum investment of €4,500.

>> **Investor:** For people who invest in a business, financial products, real estate, or other investment. Also known as golden visas, which you can read about in the next section.

>> **Freelancer:** For people who provide services as an independent contractor. Germany offers a three-month "Freiberufler" (freelancer) visa and an artist visa with an option to renew for up to three years.

>> **Marriage:** For people who get married to a citizen from a different country. Many countries also have a civil partnership visa.

>> **Medical:** For people getting surgeries or other procedures. Colombia has a Special Temporary Visa for Medical Treatment for stays of 6–12 months with an application cost of $175.

>> **Rentista:** For people who earn money from a stable or fixed income. Examples include the Portugal D7 visa, the Spain Non-Lucrative visa, and the Costa Rica Rentista visa.

>> **Retirement:** Specifically for retirees living on pensions. You can apply for the Panama and Costa Rica "Pensionado" visas if you have a retirement income of at least $1,000 per month.

>> **Startup or Entrepreneur:** For people looking to start a business abroad, rent office space, and hire employees. The Japan startup visa is for entrepreneurs who can invest at least JPY 5,000,000 or USD $38,500 in Japan. It's valid for up to one year and includes business plan support.

>> **Student:** For students looking to study abroad. Can also be used for learning a foreign language in many countries, including Hungary and Thailand. Thailand also has a Self-Defense Education visa valid for learning Muay Thai, while Japan has a Cultural Activities Visa for learning skills such as Japanese drumming (Taiko), flower arranging (Ikebana) or hosting a tea ceremony.

>> **Work:** For people looking to work for a local company. The Taiwan Gold Card is a multi-use work permit and resident visa, popular among digital nomads, that allows cardholders to live and work in Taiwan for 1 to 3 years.

>> **Working Holiday:** For people aged 18–30 who want to work while on holiday in countries such as Australia, Ireland, New Zealand, and South Korea.

REMEMBER

Many of these visas offer a path to temporary or permanent residency, which can lead to citizenship. Most countries require that you apply for a visa before arrival.

A strategy that many digital nomads on tourist visas employ is to go on a "visa run." This is accomplished by leaving a country and re-entering — even sometimes the same day. Sometimes, the act of re-entering a country is enough to extend your stay. Costa Rica is one country well known for allowing foreigners to renew their tourist visas by leaving and re-entering. However, re-entry is not guaranteed and immigration authorities have been clamping down on perpetual tourism.

Other countries have restrictions on how soon you can re-enter as a tourist after your visa expires. Tourists can stay in the EU Schengen area for up to 90 days per 180-day period (all 26 member nations included). If you stay for 90 days in a row, you must leave for 90 days before re-entering. You can also spread the days out over six months. However, it's difficult to get an extension on a Schengen tourist visa. Most digital nomads travel to a nearby European country that's not in the Schengen, instead, such as Bulgaria, Romania, Ireland, or the UK. But applying for a digital nomad visa in Europe would be a more long-term solution. (Of course, EU nationals have "free movement" to live and work in another EU country without a time limit.) You can find apps that calculate your days in the Schengen Zone in your phone's app store.

TIP

One common misconception about becoming a digital nomad is that you must give up your citizenship or apply for permanent residency to travel abroad long term or relocate to another country. However, that's not the case. Although you need permission to reside in another country, it doesn't affect your citizenship status in your home country.

Golden visas

There's a lot of buzz online about golden visas. It's not Willy Wonka's "Golden Ticket," but it's close.

A *golden visa* is a passport or residency permit you can purchase. It's called "golden," because it's expensive. Although most countries offer such a program, the cost of the investment varies dramatically between nations. However, it's usually a six- or seven-figure sum.

A golden visa provides you with long-term residency or citizenship status, depending on the type of visa you buy. A residency-based golden visa, such as the Greece Golden Visa, allows you to live, work, and study in the country for five years. Many countries offer the option to renew your visa or apply for citizenship after five years. Meanwhile, a citizenship golden visa, such as the Turkey Citizenship by Investment Program, makes you a citizen of that country, complete with a passport and local ID number.

The cost of a golden visa depends on how much demand there is to live in a country. Safe countries with low taxes, mild climates, developed economies, and a high quality of life are the highest in demand.

Sample costs of a golden visa include:

>> **Costa Rica:** $150,000 investment

>> **Greece:** €250,000 investment

>> **Ireland:** €1,000,000 investment

>> **Malta:** €30,000 government contribution and/or €250–320k investment

>> **Monaco:** Varies, but "sufficient financial resources" include at least €500K in a local bank account and a property deed or long-term tenancy agreement.

>> **Panama Investor Visa:** $40,000–80,000

>> **St. Kitts and Nevis:** $150,000 donation

>> **Thai Elite Visa:** THB 600,000 (USD $17,500) for 20-year residency

>> **Turkey:** $250,000 investment

>> **UK:** £2,000,000 investment

The main benefit of getting a golden visa is that it's a relatively fast and straightforward path to long-term residency or citizenship in a country. Having a second passport gives you more freedom and flexibility. However, it's more expensive than other long-stay options.

Some countries require that you stay there for a certain number of days per year to be able to keep your residency status, although this isn't the case if you become a citizen.

You can apply for a golden visa through an immigration authority or with the help of a local attorney. Private, third-party companies also offer golden visa services. For a downloadable list of digital nomad resources, including a list of golden visa service providers, visit www.travelingwithkristin.com/dummies.

TIP

It isn't necessary to get a golden visa or residency permit to make a country your tax domicile. You can pay taxes in a foreign country without residency or citizenship status.

Digital nomad visas

The world's first digital nomad visas were introduced in 2020 in response to societal changes caused by the coronavirus pandemic. Barbados and Estonia were the first countries to announce digital nomad visa programs for remote workers, followed by at least forty others in the two years that followed.

The concept of a digital nomad visa is exciting because it means that governments are competing to attract remote workers to boost their economies. It also means you can live and work *legally* as a digital nomad in countries you could previously only visit on tourist visas or with costly residency, work, or investment visas.

Most digital nomad and remote work visas allow you to remain in a country for up to one year but some offer an option to renew. Before traveling abroad, see whether the country you want to visit offers a digital nomad visa. Someday, I predict that every country in the world will offer a visa specifically for remote workers.

Application requirements vary, but may include:

» Possessing a valid passport

» Filling out an application online

» Showing proof of a remote job or self employment

» Submitting travel reservations and insurance info

» Paying an application fee ranging between $100 and $1,000 or more

» Appearing at an embassy or consulate for an interview

Applying for a digital nomad visa provides peace of mind that you can work remotely from your laptop while living as a tourist in another country. It also provides more time to stay in a country compared to a tourist visa, yet it's easier and more affordable to obtain compared to many of the long-term residency options mentioned in the previous sections. In some cases, you can renew a digital nomad visa for up to three years, whereas most tourist visas are valid for around 90 days.

REMEMBER

A digital nomad visa is *not* a work permit, permanent residency status, or path to citizenship. It's temporary permission to work for yourself or a remote company based *outside* of the country you apply in.

Find out about how to apply for ten new digital nomad visa programs in Chapter 20.

TIP

You can find digital nomad visa information on most countries' tourism board and/or immigration websites. I also maintain a Digital Nomad Visa Database (www.digitalnomadbootcamp.com/digital-nomad-visa-database) with information on 46 digital nomad and remote work visa programs.

Chapter **10**
Finding Housing Abroad

Finding your new home away from home is typically one of the most exciting (and daunting) parts of becoming a digital nomad. As a nomad, your home is wherever you are. You may even have more than one home base. So, it's important to find places where you'll feel comfortable, safe, and productive when working in a new city.

In this chapter, I tell you about the many housing options you'll have as a digital nomad, from chalets to sailboats. Plus, how to make the best choice every time you move. I share where you can find both short- and long-term housing, as well as suggest some untraditional ways of living nomadically, from couchsurfing to pet-sitting.

I also provide tips on negotiating prices, avoiding scams, and paying your rent across borders.

TIP

For more housing tips, you can download a rental property checklist at travelingwithkristin.com/dummies.

Checking Out the Different Housing Types

After spending so many years of my life as a digital nomad, I've lost count of how many times I've moved. But each place has been special and memorable in a unique way.

I've hung my hat from various ocean view villas in Costa Rica, a beachfront palapa in Nicaragua, a garden studio in Amsterdam, a cottage in a Montenegrin vineyard, and a cabin atop the mountains of Bulgaria. I've lived on cruise ships, in hostels, in homestays, and in co-living spaces from Europe to Japan.

In this section, prepare to explore a plethora of exciting housing options that await you as a digital nomad!

Short term: Just a few weeks or months

During your travels, you'll have the option to rent short- or long-term and private or shared accommodations. The most common type of housing for nomads is short-term housing, or anything six months or less in duration.

This category includes nightly and weekly rentals such as hotels, vacation rentals, and any type of dwelling that's offered month-to-month.

A benefit of renting short term is that you have more flexibility with less commitment compared to renting something long term. Plus, you don't have to buy any furniture! Short-term rental properties are almost always fully furnished with linens, cutlery, and appliances included. If you're lucky, your host or landlord will even include toiletries and kitchen staples such as coffee, tea, cooking oil, and condiments. You may find, however, that some short-term rentals are minimally furnished or lacking the same quantity and quality of pots, pans, pillows, and comforts you have at home.

TIP

Look closely at property photos and listing details to see what's included. If something is unclear, you can ask the owner for a copy of the property inventory.

Short-term rentals are easy to book through well-known international booking sites such as Airbnb and VRBO, as well as through local vacation rental agencies. Although short-term properties rarely require a signed rental agreement, it's a good idea to ask for one for rentals longer than a month or so.

WARNING

Short-term rentals may be deemed illegal in some locations. Barcelona and Thailand have cracked down on Airbnb bookings in recent years, while the minimum lease term in Costa Rica is technically three years. Homeowners association rules may also prohibit short-term rentals in some buildings and complexes. Do an online search or ask the host to verify before booking.

The downside to renting short term is that it's more expensive compared to properties with a longer lease term. Also, rather than paying month-to-month, a payment for your entire stay could be required up front. A general rule is, the shorter the rental period, the higher the price per night.

You can often book short-term rentals online with a credit card. Vacation rental sites also offer extra security and support in the case of a dispute.

Utilities, such as water, electricity, and Internet, are usually included in the price of a nightly or weekly rental. But, the longer the rental period, the more likely it is for utilities (especially electricity) to be additional.

Long term: Settling in for a few months or longer

Any rental that's six to twelve months or more is considered a long-term rental. As with short-term rentals, owners can decide how long of a lease term to offer their properties for and what to include in the rent. Long-term rentals can come furnished, unfurnished, or semi-furnished.

The benefit of renting long term is that it provides you with some stability as a nomadic traveler. You'll also have a physical mailing address that you can use to establish proof of residency should you need it for your job or a long stay work permit or visa. Long-term rentals are also the most affordable type of rental properties. The longer your lease, the cheaper your rent tends to be.

Renting long term does have downsides, though. Long-term rentals can have hidden costs. Utilities are almost always additional and depending on the country, you may need to pay an agency fee to a property representative or realtor. This is usually a commission or "finder's fee" equal to half a month or one month's rent.

REMEMBER

Booking a long-term rental also locks you into a long-term contract, so make sure you like the property and location before committing!

While you can book short-term rentals based on photos or videos without much of a risk, you should always visit a long-term rental property in person *before* signing a lease or wiring funds. Or send a trusted person to view it on your behalf.

WARNING

If you sign a long-term rental contract but vacate the property early, you may forfeit your security deposit and pre-paid rent. You may also have to pay a penalty. Always have a local attorney review a rental contract before you sign. Ask questions about the housing law and your rights as a tenant if you're unsure.

Some long-term rental search sources, such as classifieds websites, can be full of scams and fake properties that don't exist. Get more tips on avoiding scams in an upcoming section.

Private: Having the place all to yourself

When searching for properties online, you can choose between private or shared rentals.

Private rentals are just that — private to you! This is the way to go if you want your own space or are traveling with kids. You also have less noise and distractions compared to living with people. And you don't have to argue over who takes out the trash.

The downside to private rental properties is that they're more expensive than shared rentals. Then again, you're paying a premium to have the entire place to yourself. You could also feel lonely or less safe compared to living with others.

Private housing includes:

>> Long-term furnished and unfurnished rentals

>> Monthly furnished rentals

>> Weekly furnished rentals

>> Private sublets

>> Nightly hotels and vacation rentals

To sort for private rental properties, check the box for "private" in the search filters of any website.

Shared: Back to college dorm life

Shared housing comes in many forms. In some cases, you may opt to share a room with other people, but you can also rent a private room in a shared house or building.

The biggest benefits to renting shared housing are the cost savings and the people you meet. Sharing your rent with other people means more money for other things. You also have people to hang out with. If you live with locals, they can give you tips about the area. If you live with other travelers, you can explore together.

The downside to shared housing is a lack of privacy, more distractions, and potential personality differences or conflicts with your roommates or housemates.

Shared housing types include:

>> Renting a private room in a shared house or flat

>> Renting a shared room in a shared house or flat

>> Renting in a hostel

>> Couchsurfing

>> Co-living

Co-living: Living in a community

Co-living is slightly different than shared housing in that it's an organized form of communal living centered around a community or social experience. Co-living establishments are run by co-living operators, while shared housing is more informal, offered by private parties with a room (or couch) for rent.

Residents in co-living spaces typically have private rooms and shared leisure and common areas. But you could also have the option to rent a shared house, room, or even a sleeping pod!

A benefit of co-living is that there's usually a building manager or representative who organizes regular meetups between the residents. Co-living spaces may also come with amenities and perks such as a gym, co-working space, concierge, and restaurant or coffee bar.

Co-living is a great way to meet people — both travelers and locals alike. I've lived in co-living spaces from Norway to Japan. When I lived at Roam Tokyo, fellow residents and I co-worked together, cooked together, and hosted networking events at our building. The first day I moved in, I also had the pleasure of experiencing my first Japanese tea ceremony.

When I lived at the Arctic Coworking Lodge in Norway, my housemates and I held frequent "family" dinner parties. We also went surfing, hiking, and foraging together.

When staying at the Blue Bank in Iceland, I shared a house with entrepreneurs from New York and Finland. Each morning, we would go for a swim in the local community pool and sip coffee in the hot tub before taking a cold plunge and heading to the local co-working space. It was definitely an invigorating way to start the workday! Lucky for me, my roommate also loved baking cinnamon rolls.

As with any form of shared housing, the biggest downside to co-living is a lack of privacy compared to living alone. If you're the type of person who needs peace and quiet all the time, you might get annoyed with the guy who plays guitar in the living room at all hours of the night. Or the woman who sits in video calls all day without using headphones. So, before booking a co-living space, inquire about the layout of the accommodations and workspace, as well as any house or community rules.

Regardless, many people I've met through co-living remain my close friends to this day.

TIP

You can find co-living opportunities almost everywhere in the world. Selina (www. selina.com) is a popular co-living hotel chain catering to digital nomads. You can find smaller, local operators through location-specific online searches or by searching Coliving.com.

Travel retreats: Joining a travel tribe

Travel groups are also a form a co-living. Your home-away-from-home may end up being a group of *people* rather than a specific *place*. Plenty of mobile travel tribes roam the planet at any given time. You can join weekly, monthly, or yearly work-travel groups, depending on what you're looking for.

Examples of co-living retreat operators include Hacker Paradise (https://hackerparadise.org), Noma Collective (www.noma-collective.com), Remote Year (www.remoteyear.com), Unsettled (https://beunsettled.co), and WiFi Tribe (https://wifitribe.co).

Joining a travel tribe is a great option if you're solo traveling or just want to meet people. Imagine that it's your first time in a foreign country and you already have a built-in group of friends waiting for you when you arrive!

It's also nice to have your housing expenses and logistics simplified. Rent, utilities, and some transportation, Internet, and co-working expenses are wrapped together when you live with a co-living group. Meals and excursions are sometimes available as well.

When traveling with such a group, you also have access to a chaperone, host, or organizer to help you. It's great to have someone to go to if you have any questions about the local area.

WARNING

A downside to living with a co-living tribe is that it's usually much more expensive than renting on your own. You could pay $2,000–3,000 per week or month to live with a nomadic retreat group in a country where the monthly (total) cost of living is only $1,000.

To spend a month with Unsettled in Argentina starts at USD $3,500. However, Numbeo estimates the cost of living in Argentina at $1,500 per month. So, you're definitely paying a premium for the amenities and support that living with a community provides.

On the other hand, more conveniences are included. Remote Year boasts "comfortable accommodation," 24/7 access to a workspace, health and safety support, curated local experiences, ground and air transportation, and a local team leader.

Some providers also include airport pick-up and throw in a SIM card for your phone upon arrival.

Alternative housing: Boats, treehouses, and beyond

Whether you rent long term or short term, shared, or private, you will have a range of unique accommodation options to choose from as a digital nomad.

Have you ever thought about living in a sailboat, houseboat, treehouse, or tiny house? You can find all these options plus shipping containers, caves, domes, and more online.

In 2022, Airbnb released a feature called categories, where you can search properties by much more than their size, price, and location. Figure 10-1 shows a selection of castles you can rent around the world.

Renting a shipping container is slightly more affordable. Figure 10-2 shows a sample of shipping containers you can rent in Colombia for as low as $35 per night.

Fancy dabbling in #VanLife? Browse vans and RVs for rent on sites such as EscapeCampervans.com, IndieCampers.com, and Roadsurfer.com. Look for flexible plans that include vehicle insurance, service, preparation, and van delivery included. You may also want to test drive a van before renting it.

You can rent a tent and campsite on Tentrr (`www.tentrr.com`), GlampingHub (`https://glampinghub.com`), or Hipcamp.com.

Experience life on an organic farm by booking a stay through `Wwoof.net`.

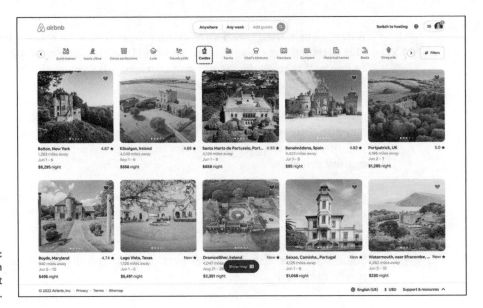

FIGURE 10-1:
Castles in different countries.

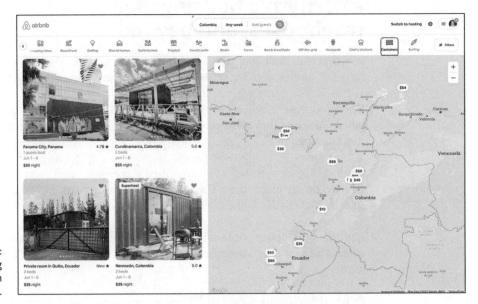

FIGURE 10-2:
Shipping containers in Colombia.

House-swapping: The modern take on trading places

If you plan on being a part-time nomad while keeping your home base, consider house-swapping.

Rather than paying to rent a second property, you can trade your current home with fellow homeowners either domestically or abroad.

Love Home Swap (www.lovehomeswap.com), Holiday Swap (www.holidayswap.com), and Home Exchange (www.homeexchange.com) are three websites where you can list your house and find people to trade with. An annual membership ranges between $100–200 per year.

When home-swapping, it helps to be flexible with your travel dates to find the most opportunities. Double-check your insurance coverage and discuss details with the people you're trading with before confirming. And of course, treat others' homes as you'd like yours to be treated.

House-sitting: Taking care of someone else's place

Does living rent-free sound good to you? If so, house-sitting could be for you. People need house-sitters for many reasons, from watering their plants to taking care of their pets (more on that in the next section).

You can find house-sitting opportunities on HouseSitter.com, Nomador (www.nomador.com), and MindMyHouse (www.mindmyhouse.com). You may even end up house-sitting for fellow digital nomads!

House-sitting is a great option for long-term slow travelers looking for a comfortable place to live without breaking the bank. But short-term travelers can also find unique last-minute opportunities on any of these sites.

If your travel plans are flexible, give house-sitting a try! I once met a digital nomad who house sat around the world for nine years. Quite a feat!

Pet-sitting: Loving someone else's fur baby

Many homeowners who you'll find on house-sitting sites are also pet owners.

With pet-sitting, you take care of someone else's furry friend in exchange for free accommodation.

The only cost to pet-sitting is either a website membership or a nominal booking fee.

TrustedHousesitters (www.trustedhousesitters.com) is a great resource to find pet-sitting opportunities worldwide. It has hundreds of listings in cities including New York, Sydney, and London.

Whether you're tending to someone's horses in Scotland, befriending a "best mannered hipster doggy" in Zambia, or taking care of an "affectionate rescue cat" in Azerbaijan, pet-sitting can be a unique experience — no doubt about it!

Homestays

Living in a homestay — living with a family for a fee — is a great way to get to know the local people in your destination while immersing yourself in their culture and language. If you're yearning for an authentic travel experience, living in a homestay could be for you.

The first time I ever lived overseas was as a study abroad student in Costa Rica. My language school arranged a home stay for me, and it changed my life forever. I probably would have never learned Spanish, fallen in love with Costa Rica, or ultimately have become a digital nomad if I didn't have that experience.

Living in a stranger's house can seem awkward at first, but they won't be strangers for long! You'll soon bond with your hosts (and neighbors) over morning coffee, meals, and late-night chats on the porch.

The best way to find a homestay is through a language school. You can also check Facebook groups and websites such as Homestay.com or Couchsurfing.com.

Planning Your Housing Search

Before jumping into your housing search, take some time to envision what you're looking for. Consider the following:

> **»** **Your priorities and goals:** What's most important to you in a rental property? Is it the price? Being walking distance to amenities? Living with people? Having a balcony or view? High speed Internet? A pet-friendly or accessible property?
>
> Write down three non-negotiable things you are looking for in a rental property:
>
> 1._____
>
> 2._____
>
> 3._____

>> **Your rental budget:**

- If you have a tight budget, you might have more time than money to spend. If that's the case, your search strategy may include scouring classifieds sites and Facebook groups to find the best deals. Or, planning your travel around pet- and house-sitting opportunities.

- If you have a flexible budget, you have more options. You could start your search through online booking portals or contact rental agencies or estate agents to find properties for you.

>> **Your lease term:** Are you looking for a short-, mid-, or long-term rental?

>> **Your destination:** Some websites, such as Airbnb, Craigslist, and Booking.com, are available almost anywhere in the world. Others are specific to different cities and countries. For example, Kijiji is based in Canada while Malta Park is exclusive to properties in Malta.

>> **Your timeline until arrival:** When should you start looking for housing? That's up to you, but many people book up 6-9 months in advance. For more flexibility, book 1-3 months ahead.

The longer you wait to book a rental property, the less availability there will be and the higher the prices.

Knowing what to look for in a rental property

Before starting your property search, keep the following in mind:

>> **Money, money, money:** Is the property in your budget? Is a security deposit required? Is the price negotiable? Chapter 3 helps you calculate your digital nomad budget.

>> **Location, location, location:** Besides the country or city location, consider a property's safety, walkability, and proximity to restaurants, co-working spaces, public transportation, and amenities. (See the next section for how to evaluate a location.)

If you're sensitive to noise, ask if the property is next to a church, school, nightclub, or construction site.

>> **Safety and security:** Safety is partly dependent on the neighborhood a property is in, as well as the country. In more high-risk destinations, you may want to ensure that you stay in a secure building or a gated community. In other locations, you may be perfectly safe in a regular house.

TIP

The travel app, TripIt, has an international feature where you can look up a city's safety score. Figure 10-3 shows an example in New York, as well as a comparison of the same neighborhood during the day and night.

More things to look for include:

- A concierge or security guard.

- A gate to enter the property.

- Security bars or reinforced windows, when applicable.

- A safe to store valuables.

- Method of entry: Is there a regular key, lockbox, or code to get in?

FIGURE 10-3: The NYC safety score on TripIt.

» **Remote work-friendly:** If you'll be working from home, is there a comfortable table or dedicated workspace you can use?

TIP

Some properties only have a bar with barstools to sit at, or a coffee table without dining room chairs. Make sure there's a comfortable place for you to sit. If there's nowhere to work within the property, continue your search or find nearby co-working spaces on Coworker.com.

>> **Wi-Fi status:** What's the Internet speed? Beware of the term, "high-speed Internet." *What does that mean?* Look for the exact upload/download speed in the description or ask the landlord to send you a screenshot of the speed test.

>> **Comfort and amenities:** Scan the description and photos for any other must-haves, such as an elevator, king-sized bed, flat screen TV, feather pillows, a particular brand of coffee maker, or an in-house washer, dryer, and dishwasher.

REMEMBER

A property rarely meets 100 percent of the features you're looking for. Be flexible but also watch out for any deal breakers. Make a list of non-negotiables and read reviews to avoid any unpleasant surprises.

TIP

If you're short on time and can afford help, consider hiring a virtual assistant (VA) to help with your search. You can find VAs through freelancing sites such as Fiverr, Upwork, Onlinejobs.ph, Chatterboss, or TaskRabbit.

Learning about a location

To decide where you want to rent within a city or town, it helps to familiarize yourself with the different neighborhoods in the area. Doing this can help you narrow your search before you start.

Find a destination in your favorite maps app. Look for neighborhood names, and then research those neighborhoods online.

Or, simply search for "the best neighborhoods in *your destination*." For example, Paris, France, as shown in Figure 10-4.

The more you zoom on a section of the map, different neighborhoods will appear (examples circled in red).

Sources you can use to research neighborhoods around the world include:

>> Airbnb Neighborhoods Database (www.airbnb.com/locations): Airbnb offers descriptions of the different neighborhoods in most cities.

>> Culture Trip (https://theculturetrip.com): Culture Trip has helpful neighborhood guides of the most popular cities in the world.

>> Hoodmaps by NomadList (https://hoodmaps.com): Publicly crowdsourced maps good for figuring out what your neighborhood vibe will be like; for example, High-End, Hipster/Gentrified, Touristy, Normie.

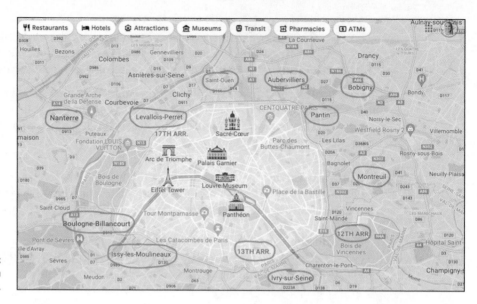

FIGURE 10-4:
Finding Parisian
neighborhoods.

TIP

Look up a location on Walkscore.com to help you get an idea of what your local day-to-day life will be like living there. A "walk score" of 100 is perfect, where daily errands do not require a vehicle. A walk score of 70 means that the city is somewhat walkable or bikeable (but some errands require a car). A walk score of 20 would mean that having a car is almost a necessity.

Searching for Housing

Your next step is to start your housing search.

Simply read the description of each search method, choose the one that's best for your needs, and happy house hunting!

TIP

Check out my YouTube channel (https://youtu.be/gQ87f0ZyzFI) for a video tutorial that walks you through 27 ways to find housing as a digital nomad.

Short-term vacation rentals websites

You can find short-term rentals on almost any property website, from nightly booking sites such as Booking.com or Hotels.com to sites that specialize more in weekly and monthly accommodations, such as Airbnb and VRBO.

Short-term vacation-rental portals include:

>> 9Flats: "The alternative to hotels" with six million homes worldwide

>> Airbnb: Nightly, weekly, and monthly private and shared rental properties

>> Booking.com: Find everything from bed & breakfasts to luxury hotels

>> Flatio: For "a few months long" accommodation

>> FlipKey: A place to find "the perfect vacation rental"

>> Housing Anywhere: Mid- to long-term rentals in 400+ cities

>> Nestpick: One of the world's largest websites for furnished apartments

>> Plum Guide: Stay in an "expertly curated" home

>> Sublet.com: Furnished rentals and rooms for every price range

>> Tripping.com: A vacation rental comparison site with listings in 190 countries.

>> Trivago: Price comparison website for searching hotels and rental properties

Housing subscription services are an excellent way to find short-term housing. Take a look at HelloLanding (`www.hellolanding.com`) and Blueground (`www.blueground.com`). Both sites allow you to rent properties in different cities and countries for one flat, monthly fee. Figure 10-5 shows the features of the Blueground Pass.

FIGURE 10-5: Blueground Pass.

TIP

Selina (www.selina.com), a global hotel chain for digital nomads, is a short-term rental option that includes access to a workspace and community. It offers a range of accommodations and price points for backpackers, luxury travelers, groups, and more. You can even rent hammocks!

TIP

Budget-friendly picks for short-term rentals include Hostelworld (www.hostelworld.com), Couchsurfing (www.couchsurfing.com), and Sublet.com (www.sublet.com).

Finding long-term housing

For lease terms of six months or more, classified sites are a good way to find the best deals and to book directly with owners. Craigslist is an obvious choice, but the upcoming section on classified ads explains how you can use them to your advantage.

Some websites specialize in mid- to long-term rentals for nomads. Flatio offers "a few months long accommodation" and Anyplace (www.anyplace.com) offers digital nomad-friendly apartments for stays of one month or longer. Figure 10-6 shows a typical property you can rent on Anyplace.

FIGURE 10-6: An Anyplace property.

WARNING

Avoid looking for long-term rentals on vacation rental sites, as you'll pay a premium.

Reaching out to property developers and condo administrators to inquire about long-term rates is another strategy. Just make sure to specify that you're looking for *furnished* properties.

Real estate offices also frequently have long-term rentals. Read more about finding properties through real estate offices in an upcoming section.

Many nomads score long-term housing by searching the Facebook Marketplace or in Facebook groups, which you can read about next.

Facebook groups and forums

Searching Facebook groups is a time consuming but rewarding strategy for finding all types of housing: short-term, long-term, shared, and sublets. One group, called Chiang Mai Buy/Sell/Rent/Swap has nearly 2,0000 people in it. You can browse listings passively or post what you're looking for and see who responds.

Figure 10-7 shows the Facebook group search results for Chiang Mai rental properties.

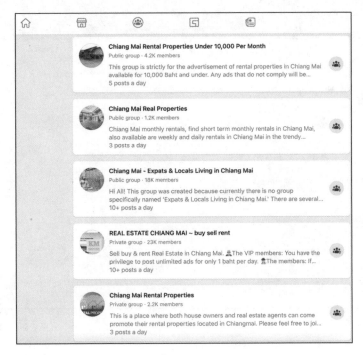

FIGURE 10-7:
A Facebook search for Chiang Mai rental property groups.

Tips for finding properties on Facebook:

>> Filter your search for "groups" rather than "all results" that include people, pages, and posts.

>> Check a group's activity before joining to make sure it's been active in the last few days.

>> "Take Over My Lease" Facebook groups are excellent ways to find sublet opportunities.

>> General groups for expats, foreigners, and digital nomads in a specific city or country can also be a good resource for finding rentals.

Beyond Facebook, you may be able to find a place to stay using a digital nomad forum, such as Nomad List.

TIP

JustLanded (www.justlanded.com) has a community forum, housing portal, and classifieds listings in cities around the world. Figure 10-8 shows properties in Kuwait listed on JustLanded.

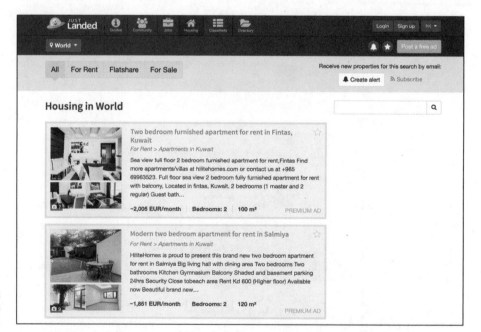

FIGURE 10-8:
Kuwait properties
on JustLanded.

Local classifieds listings

Besides international classifieds sites such as Craigslist, local classifieds pages offer plenty of housing options. You can find properties to rent or buy this way, often at local prices.

Say you want to find a two-bedroom apartment in Nairobi, Kenya. You could book through VRBO and pay a premium, but you could also find some great deals on Pigiame.co.ke, a Kenyan classifieds site with property rentals and sales listings.

Perhaps you're interested in spending three months in Medellín, Colombia. You could find a place on Airbnb, or you can search local listings on Encuentra24.com, Olx.com.co, or Allanuncios.com.

To find a local classifieds site in your destination, search online for "classifieds *the city you're looking for*." Translate "classifieds" into the local language for better search results. For example, search for "clasificados Playa del Carmen".

There is usually a way to switch the language and search results of a classifieds site to English. If you use Google Chrome web browser, it might translate automatically for you. However, sometimes that feature is buggy, and it doesn't work. In that case, Google Translate is your friend.

TIP

If prices appear in the local currency, use a search engine or XE.com to convert into your home currency.

TIP

Check the listing details to see when a property was published before inquiring. Some properties may be months or years old. You can also sort by most recent. If you find an old rental listing where the property has been vacant for a long time, you might be able to negotiate a better rate.

TIP

Search engine strategies

Don't be afraid to use a search engine to uncover small or privately owned websites offering housing in different cities.

To find websites not listed in this book, search different combinations of keywords, such as "furnished rentals *the city/country you're looking for*."

If you were to search, "furnished rentals St. Lucia," you would find 368,000 results, including a local agency called "St. Lucia Apartment Rentals" (which may or may not have listings on Airbnb or Booking.com).

You would also get results for specific buildings with apartments for rent, such as Agusta's Apartments in St. Lucia. Figure 10-9 shows a map of the rental properties available in St. Lucia.

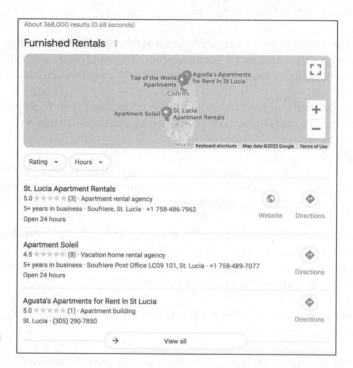

About 368,000 results (0.68 seconds)

Furnished Rentals ⋮

Top of the World Apartments · Agusta's Apartments for Rent In St Lucia · Castries · Apartment Soleil · St. Lucia Apartment Rentals · Vieux Fo · Keyboard shortcuts · Map data ©2022 Google · Terms of Use

Rating ▾   Hours ▾

St. Lucia Apartment Rentals
5.0 ★★★★★ (3) · Apartment rental agency
5+ years in business · Soufriere, St. Lucia · +1 758-486-7962
Open 24 hours
🌐 Website   ◈ Directions

Apartment Soleil
4.5 ★★★★★ (8) · Vacation home rental agency
5+ years in business · Soufriere Post Office LC09 101, St. Lucia · +1 758-489-7077
Open 24 hours
◈ Directions

Agusta's Apartments for Rent In St Lucia
5.0 ★★★★★ (1) · Apartment building
St. Lucia · (305) 290-7850
◈ Directions

→   View all

FIGURE 10-9:
St. Lucia rentals.

Get creative and see what you find!

TIP

If you have a flexible budget, try searching for "executive housing" or "corporate housing" that is geared toward business travelers. It's sometimes more expensive than renting leisure properties, but executive rentals are usually fully equipped with everything a remote worker would need — especially high-speed Internet! One executive rentals site I use often is CorporateStays.com.

Property management companies

Property management companies represent a large inventory of properties. They might not have the lowest prices you'll find online but using them as a resource is a quick way to find a property almost anywhere in the world.

I used to manage rental properties when I lived in Costa Rica and recognize the value that property agents provide. And when I became a digital nomad, I used property managers to find rentals in Hong Kong, Bulgaria, and beyond.

You can find property managers through online searches, Facebook groups, and by contacting local real estate offices.

Real estate offices

Many real estate agencies offer properties to rent as well as to buy. If you get stuck and can't find a property you like online, contact a few real estate offices to see whether they have any short- or long-term listings in their inventory. Sometimes they can also refer you to a local rental agent or agency with additional properties.

TIP

You can find real estate agents on a country's Multiple Listing Service or MLS website.

In-person searching

If you have extra time to invest in finding the perfect property for you, book a hotel or short-term rental so you have somewhere to stay while you look for a long-term rental.

Looking in person could mean walking, driving, or biking around, looking for signs, and making phone calls.

Another strategy that pays off in digital nomad hubs such as Thailand is contacting building administrators or managers to ask about vacancies.

These strategies can be more labor-intensive than searching online but can result in finding some hidden gems. It also gives you the opportunity to negotiate rates with people in person rather than paying the listing price online.

Reserving and Booking Your Housing

Once you find a property you like, it's time to book it! This section gives you tips on negotiating and paying for your housing, as well as recovering your security deposit.

WARNING

Make sure you aren't renting a property for longer than you're able to stay in the country for. I once pre-paid a three-month rental in Malta but left after two months because my Schengen visa expired. I was out €1,200 plus my security deposit.

Negotiating the best price

Your negotiating power depends on the time of year you're renting in (peak, shoulder, or low season) and the market conditions there at the moment. You'll have more negotiating power in the off season than the high season.

For example, if you're going to Barcelona for a week in the middle of summer, prices will be much higher than if you're going for a month during winter. See Chapter 8 for more about how seasonality impacts travel.

You'll also have more wiggle room if you're renting long term versus short term.

If you're renting a short-term rental for a long period of time, ask the owner if they offer a long-term rate. If you're renting a long-term rental for a shorter period of time, be prepared to pay more.

Tips for saving money on rentals:

>> Travel slowly and off-season.

>> Ask about long-term rates that might not be advertised.

>> Offer to pay up front for a discount (if you're sure you want to stay there).

>> Know when to walk away. Sometimes, it's better to move onto the next property.

Paying for housing

How you pay your rent depends on where or who you rented the property from.

If you rent online, you should be able to pay by credit card through the site you used to book.

If you rent through a private party or agency, you may need to transfer funds to a domestic or foreign bank account.

If your landlord has a bank account in the same country, you can send a check, domestic wire, or local transfer.

If your landlord has a bank account in a different country, you can send a bank wire or use an online money transfer service such as Wise, Revolut, or PayPal. (See Chapter 11 for more about banking and credit card services.)

Never pay for housing without some form of a written agreement.

Always read the terms of your rental agreement before paying. Inquire about the penalties for terminating a lease early and the options for extending it, should you want to stay longer. Hire a legal professional to review your agreement if you have questions and note that an English version of the contract may not be enforceable.

Avoiding scams

Renting through reputable agencies and booking sites is the best way to avoid scams. If a property on a classifieds site or in a Facebook group looks too good to be true, it probably is.

To reduce the risk of getting ripped off, avoid any properties where the rep says they will "mail the key" to you.

Before sending money to someone you don't know, request a video tour or view the property in person, first. You can also send an assistant or rental agent to view a property for you.

Use a credit card or payment method with vendor's insurance, such as PayPal or Venmo, which allows you to dispute a fraudulent charge.

Never send money by cash, check, bank transfer, or Western Union to an unknown source.

Always ask for a receipt or proof of payment.

Getting your security deposit refunded

A security deposit is usually equal to one month's rent for long-term rentals and varies for short-term rentals, from a few hundred dollars or nothing at all. If you're booking through a short-term rental site, the property description should indicate what the amount and terms of the security deposit are.

When it comes to getting your security deposit back, prevention is the best remedy. Always review the terms of *when* and *how* your security deposit will be returned *before* paying it.

IDEAS FOR FINDING YOUR PERFECT HOUSING

Here are a few examples of different housing strategies I've used in the past. Feel free to borrow one or more of them to kick off your property search!

Exhibit A: You want to see the world as fast as possible. Housing options for you could include:

- Renting a property on Airbnb or another vacation rental site.
- Signing up for organized travel retreat groups.
- Backpacking around and booking hotels on the fly.

Exhibit B: You want to travel slowly, go with the flow, and see where you end up. Housing sources for you include:

- Renting a one-month rental to start on a short-term rental website.
- Getting to know the local area and keeping an eye out for "for rent" signs on properties that appeal to you.
- Searching Facebook groups for long-term housing.
- Inquiring about rentals with local real estate and rentals agencies.
- Searching classifieds websites for sublets and local deals.

Exhibit C: You don't care where you go or how long you stay, as long as you're with cool people. Try:

- Starting your digital nomad journey in a popular nomad hub or at a conference or event where you can meet people quickly.
- Signing up for organized travel retreat groups.
- Staying in hostels.

Exhibit D: You're focused on your business, being productive, and immersing yourself in the culture of one place. Check out:

- Local classifieds websites for housing.
- Local realtors and rental agencies.
- A monthly or long-term co-living arrangement.
- A homestay.
- Long-term house-sitting options.

Chapter **11**

Managing Travel Logistics

Every digital nomad voyage involves a lot of moving parts. But if you know what to expect, you can manage your logistics efficiently and with confidence.

If you feel overwhelmed by the logistics of taking your first trip as a digital nomad, this chapter is your guide. I cover how to prepare for your departure and arrival (including if you're traveling with a pet), where to find the best flights, what to pack, and how to stay in touch using your international phone and Internet plans. Let's go!

Making Your Adventure a Reality

After deciding where to go (Chapter 8), booking your accommodation (Chapter 10), and applying for a travel authorization or visa, if applicable (Chapter 9), it's time to start preparing for lift-off! In this section, I help you find the most affordable and comfortable flights, pack just enough for your journey, plan your arrival, and bring your furry friend with you.

Purchasing travel and health insurance

Travel insurance is mentioned a few times in this book because it's important. Always purchase emergency travel insurance and update your health insurance policy *before* leaving home. See Chapter 12 for the run-down on international and domestic travel and health insurance plans and a list of providers. Having travel insurance gives you peace of mind so you can sleep well and avoid the worries shown in Figure 11-1.

FIGURE 11-1:
A digital nomad's nightmares.

Source: Giang Cao / Very Nomad Problems

Joining travel rewards programs

Before booking travel, I recommend signing up for rewards and loyalty programs with travel providers you expect to use often.

Enrolling in travel rewards programs is a fun way to save money on travel. The benefit is that you earn points or miles every time you book travel. Points can be redeemed for free flights, nights, cash, upgrades, or travel credits.

Most airlines, car rental agencies, and hotels offer loyalty programs. Some also offer a branded credit card that allows you to earn points faster.

I've been a frequent flier with Delta since 2006. I have the SkyMiles Reserve Card, which costs $550 per year, but comes with benefits such as complimentary Sky Club lounge access, priority check-in, a fee waiver on your first checked bag, and bonus points when you reach different spending thresholds.

You can also opt for a general travel credit card that allows you to earn points that can be exchanged for travel with any company. See Chapter 9 for examples of travel rewards cards.

Checking health requirements

It's no secret that the COVID-19 pandemic changed the way we travel — possibly forever. During 2020–2021, many countries closed their borders to travel and tourism. Over time, the world started re-opening, but with new travel and entry requirements.

Although travel restrictions change often, it's good to get an idea of what you might need to do before choosing a destination.

Possible entry requirements include:

>> Testing negative for COVID-19 (sometimes more than once).

>> Showing proof of immunity or full vaccination status.

>> Downloading or printing a country's health passport app.

>> Filling out a passenger health form.

>> Purchasing local or international insurance.

>> Quarantining at a government-designated facility.

>> A combination of all these.

You can look up your destination country's entry requirements by checking with your airline, the tourism board, or government portals (for example, the Department of Health or Immigration). You can also check third-party websites. Two I like to use are IATA's Travel Map (www.iatatravelcentre.com/international-travel-document-news/1580226297.htm) and SafetyWing's Borderless (https://borderless.safetywing.com).

Booking your flight

There are countless strategies for booking a cheap plane ticket. But you can rely on the principles in this section time and again.

Although the sheer number of flight booking sites can make your head spin, you only need to check a few to find the best deals. My top three favorites are Google Flights (www.google.com/travel/flights), Kiwi (www.kiwi.com), and Skyscanner (www.skyscanner.com). These sites offer the biggest variety of airlines, routes, and prices. They also have advanced filters and search options.

Beyond these three sites, you'll probably find more of the same results. The more time you spend looking at flights online, the higher the real cost is in time and energy. Rather than refreshing private browser tabs, searching from different devices, and comparing results, you could be working or relaxing. That's why I caution against spending endless hours looking for cheap flights. It might cost you more in the long run.

TIP

Use these strategies when booking flights:

>> **Be wary of low-cost providers.** Cheap tickets are often more expensive when you add up booking fees, taxes, seat selection, baggage fees, and restrictions.

>> **Choose an airline alliance to remain loyal to.** You can share status and earn or redeem frequent flier miles across airlines in the same alliance. SkyTeam, OneWorld, and Star Alliance are three popular options.

>> **Use search filters to your advantage.** Search using fare calendars or flexible dates to find the best deals. Changing your travel dates by a few days can save you hundreds or thousands of dollars.

>> **Consider alternative forms of transportation.** It could be cheaper and just as comfortable to take a train or bus, especially when you factor in layovers and in getting to the airport early.

>> **Opt for direct routes.** The cheapest flights are usually the longest routes with the most layovers at the worst times. Suffering through a miserable flight route can kill your mood and productivity, costing you more in the long run.

>> **Sign up for mileage programs.** Frequent fliers enjoy better customer service, shorter phone hold times, free drink vouchers, and other perks.

>> **Spend as little time as possible searching for flights.** The more time you spend looking at and comparing/evaluating flights, the higher the true (hidden) cost of the plan ticket.

>> **Use automation and robots to your advantage.** Sign up for flight alerts on a site such as Scott's Cheap Flights or consider outsourcing your flight search to a virtual assistant. Scott's Cheap Flights offers a membership program that can save you up to 90 percent on flight prices. Scott's team of Flight Experts monitors fares and send you an email for routes and destinations you're interested in. There are three membership tier levels: free, Premium ($49/year), and Elite ($199/year).

TIP

An alternative method to booking your flight is not to fly. Websites such as Kiwi and Rome2Rio show you the fastest and most economical transportation options between two destinations, including bus, plane, train, rental car, and ride-share options.

THE HIDDEN COSTS IN CHEAP FLIGHTS

The prices of flights with low-fare carriers can be deceiving. Say you're looking at flights from London, England to Bucharest, Romania. One discount carrier shows a base fare of $104. But that doesn't include fees such as:

- Carry-on bag fees
- Check-in fee at the airport (if you don't check in early)
- Extra layovers with the risk of delays and eating in airports
- Seat selection fees
- Transaction fees for using a U.S. debit or credit card

Adding these fees could double or triple the cost of a "cheap" flight.

If you book with a bigger airline, you might pay the same amount or less and have a better experience. A competitor airline shows the same flight for $302 but seat selection and baggage fees are included. It's also a direct flight with no layovers or check-in fees.

Which flight-booking experience would you prefer? The decision is up to you.

Remember to do the following when looking at travel:

- Double check the carry-on and checked luggage policy and fees before you book.
- Give preference to airlines you have loyalty/rewards with for better seats, lower baggage fees, and to accumulate points/miles (when fares are similar).

As a digital nomad, when your travel dates are flexible, you can always choose the most comfortable and economical way to travel between two cities.

Packing your bags

Packing as a digital nomad is as much about what you *don't* bring with you as much as what you *do*. Suffice to say, many people err on the side of packing too much (myself included).

See Figure 11-2 for a humorous look at the packing process for a nomad.

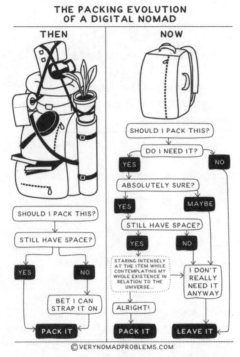

Source: Giang Cao / Very Nomad Problems

FIGURE 11-2: The evolution of packing.

Ideally, you should aim to travel carry-on only, without a checked bag. By packing light, you save on luggage fees, time and energy at the airport, and reduce or eliminate the risk of having a lost, damaged, or delayed bag.

The first time I went to Bali in 2009, I overpacked and ended up storing most of my stuff with the owner of a local homestay. My travel companion and I survived for a month with nothing but a set of backpacks, surfboards, bikinis, and mopeds.

At the end of my trip, I mailed a box of stuff home using sea freight and sold my surfboard on consignment so I didn't have to pay excess baggage fees on the way home.

As a digital nomad, less is more. Few people have ever uttered the words, "I wish I brought more stuff." You're more likely to want to leave things behind than you are to wish you had packed more. You can always add more to your must-haves, but it's harder to edit once you have an overflowing bag with you.

Digital nomad packing lists can be hundreds of items long. But I'm here to simplify the list for you.

TIP

Travel writer, Rolf Potts, once documented traveling around the world without any luggage at all! Read about the No Baggage Challenge at www.rtwblog.com.

Things you will find useful to pack:

Travel Basics

- [ ] Travel documents (passport and visas; and copies of both)
- [ ] Travel insurance policy and card
- [ ] Debit and credit cards and some cash
- [ ] Rain poncho and/or travel umbrella
- [ ] Sunglasses and case
- [ ] Glasses or contact lenses and case
- [ ] Vitamins, medications, and prescriptions
- [ ] Luggage tags
- [ ] Packing cubes
- [ ] Luggage lock
- [ ] Waterproof bag
- [ ] Sleeping mask and ear plugs
- [ ] Travel pillow
- [ ] Refillable water bottle
- [ ] Snacks for the flight
- [ ] Emergency contact info and file
- [ ] Travel health kit or first aid kit

Technology

- ☐ Carry-on backpack or laptop bag
- ☐ Laptop with external keyboard, monitor, mouse, and laptop stand
- ☐ Smartwatch
- ☐ Tablet
- ☐ External hard drive
- ☐ Unlocked smartphone and charger
- ☐ Unlocked Wi-Fi hotspot or travel Wi-Fi device
- ☐ Miscellaneous cables and cable organizers
- ☐ International electricity adapters
- ☐ Ethernet cable
- ☐ Universal card reader or multi-use laptop port
- ☐ Noise-cancelling headphones
- ☐ Portable laptop and portable device chargers
- ☐ Power strip with surge protector
- ☐ Batteries
- ☐ Portable Bluetooth speaker
- ☐ Camera equipment

Clothing

- ☐ Daily uniform (basics, merino wool, and clothing you can layer)
- ☐ Comfortable walking shoes for everyday use
- ☐ Nice outfit and versatile shoes to wear at night or for business meetings
- ☐ Workout clothes and athletic shoes
- ☐ Flip flops or sandals
- ☐ Hoodie or sweater/cardigan
- ☐ Down jacket
- ☐ Raincoat
- ☐ Swimwear

❏ Weather-appropriate clothing: anything you need, from a sarong to thermal underwear

REMEMBER

Check the weather forecast before you pack. Sometimes I pack two bags — one for warm weather and one for cold weather and I leave one in storage. That makes it easy to swap out bags when I come home for a visit.

TIP

If you want to mix up your wardrobe while traveling, consider enrolling in a monthly subscription plan through a stylist website such as Rent the Runway, Gentleman's Box, or Stitch Fix (options may vary by country). A Rent the Runway plan mails you eight items per month for $145/month, while Stitch Fix lets you pay per item. Another strategy is to shop at secondhand stores in your destination and sell them back when you leave. You can also trade items of clothing with other travelers you meet along the way.

Hygiene

❏ Toothbrush, dental floss, and travel-sized toothpaste

❏ Shampoo and conditioner bar

❏ Brush/comb

❏ Lip balm

❏ Travel towel set

❏ Travel-sized deodorant, bug repellent, and styling products

❏ Antibacterial gel and wipes

❏ Tweezers, nail clippers, and vanity set

❏ Toiletry or make-up bag with mirror or compact

Things you might find more optional:

» Books, journals, and planners (you can donate or trade your books when you leave)

» Extra clothes for more diverse settings, such as formal events or trekking

» More shoes, such as dress shoes and hiking shoes

» Technology: GoPro, camera, and any other hardware you want to bring that you need to do your job better

TIP

Find more ideas for what to pack in my Amazon Travel and Remote Work Store (https://www.amazon.com/shop/travelingwithkristin).

THE CAPSULE WARDROBE

"Capsule wardrobes" are popular with many professionals and entrepreneurs but also work well for digital nomads who want to pack light yet have a versatile wardrobe for multiple occasions. The idea behind a capsule wardrobe is to decrease the amount of time you spend thinking about what to wear every day.

Humans have a limited amount of willpower and decision-making capacity per day. Your brain treats the decision of what to eat for lunch with the same weighting as a much more important decision, such as when to press the nuclear launch button.

Barack Obama, Steve Jobs, and Mark Zuckerberg are a few public figures who wear the same thing every day. Obama always wore a dark blue suit while president. Jobs was known for his black turtleneck, jeans, and white sneakers. Facebook's founder is often seen in a gray tee and jeans.

According to Ryan Holiday, the average person spends over 150 hours per year choosing what to wear to work. Mortified by this figure, Ryan created a capsule wardrobe for himself. It consists of a tee shirt, jeans, a belt, and running shoes. He wears the same thing every day at his home and office in Texas, unless he has a meeting or speaking engagement.

Traveling with pets

A pet is like a family member. If you have a furry friend, you almost certainly want to bring them with you! You can travel almost anywhere with your pet, as long as you leave enough time to take care of the requirements. Talk with a veterinarian at home and in your destination before leaving. Also review your airline's pet regulations.

The common requirements for traveling across borders with pets include:

>> A pet passport or health certificate

>> Blood tests

>> Customs clearance fees

>> Microchipping and tagging

>> Pet carrier

>> Pet quarantine period

>> Transportation costs

>> Vaccinations

WARNING

All countries have varying pet import laws, which may change regularly. Check with the customs authorities, health department, or other appropriate government agency in your destination at least three months before your departure date. Certain animals or breeds of dogs may be banned altogether.

WARNING

Sometimes pet documents must be apostilled, or translated and notarized and certified, depending on the country of destination.

If you're unsure that you've met all the requirements to travel with your pet, consider hiring a pet relocation company to help you. Airpets International (`https://airpetsinternational.com`), Happy Tails Travel (`www.happytailstravel.com`), and Starwood Animal Transport (`www.starwoodanimaltransport.com`) are three options.

Preparing for Departure and Arrival

Before leaving home, there are a few things you can do to ensure your arrival goes smoothly.

Tips for departure and arrival:

TIP

>> **Book your airport transportation in advance.** Decide how you will get from the airport or train station to your rental property or other accommodations. Use Rome2Rio, your maps app, or consider hiring a private driver or tour guide to help you get where you're going quickly and easily.

See whether there is an airport express bus or tourist bus in your destination for an affordable way to get around. Amsterdam Schipol Airport has the Amsterdam Airport Express bus, while the Aerobús is a comfortable way to get between El Prat Airport and Barcelona city center.

>> **Bring some cash with you for tipping or miscellaneous expenses.** You can also withdraw local currency at an airport ATM.

>> **Coordinate your arrival on a day where you can take a few days off to adapt to your surroundings.** Saturday is usually a nice day to arrive, so you have Sunday to relax before the work week. However, if you arrive on a weekend, some stores and banks will be closed.

>> **Ensure you have a return flight or proof of onward travel (bus or train ticket) if traveling on a tourist visa.** Your airline will ask for this at check-in. If you're traveling on a one-way ticket, companies such as Onward Ticket (https://onwardticket.com) or BestOnwardticket (https://bestonwardticket.com) can provide a real reservation for you.

>> **Reconfirm your arrival time and the check-in process with your landlord or host.**

WARNING

Try to avoid arriving peak times of day, which can mean long lines in immigration, baggage claim, and in rush hour traffic.

>> **Download handy travel apps to your phone.** You can find a list of digital nomad-friendly travel apps in the next section.

Downloading Digital Nomad-Friendly Travel Apps

Plenty of digital nomad–friendly apps help make your travels easier. Here they are, organized by category:

>> **Accommodations:** Download Airbnb plus at least one hotel app such as Hotels.com, Booking.com, or Agoda.com so that you can always find short-term accomodations.

>> **Airlines:** By downloading your carrier's app, you can check in for your flight, make flight and seat changes, look up airport maps and amenities, and receive important updates and push notifications. Also download a general flight booking app, such as SkyScanner.

>> **Banking, budgeting, and finance:** Download your bank's app as well as Wise, an international money transfer app, and a foreign exchange app, such as XE.

>> **Communication:** Download a translation app, such as Google Translate, as well as the messaging apps of your choice (for example, Messenger and WhatsApp). Skype is good for international calls. Signal is good for checking Wi-Fi availability, and Solis is the app for activating Internet packages on the Solis Wi-Fi hotspot.

>> **Community:** Download dating and friendship apps such as Bumble, Hinge, Fairy Trail, and Tinder. Also download social networking apps such as Facebook and events apps such as Eventbrite and Meetup.

>> **Health and wellness:** Download a health passport app as well as nutrition and exercise apps. Timeshifter is good for combating and preventing jet lag. Stay up to date with general trends and news with the World Health Organization app.

>> **Travel:** Download a maps app such as Google or Apple Maps, a travel planning and organization app such as TripIt, and an app with travel guides sourced from travel bloggers and content creators, such as Thatch. Also download TripAdvisor for ratings and reviews and a reservations app such as Expedia, Orbitz, or Priceline.

TIP

The Maps.Me app has a great selection of international maps available offline.

>> **Utilities:** Download a weather app, world clock or time zone converter, and app to check Internet speeds, such as Speedtest.

Lining Up Essential Services in Your Destination

Once you arrive in your destination, your most basic necessities for survival (besides food and water, of course) are accessing money for your living expenses and Internet. In this section, I share with you the simplest ways to get online and send, spend, or receive money anywhere.

Buying a SIM card

Upon arrival in your destination, purchase a pre-paid local SIM card.

A local SIM card provides you with a domestic phone number for your phone. You can purchase them at airport kiosks, phone stores, and some supermarket and convenience stores. Always buy a local SIM card at your destination instead of renting a tourist phone or Internet device online. Local SIMs are always the most affordable option for local calling and data (with the fastest speeds available). Research the telecommunications providers in your destination before departure.

If you plan on staying in one country for months at a time, inquire about getting a post-paid monthly plan instead of a pre-paid plan. However, post-paid plans may only be available for local residents.

Always have a back-up Internet connection in addition to a local SIM card. You could use a phone with an international Google-Fi plan or purchase a plan from Solis or EZ Mobile Data.

Exchanging money

Back in *ye olden days*, exchanging money in different countries was a challenge. If you used to travel with paper maps, you may also have traveled with travelers' checks. In the digital nomad era, however, exchanging money is as simple as tapping the screen of your phone or ATM.

To withdraw foreign currency at an ATM, use your bank debit card or a debit card from your money transfer app, such as Wise or Revolut.

If you're prompted to select between two exchange rates at an ATM or point-of-sale in a store, always *decline* to take the local rate (converting automatically). Select your bank's exchange rate with the *delayed* conversion, instead, as it's the lower of the two.

If you're carrying cash, avoid exchanging money at the airport, where the rates are expensive. Instead, opt for using a bank or authorized vendor with a retail storefront and a website. Steer clear of individuals offering to exchange money for you on the street or unofficial money exchange stalls, which are known for scams.

Before exchanging money, look up the current exchange rate online or an app such as XE.com.

4

Living a Full and Healthy Life as a Digital Nomad

Understand the different types of travel and medical insurance.

Care for your mental and physical health.

Navigate healthcare abroad.

Meet people and stay social.

Adapt to foreign cultures.

Sustain the digital nomad lifestyle long term.

Chapter **12**

Maintaining Your Health and Wellness

When you're constantly on the move, your health and wellness can take a backseat to travel, work, and adventure.

As a digital nomad, you'll be eager to see the wonders of the world and meet new people. The thing is, jet lag, working long hours, and constantly adapting to new environments can wreak havoc on your immune system. Plus, socializing usually takes place around food and alcohol — neither of which are so great for your waistline.

It takes extra intention to keep up with your sleep, diet, exercise, and work while traveling full time. Apparently, there's such a thing as eating too many chocolate croissants (who knew!?). But follow the tips in the upcoming sections and your body will thank you.

You can leverage your newfound freedom to make changes that result in *better* health (not worse). This chapter shows you how.

WARNING

I'm not a doctor or insurance provider. Please consult with a licensed medical professional and insurance company before making medical decisions or purchasing a healthcare or insurance plan.

Staying Healthy on the Road

Staying healthy as a nomad starts before you leave home. In this section, I tell you some ways to prepare for your journey and what to expect along the way.

Being insured

Every digital nomad should have two types of insurance coverage that protect your well-being: emergency travel/medical insurance and an international or local health insurance plan. You never know when you'll need it.

I've used my travel medical insurance to get reimbursed for spraining my ankle in Prague, getting stitches in Costa Rica, and contracting diphtheria in the Dominican Republic (which landed me in the hospital). Those are just a few of the *many* times I've relied on my travel medical insurance plans in the past.

The most popular international travel/medical insurance options for nomads include:

>> SafetyWing Nomad Insurance (https://safetywing.com)

>> World Nomads (www.worldnomads.com)

>> Insured Nomads Travel Insurance (www.insurednomads.com/travel-insurance)

You should also have a general health insurance plan in your home country, abroad, or both, that covers you for regular healthcare and pre-existing conditions. An upcoming section in this chapter explains the coverage, prices, and differences between international emergency travel/medical and health insurance plans.

Practicing good hygiene

You've heard it before, but washing your hands is one of the best ways to prevent the spread of infection and disease. The CDC reported that hand washing reduces the risk of contracting a cold by 20 percent and getting sick with diarrhea by 30-40 percent. Wash your hands often and travel with hand sanitizer. (But you already knew that!)

Using protection

You may encounter a range of new environments as a digital nomad. Do your best to protect yourself from the elements, whatever they may be. For example

>> Use sunscreen with at least a 30 SPF to protect your skin from the sun in tropical climates or at high altitudes.

>> Use bug spray and wear long sleeves and pants to repel mosquitos, ticks, and other insects while out in nature.

>> Use condoms and contraception to protect against unwanted pregnancy or sexually transmitted disease.

TIP

Pack a first aid kit or travel health kit in your luggage. The CDC provides a "Pack Smart" list at wwwnc.cdc.gov/travel/page/pack-smart.

Drinking the water (or not)

You should always stay hydrated. But drinking contaminated water (or eating food that's been washed in contaminated water) can put a damper on your trip (or worse).

I once met a traveler in Bali who had been suffering from "Bali belly" for over a year. Follow these tips to minimize the risk of contracting food poisoning, parasites, or other stomach bugs:

>> Research online if it's safe to drink the tap water in your location. When in doubt, drink bottled water.

>> Avoid swimming in water that may be contaminated, especially near river mouths.

>> Be wary of ingesting food or drinks that may have been prepared with contaminated tap water. Salads, juices, smoothies, ice, and frozen treats are common culprits.

>> Don't brush your teeth with tap water if you're unsure about the water quality.

>> Travel with a water purification straw or filter. LifeStraw makes a range of products for home or travel. Steripen makes a UV water filter that kills bacteria. I also travel with water purification tablets, just in case.

TIP

Boiling your water for at least 1-3 minutes can kill parasites and pathogens.

Minimizing jet lag

Perpetual border hopping and jet-setting can throw off your body's circadian rhythm. While some jet lag while traveling is unavoidable, you can minimize its effects by following a few strategies, remembering that what works for one person won't work for everyone.

>> **Travel slowly.** The more you travel, the more you'll experience jet lag. So, travel wisely! Reducing how often you fly naturally reduces jet lag. Some nomads opt to travel by cruise, ferry, or land to adapt to time zones better.

>> **Choose optimal flight times.** Some people like to fly overnight and sleep on the plane. I like to fly during the day, stay awake, and sleep when I arrive in my destination.

>> **Stay hydrated.** I've found that drinking water instead of alcohol on flights works wonders for my recovery time upon landing. If you're feeling dehydrated, hungover, or jet-lagged, search for the nearest IV hydration bar for a dose of vitamins, minerals, and pain killers.

>> **Hit the ground running.** Get outside and walk or do some light exercise when you arrive. Avoid long naps. A little bit of caffeine to stay awake also helps!

LIVING IN BLUE ZONES

Imagine living in one of the healthiest places on the planet. That dream can become a reality when you're a digital nomad.

Blue zones are regions of the world that are known for longevity, with the highest quantity of centenarians (people who live to be 100).

The world's top blue zones are:

- Ikarios, Greece
- Okinawa, Japan
- Sardinia, Italy
- Loma Linda, California
- Nicoya Peninsula, Costa Rica

Blue zones attract digital nomads for a reason. For example, residents in Nicoya are twice as likely as U.S. citizens to reach the age of 90. You can find out more about blue zones at www.bluezones.com.

TIP

If you aren't sure what to do or when, the Timeshifter app can help keep your circadian rhythm in check. It gives you recommendations on when to sleep, when to see sunlight, when to avoid blue light, and when to consume or avoid caffeine and sleep aids such as melatonin.

Maintaining Your Physical Health

Health means different things to different people. But regardless of your interpretation of the term, staying healthy as a digital nomad has a lot to do with maintaining healthy habits and knowing your limits.

Fortunately, the flexibility of a location-independent lifestyle allows digital nomads more control over their time compared to traditional, location-based workers. You can set your own schedule, exercise more, and avoid the stresses of a daily commute.

You can also choose a destination that naturally supports a healthy lifestyle, by providing access to plenty of sunshine, fresh food, and clean air.

The following are some ways that you can take advantage of your freedom and flexibility to have a positive impact on your health.

Eating healthy

Everyone knows it's important to eat healthy, but if you've ever been on a cruise or to an all-inclusive resort, you know how easy it can be to overindulge.

The digital nomad lifestyle can feel often like living in the pages of Food & Wine magazine, with French baguettes stacked on your left and bottles of Bordeaux on your right. Moderation is ideal, but willpower can be limited — especially when you live in Italy and there's a gelato shop on every corner.

It's also harder to cook in a temporary rental property compared to your home. That is, if you have a kitchen at all. Cooking could be near impossible if you're staying at a hotel or hostel.

Fortunately, eating out can be healthy and affordable in some destinations. You can buy a meal for $2 in low-cost digital nomad hotspots such as Chiang Mai or Bali.

Here are some healthy eating tips to help you out:

>> Book accommodations within walking distance to a supermarket to make it easy to eat at home.

>> Find out what the delivery food options are in your area. Search online to enroll in a healthy meal plan subscription service. Fit Food Home delivers nutritious meals to homes and offices in Japan.

>> Find a smoothie or juice bar near your home or workspace.

>> Look for salad or hot bars in local supermarkets.

>> Try intermittent fasting or a healthy eating plan to challenge yourself.

>> Schedule alcohol-free "dry months" or abstain from drinking altogether.

>> Stay hydrated! Drink plenty of water and carry a refillable water bottle with you (a built-in purification filter is a bonus).

>> Shop at outdoor markets, when possible, where you can find fresh, local, often organic produce at affordable prices.

REMEMBER

Nutrition is especially important for remote workers who travel a lot or sit in front of screens for long hours. Researchers at Columbia School of Health found that business travelers rank worse on health indicators such as Body Mass Index, HDL cholesterol, and blood pressure compared to people who travel less often. Researchers attribute these findings to poor food choices and long hours spent sitting in cars or planes.

Sleeping well

In the book, *The Sleep Revolution*, media mogul Ariana Huffington asserts that the modern day workforce is in a "sleep deprivation crisis."

Sleep is a critical component of good health. But travel, jet lag, and screen time can wreak havoc on your sleep cycle. To get better sleep:

>> Reduce jet lag as much as possible. Travel slowly, choose flight routes that fit your sleep schedule, and use an anti-jet lag app such as TimeShifter to help your body adapt to a new place.

>> Avoid staying in hostels and pod hotels with loud environments.

>> Ask your host or landlord whether there is a construction site, church, school, or nightclub next door to your prospective future home (*before* you rent it).

>> Check reviews for noise complaints before reserving a hotel or apartment.

>> Travel with ear plugs, noise-cancelling headphones, and an eye mask. (I also travel with a feather pillow.)

>> Choose destinations in time zones that align with your optimal work hours. (See Chapter 7 to figure out your peak times to work.)

>> Experiment with herbal teas, calming essential oils and nutritional supplements, and natural sleep aids, such as melatonin.

>> Drink less coffee and avoid caffeinated drinks late in the day.

>> Use a smartwatch or app such as Sleep Cycle to track sleep quality and patterns.

Blue light exposure can also adversely affect your sleep quality. Because digital nomads and remote workers spend a lot of time glued to their screens, it's important to know how to curb its adverse effects.

The best way to reduce blue light exposure is to reduce your screen time. While that may be easier said than done, you can adjust your phone settings to track your screen time and send you reminders or notifications.

Another way to reduce blue light exposure is to make sure your computer display is programmed to change color at night. It should adjust automatically from blue to warmer tones. If your computer doesn't offer that setting, install an app that accomplishes the same thing, such as f.lux. Or purchase a pair of blue light–blocking glasses.

Finally, set a nightly cutoff time for screens. I know, I know — it's hard. But unwinding before bed with phone time or Netflix isn't doing you any favors. Experts recommend avoiding blue light for at least *three hours* before bedtime.

Exercising your way around the world

Your next destination can inspire a new exercise routine.

When I lived in Japan, snowboarding was my preferred way to get a workout. In Costa Rica, it was surfing and yoga. In Peru, it was hiking. And in Europe, it's walking and bike riding.

Take advantage of your newfound flexibility as a nomad to mix up your workout routine according to seasons and destinations. Many digital nomads choose to live in Thailand or Brazil to practice martial arts such as Muay Thai, capoeira, and jiu-jitsu. Others move from cities and suburbs to outdoor destinations such as Colorado, Utah, or Wyoming.

Regardless of where you live, follow these tips to get a good workout anywhere in the world:

>> Book a rental property with fitness amenities in the building or rent a place within walking distance to a gym, Pilates studio, or bootcamp.

>> Join local health-centric meetup groups or running clubs.

>> Search free exercise classes on YouTube or get a remote online fitness membership that you can do from anywhere. Examples include Future Remote Fitness and Personal Training (www.future.co) and Obé Fitness On-Demand Workouts (https://obefitness.com).

>> Try Classpass (https://help.classpass.com), OneFit (https://onefit.com), Gymhopper Europe (https://gymhopper.com), and Zeamo Fitness App (https://zeamo.com) to book day passes at gyms in different countries.

>> Travel with a jump rope, water weights, and exercise bands.

>> Take frequent, five-minute breaks throughout your remote workday to do push-ups, sit-ups, or squats.

Set a reminder on your computer or phone to stand up and walk around at least once per hour.

>> Use an ergonomic chair and laptop stand for good posture when working. Some co-working spaces and digital nomad apartments also have standing desks.

TIP

Getting sufficient sunshine and vitamin D

Vitamin D deficiency is associated with a range of health risks, including diabetes, heart disease, cancer, and multiple sclerosis. It can also lead to "depression-like symptoms," according to WebMD.

You can get Vitamin D through sunlight or supplements.

The Mayo Clinic recommends getting between 600–800 international units (IU) of Vitamin D per day (15–30 minutes of sun exposure). However, you may need up to 4,000 IU to correct a deficiency.

If you're a digital nomad living in a cold place like Northern Europe or Canada during winter, you might not be getting enough Vitamin D. Check with your healthcare provider to find out.

Reducing your alcohol intake

It seems like socializing and drinking go hand in hand. In fact, I'd bet you've been to plenty of business dinners and networking events that involved alcohol. You may have even been to conferences where they gave you free alcohol tickets!

When you become a digital nomad, you'll naturally want to get out and meet people. Oftentimes, it will be by going out to eat or going to a conference or event. Be cognizant that such activities will usually include alcohol.

This is especially true if you're hanging out with travelers who are in "vacation mode." They might be indulging more they would at home. You, on the other hand, are living your new version of "normal." That may or may not include bottomless margaritas.

Temptations are everywhere, but especially in popular tourist destinations such as Bali, Croatia, Greece, or Mexico. When everyone else is drinking and partying, it's easy to get swept up in that mindset.

So be aware of the tendency to socially drink when you're with other travelers or because it's happy hour at the local WeWork.

Alcohol is a depressant. And everyone has their limits. If you feel sluggish or low energy, it could be the culprit.

Maintaining Your Mental Health

Although living a lifestyle of nomadic world travel may look glamorous from the outside, it's not all private jets and piña coladas. Nomads experience the same ups and downs of life as everyone else.

Traveling the world, while fun at times, won't solve all your problems. In fact, it can create new problems and challenges, such as loneliness, over-work, and burnout.

If you feel down as a digital nomad sometimes, it's normal. After all, you're only human! No matter how dynamic or exciting life gets, everyone knows what it's like on the roller coaster of life. This section gives you tips on caring for your mental health.

Staying mindful

Having a meditation or mindfulness practice can help you stay grounded in a lifestyle based around travel and technology. I've been meditating for almost ten years, and it's helped me cope with the demands of remote knowledge work and entrepreneurship. According to the meditation app, Headspace, studies show that meditation reduces symptoms of depression, anxiety, and stress, while increasing focus and resilience.

By downloading a meditation app such as HeadSpace or InsightTimer to your phone, you can meditate anytime, anywhere. I've even meditated while sitting on the New York City subway!

Embracing human connection

One of the most important aspects of being a human is connecting with other people, and being a digital nomad is no exception. Working from home or from a foreign country alone can be isolating and lonely. Make sure to hang out with other humans and call home sometimes.

See Chapter 14 for tips on meeting people, making friends, and staying in touch with family as a digital nomad.

Talking it out

Talking with a professional counselor, life coach, or therapist can help you work through issues that may be bothering you. TalkSpace (www.talkspace.com) is an online therapy app you can access from anywhere. BetterHelp (www.betterhelp.com), the world's largest therapy service, is also 100 percent online.

Taking time off for rest and self-care

Have you ever needed a vacation from your vacation? Even if you're traveling or living in exotic locations as a digital nomad, it's still important to take time off and go on vacation sometimes.

In between sabbaticals, make time for regular rest, relaxation, and self-care.

Whether self-care to you means going for a walk, taking a bubble bath, or cooking chicken noodle soup, make time for it. Set fixed work hours, turn off email and Slack notifications, and keep your weekends free (even if your Wednesday is your weekend).

TIP

Also schedule regular check-ups with your healthcare provider.

Look up alternative or holistic treatments in your area, such as acupuncture or an infrared sauna.

TIP

Cheering yourself up

Here are some ways to troubleshoot or boost your mood when you're feeling down:

» Get tested for food allergies and insensitivities; try an elimination diet.

» Get out into nature.

» Make sure you're getting enough exercise, sunlight, Vitamin D, and other essential nutrients, such as healthy fats and green vegetables.

» Take a cold shower. There are numerous psychological and physiological benefits of cold therapy.

» Write. Start journaling each morning to capture your thoughts and release worries.

» Laugh or watch comedy.

» Read philosophy or an inspiring book.

» Watch a motivational video on YouTube.

» Volunteer your time.

» Video call a friend or family member to chat.

» Reach out to digital nomads who understand what you're going through.

» Reflect on everything you're grateful for. Better yet, start a daily gratitude journal.

» Slow down on travel if you're feeling tired.

» Indulge in something you love to do, even if it means doing nothing!

I like the idea of an "Artist's Date," from Julia Cameron's book, *The Artist's Way*. Artists Dates are dates with yourself. It can be watching a movie, taking yourself out to dinner, or spending the day at a spa. Let your creativity be your guide!

Comparing and Contrasting Health and Medical Insurance

Although you may be able to pay out of pocket for some medical procedures abroad, it's still important to have insurance as a digital nomad.

You should have a regular healthcare plan that covers pre-existing conditions as well as an emergency travel/medical plan that covers things such as lost luggage and medical evacuation. This section explains the differences between international travel and health insurance plans.

International emergency travel medical insurance

Many new nomads confuse emergency travel/medical or trip insurance with general health insurance.

Travel insurance provides reimbursement for lost or damaged luggage, trip interruption or cancellation, and other travel-related issues.

Figure 12-1 shows typical coverage with travel insurance.

Travel medical insurance covers you if you get sick or injured while traveling or need emergency medical evacuation.

Figure 12-2 shows typical coverage with an emergency travel medical plan.

In other words, emergency travel medical insurance covers *emergencies* — not pre-existing conditions or long-term healthcare. That's where your regular health insurance plan comes in, which should cover your doctor's appointments, specialists, surgeries, dental work, and prescription medicine. (More on that in the next section.)

Emergency travel medical insurance can cover you for food poisoning, a broken arm, or trip cancellation, but not a root canal.

REMEMBER

Having an emergency travel/medical plan is non-negotiable as a digital nomad.

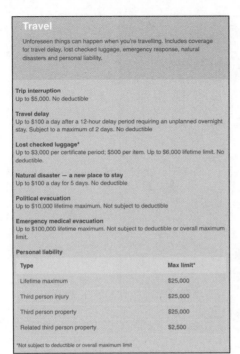

FIGURE 12-1: This is what's included in a typical travel insurance policy.

Source: Safety Nest, Insurance for nomads, Safetywing.com

The most popular international travel/medical insurance options for nomads include:

>> SafetyWing Nomad Insurance (https://safetywing.com)

>> World Nomads (www.worldnomads.com)

>> Insured Nomads Travel Insurance (www.insurednomads.com/travel-insurance)

Prices and deductibles vary widely according to your destination, age, and trip length. Inquire with each site directly for exact rates. But, for a ballpark figure, Nomad Insurance through SafetyWing starts at $42 per four weeks. Depending on your plan, you could get emergency travel medical coverage for less than $1,000 per year.

TIP

For even more travel insurance options, compare plans from different providers in the Insuremytrip.com marketplace.

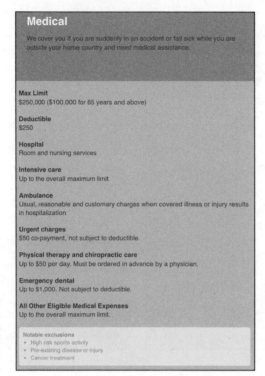

Medical

We cover you if you are suddenly in an accident or fall sick while you are outside your home country and need medical assistance.

Max Limit
$250,000 ($100,000 for 65 years and above)

Deductible
$250

Hospital
Room and nursing services

Intensive care
Up to the overall maximum limit

Ambulance
Usual, reasonable and customary charges when covered illness or injury results in hospitalization

Urgent charges
$50 co-payment, not subject to deductible.

Physical therapy and chiropractic care
Up to $50 per day. Must be ordered in advance by a physician.

Emergency dental
Up to $1,000. Not subject to deductible.

All Other Eligible Medical Expenses
Up to the overall maximum limit.

Notable exclusions
• High risk sports activity
• Pre-existing disease or injury
• Cancer treatment

FIGURE 12-2:
This is what's included in a typical travel medical insurance policy.

Source: Safety Nest, Insurance for nomads, Safetywing.com

International health insurance

Regardless of where you live, you need general health insurance coverage. As a digital nomad, you may opt to keep your home country insurance, sign up for a local plan wherever you are, or get an international policy that covers you in many countries. This section explains international health insurance options, good for when you are traveling or living in multiple countries per year. (If that doesn't describe you, move to the next section on local insurance or keeping your home country insurance).

REMEMBER

You should have general health insurance in addition to an emergency travel medical plan. Whether you get an international health insurance plan, a local health insurance plan, or keep your home country plan is up to you.

International health insurance differs from emergency travel medical plans, in that it covers you for ongoing care and pre-existing conditions as well as medical emergencies.

If you need stitches or your flight gets delayed, your trip insurance can cover it. But if you want full coverage for ongoing healthcare, such as periodic exams and screenings, prescription medicines, dental care, pregnancy, or surgery, you need an international healthcare plan. Figure 12-3 shows typical coverage with an international healthcare plan.

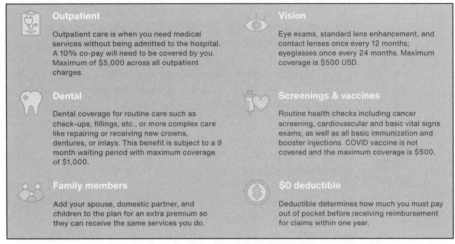

Source: Safety Nest, How much does Remote Health cost?, Safetywing.com

FIGURE 12-3: This is what's typically included in an international healthcare policy.

International health insurance options for nomads include:

>> SafetyWing's Nomad & Remote Worker Health Plan (https://safetywing.com/nomad-health)

>> Cigna Global (www.cignaglobal.com)

>> IMG Global (www.imglobal.com/international-health-insurance)

>> Pacific Prime (www.pacificprime.com/health-insurance-plans/international-health-insurance-plan)

>> Insured Nomads Global Health Insurance (www.insurednomads.com/global-health-insurance)

Prices for international health insurance plans vary according to your age, destination(s), deductible, and plan. But to give you an example, SafetyWing's Remote Health plan for nomads and remote employees starts at $206/month. I have often received quotes for $500–600 per month for a global healthcare plan for a single person.

If you plan to travel to multiple countries per year, having an international health policy is a good idea.

Local tourist insurance for foreigners

Instead of purchasing international travel/medical or health insurance, purchasing a domestic policy in your destination country is also an option. Consider buying a local insurance policy abroad if you want to be insured in one destination. (Or if you prefer the coverage compared to an international plan.)

A local insurance plan can either supplement or replace an international plan. You can purchase an emergency travel/medical policy for tourists abroad. Or you can purchase general health insurance through a local provider.

A local insurance plan only covers you in the country where you purchase the policy. If you plan to travel and change locations often, an international plan provides more comprehensive coverage wherever you go.

For example, the Costa Rican company, Sagicor, offers tourist insurance options for individuals, couples, and families. A 30-day tourist policy with Sagicor for an individual under 70 years old is $309. A 30-day policy for an individual over 70 years old is $618.

Sample coverage includes:

>> Medical expense, including medication: $20,000

>> Lodging expenses due to sanitary isolation: $4,000 (max. $300 per day)

>> Sanitary/funerary repatriation: $18,000

>> Pre-existing condition medical expense: $300

>> Loss of passport: $100

As you can see, a tourist policy includes basic coverage, but is not a comprehensive long-term option. When I lived in Bansko, Bulgaria one winter, I enrolled in a short-term emergency medical policy for foreigners and tourists at a local insurance office. At the time, I was also covered by an annual international travel insurance plan through World Nomads. It wasn't necessary to get two plans, but I felt better having extra coverage and care options in case I got in a snowboarding accident.

If you're applying for long-term or permanent residency in your destination country (see Chapter 9 for how to get visas and permits), you might be required to enroll in a local insurance plan. Check with the immigration or health department in your destination for more info. Or ask your immigration lawyer.

Some countries require that tourists sign up for a local insurance plan specifically related to pandemic coverage. At the time of writing this book, Sri Lanka requires a mandatory COVID-19 insurance policy for all travelers (vaccinated or not). Check with the local tourism board or health department in your destination to confirm.

Keeping your home country health insurance

Now, you may be wondering what to do with your domestic health insurance plan if you become a digital nomad. I can't tell you what to do, but I can give you some tips.

First, always consult with your doctor or healthcare provider. Note that in addition to having emergency travel medical coverage and an international health insurance plan, many digital nomads keep their home country health insurance, too. That means potentially holding *three* insurance plans!

Consider keeping your regular home country plan or downgrading to a bare bones "catastrophic" plan if you plan to use health services there in the future.

If you have healthcare coverage through an international health insurance provider (such as IMG Global) and you plan to stay abroad long term, you can potentially let your domestic plan lapse and re-enroll if or when you return.

If your employer or government offers health insurance, it would be ideal to keep it, if possible. However, financial or other costs may be associated with keeping it. Your government may require you to pay taxes or reside in your home country for a certain number of days per year to keep your health insurance.

Regardless, it's a good idea to keep the coverage that you're familiar with for the first few years that you're a digital nomad. At least until you feel comfortable with your international insurance options and healthcare providers.

Depending on your country of citizenship, you may qualify for a regional insurance plan. For example, the European Health Insurance Card (EHIC) gives EU residents access to "medically necessary, state-provided healthcare during a temporary stay in any of the 27 EU countries," plus Iceland, Liechtenstein, Norway, and

Switzerland, under the same cost as your home country (or for free). A European Health Insurance Card is not a replacement for travel insurance, and it does not guarantee free medical care.

Travel medical and health insurance for seniors

Unfortunately, most insurance providers have age limits for their coverage. Finding plans for people over age 60 or 70 may be more expensive or have some coverage limitations and exclusions.

Companies that cater to travelers 50+ include:

>> Freedom Travel Insurance (www.freedominsure.co.uk)

>> Generali Global (www.generalitravelinsurance.com/csa-travel-protection.html)

>> JD Health Insurance (www.jdtravelinsurance.co.uk)

>> Saga Health Insurance (UK) (www.saga.co.uk/insurance/health-insurance)

>> Travelex (www.travelexinsurance.com/travel-insurance/traveler/seniors)

>> Travel Guard (www.travelguard.com/travel-insurance/plans/annual)

Best practices for purchasing insurance

Here are a few more tips for successfully navigating the world of international insurance:

>> Some plans allow you to purchase a policy after you arrive in your destination. But for peace of mind, research insurance providers and select a plan before you leave home.

>> When applying for coverage, disclose as much information as possible about your trip and coverage needs.

>> Always read the entire policy before purchasing. It's important to know what you're buying.

>> To potentially save money, opt for long-term policies over individual, per-trip plans that you might see when you purchase an airline ticket.

>> Contact providers with your questions and try to get your answers in writing for easy reference.

Navigating Healthcare Systems in Foreign Lands

Despite taking precautions, sometimes you will need medical care abroad. The cost and quality of medical care varies by country, although the United States, Canada, Australia, Switzerland, and other European countries tend to be the most expensive, according to the OECD.

Before traveling to a new destination, research the local healthcare system and costs, so you know what to expect. Ask your emergency travel/medical or health insurance provider whether there are any restrictions on where you can go for care abroad.

Finding medical care abroad

Once you've arrived in your destination, you have the option between public and private medical care. The public system is usually funded and managed by the government, while private care is for profit.

If you are a local resident or citizen, you may have health insurance through the public healthcare system. See Chapter 9 for more about getting long-term residency or citizenship status.

If you are a tourist, you could pay out of pocket for private care or submit a claim through your insurance provider. I discuss insurance options in the earlier section "Comparing and Contrasting Health and Medical Insurance."

Many digital nomads inadvertently become medical tourists — people who pay out of pocket for healthcare abroad. If you pay out of pocket, tests, lab work, surgeries, and other procedures overseas are typically a fraction of the price of the United States. (That doesn't mean it's cheap, though.)

Latin America, Eastern Europe, and Southeast Asia are three of the most popular medical tourism destinations, especially Mexico, Costa Rica, and Thailand. A dental cleaning could run you between $100–200 in the United States versus $15–50 abroad. An annual check-up at a physician's office that starts at $100–250 in the United States could cost as low as $20-60 in another country.

You may also be pleasantly surprised with the high quality of healthcare abroad, as well as the good customer service and access to doctors. I've often been given my international doctors' cell phone numbers so I can reach out on WhatsApp with questions. (However, that's not always the case.)

Before seeking medical care abroad, try to find out whether your healthcare provider is accredited by an international body, such as DNV GL Healthcare (www.dnv.com/assurance/healthcare/accredited-hospitals.html). Also inquire whether your provider speaks the same language. If not, hire a local interpreter or use an online translation service.

Pharmaceutical drugs may be more widely available over the counter compared to in your home country. Or they may be more restricted. Check with your doctors and pharmacists at home and abroad to inquire before leaving home.

Here are some ways to find healthcare providers abroad:

>> Search the International Society of Travel Medicine's Online Clinic Directory (www.istm.org/AF_CstmClinicDirectory.asp).

>> Search online or in your phone's maps app to look up the closest public and private hospital in your area.

>> Search for a local primary doctor and dentist for regular check-ups. Or contact your insurance company to find providers in network.

>> Search online for a "tourist doctor" or "hotel doctor" in your area to find English-speaking doctors who offer a variety of services, including 24/7 assistance, home visits, lab analysis, immunizations, prescription drugs, and more. Examples include www.playadoctor.com in Playa del Carmen, Mexico and www.mydoctorinmadrid.com in Madrid, Spain.

>> Contact your country's embassy or consulate for a list of local medical providers. Getting recommendations from other expats, foreigners, and digital nomads you trust is also helpful.

>> Find a remote doctor. Examples include Teladoc Remote Doctor (www.teladoc.com) and MD Live Virtual Healthcare (https://mdlnext.mdlive.com).

>> Find a list of hospitals in different countries worldwide at www.internationalinsurance.com/hospitals.

>> Holistic and alternative medicine providers are also an option. Always do your research and stay safe. Do what you feel is best for you!

TIP

Always bring your passport with you for identification when going to a hospital or doctor's office in a different country, as well as your health insurance card(s).

Chapter **13**

Finding a Productivity and Work Life Balance

O nce you get acclimated to a digital nomad lifestyle, it's nearly impossible to go back to the "old way" of living. That's why it's so important to get your work done so you can continue your location-independent journey. In this chapter, I offer guidance for how to plan your workday, stay productive, and find work-life balance.

TIP

Download a list of productivity tools and apps for digital nomads at www. travelingwithkristin.com/dummies.

Achieving Peak Productivity as a Digital Nomad

Although you don't necessarily have to work 9-5 if you aren't in a 9-5 job, it's important to have structure to your day to balance the freedom and spontaneity of a nomadic lifestyle. And if you want to *truly* disconnect from work sometimes, you'll need to be able manage your time and meet deadlines without anyone looking over your shoulder.

In this section, you find out how to organize your digital nomad workday for peak productivity while avoiding some common productivity mistakes.

Determining how much to work

Time — we all have the same amount but working remotely can free up a lot of it. According to my calculations, working from home can save up to 150–200 hours per month that's typically lost to commuting, meetings, and office distractions. That's good news for digital nomads, who have a lot of control over how they spend their time.

How much you should work as a digital nomad depends on the nature of your job, who you work for, and your income goals.

If you're a remote employee, you may be expected to work a 40-hour work week. Some employers will want you to be online at certain times, while others are more flexible, as long as your work gets done.

If you're a self-employed freelancer or online business owner, your schedule may vary. You could work overtime if you're managing multiple clients, racing toward a deadline, or launching a new product. During other times of the year, you may have a lighter schedule. And if most of your earnings come from passive income streams, you might *never* work, or clock a few hours per week.

To figure out how much you should work, evaluate your workload, income, cost of living, and short- and long-term goals. Make adjustments when necessary.

REMEMBER

Where you live could determine how much you have to work to pay the bills. If you typically earn €2,500 per month as a full-time freelancer in Germany, your money will go farther living in Bolivia, where the average cost of living is closer to €900 per month. If you moved to Singapore, however, your expenses could triple.

When living in an expensive destination, you may have to work more hours, raise your prices, or create new income streams to offset the increased cost. Likewise, if you want to work less, moving to a less expensive place is one way to cut back on your hours without decreasing your profits.

Get a guide for calculating your budget and cost of living in Chapter 3.

Planning your remote workday and daily routine

Humans thrive on consistency and routine, but there's a fine line between having too much structure or none at all. Commuting to an office might not be your idea of a good time, but it has the benefit of creating an anchor for your daily routine. When your laptop is your office, however, it takes extra intention to organize your day.

Without a routine, you can end up wasting a lot of time and energy on things you didn't think about before you became a nomad, such as what time to wake up, where you'll be working from, and what the Wi-Fi password is, (See Chapter 7 for how to choose a workspace.)

Luckily, becoming a digital nomad is a great opportunity to create a balanced routine, without the stress of a daily commute.

When it comes to working remotely, output is more important than hours worked. Rather than assuming that you'll always work an eight-hour day, approach your schedule in terms of when you enjoy working, what needs to get done when, and how long it will take. This is also known as a *Results-Oriented Work Environment (ROWE)*. There's no set schedule in a ROWE. You get to design it.

To plan your workday schedule:

REMEMBER

>> Define your work week and which days you'll take off. How many days per week will you work? Do you prefer working M-F with weekends off, or perhaps you want to work 3-4 days per week?

Look ahead in your calendar and try to identify weeks or months that will be busier than others. Also look for periods that would be optimal to travel or take time off.

>> Determine what your work deliverables and responsibilities are. Identify upcoming deadlines or recurring meeting times.

>> Estimate how many hours you'll need to be available to other people each day and in what time zone(s).

TIP

Use a website such as WorldTimeBuddy.com to convert differences in time zones.

>> Get to know your most productive time of day. Are you a night owl or an early bird? Chapter 7 helps you figure out your peak attention hours.

>> Set a start and end time to your workday.

TIP

>> Identify where you will work. Your Airbnb? A co-working space? A coffee shop? See the next section for how to choose your best work environment and Chapter 7 for how to find a co-working space.

Do your most important or demanding work during your peak attention hours when you're most alert. Batch shallow work that requires less focus to your least productive hours of the day. Chapter 7 helps you figure out if you're a night owl or an early bird.

>> Set aside time each morning for a ritual such as journaling, reading, exercise, or meditation to start your day.

>> Schedule in time for breaks, meals, or taking a walk.

Once you find a schedule that works for you, you can choose your destinations around your ideal workday. If you like to start your workday in the afternoon, you can move somewhere that's a few hours ahead of people you work with.

Likewise, be wary of time zone conflicts that would require you to work during hours that you'd rather be sleeping.

REMEMBER

Don't be afraid to embrace an "odd" or untraditional work schedule (whatever that means to you). You'll also want to adjust your schedule to take advantage of once-in-a-lifetime opportunities.

Designating a workspace

If you're transitioning to a nomadic lifestyle from a traditional or work-from-home job, you're probably used to working in the same place every day. But when you become a digital nomad, you may change homes and workspaces often.

Moving to a new place creates a pattern interrupt in your daily routine that can work for you or against you. Changing locations eliminates the cues that triggered old behaviors and gives you the opportunity to build new habits.

The key is to use your new environment to your advantage. Every time you arrive in a new place (or before you get there), decide where you will work — either within your apartment or in your new neighborhood.

In the book, *Willpower Doesn't Work*, author Ben Hardy explains how you can increase your productivity and enter a flow state faster by linking your work activities with a certain location. For instance, Ben likes to write in his car in the mornings. You might like to work from your couch, a coffee shop, or a co-working space.

Where you work isn't important, as long as it works for you. You might even work from multiple places. Perhaps you like to attend virtual meetings from your Airbnb in the mornings and code from a café in the afternoons. I particularly love working in libraries, but I often journal from a hotel lobby or answer email from a museum café. Think about what would inspire you the most and go for it.

Chapter 7 has tips on how to find a co-working space or office worldwide. But Coworker.com and Croissant are two places to start. Penty of co-working spaces and cafés can be found on TripAdvisor or your phone maps app. When in need, WeWork offers a $275/month flex desk plan in almost every major city in the world.

You can also find recommendations on where to work through local tourism boards, business bureaus, and digital nomad groups. The Croatia Digital Nomad Association offers resources and support to new arrivals, while the Croatia Tourism Board has an online guide with tips for how to create a new office space.

REMEMBER

Anywhere can be an office if you bring a Wi-Fi hotspot with you. See Chapters 9 and 10 for how to adapt your phone and Internet to a digital nomad lifestyle. Use an app such as WiFi Map to find public networks, although make sure to use a VPN for security. I've logged into work in parks from Portugal to Panama.

Optimizing your productivity

Regardless of when, where, or how long you work, there are a few best practices for remote productivity:

>> Follow a consistent work schedule and routine.

>> Consider designing a startup and shut-down ritual for your workday.

>> Schedule your most difficult tasks for your peak hours of the day.

>> Choose no more than three "Most Important Things" (MIT) to do per day.

>> Try time blocking. Minimize time and attention lost to "task switching" by batching similar work into one day or time block.

>> Use the Pomodoro method to help you focus on one task for 25 minutes at a time.

>> Track your time with a tool such as Toggl, Harvest, or in a project management system.

>> Download an app such as Freedom to block distracting apps and websites.

>> Delegate anything that doesn't directly contribute to your bottom line. Find freelancers and virtual assistants on Fiverr or Upwork.

>> Take intermittent breaks outside or away from your screen.

>> Turn off notifications. Respond to email once or twice per day.

>> Plan tomorrow's to-do list today. Take five minutes at the end of each day to write down what you want to achieve tomorrow.

>> Reward yourself. Plan a fun outing or excursion for when you finish your work. I'll never get tired of ending my workday with a stroll on the beach or a dip in the Adriatic Sea.

REMEMBER

Part of being a productive and responsible digital nomad is also about knowing when to disconnect and take time off. Self-employed entrepreneurs and freelancers may end up working more hours for themselves than they did when they were salaried workers. This is especially true if you're working in multiple roles at the same time or have a side hustle.

Avoiding common productivity mistakes

Productivity is subjective. Only you know what it means for you. However, a few productivity mistakes digital nomads sometimes make (myself included) include:

>> **Working with your phone on your desk.** Social media apps and notifications are designed to be addictive. The *Journal of the Association for Consumer Research* found that your phone can distract you even if it's turned off! Protect your attention span by leaving your phone in a different room while you work.

>> **Traveling too fast.** How you define "fast" is up to you. But, at some rate, travel will cut into your productivity.

>> **Traveling with too many people.** Working alongside cool people is often inspiring and enjoyable. But it can also become distracting. If you begin to suspect that socializing is adversely affecting your job, balance things with some alone time.

>> **Wasting time looking for Wi-Fi.** Always bring your Internet with you. Public Wi-Fi networks can be few and far between. Or slow and unreliable. Travel with an international Wi-Fi hotspot or unlocked device that you can use with local SIM cards.

>> **Working when you don't need to.** Put the idea that you need to appear busy or fill the time until you clock away. As a digital nomad, you won't want to waste time at work because there are so many fun things to do when you finish!

>> **Working all the time.** Some nomads *never* disconnect from work. They'll join a conference call from the Acropolis or answer email while trekking Machu Picchu. Do what you feel, but remember to unplug and be present sometimes.

Establishing a Healthy Work-Life Balance

Becoming a digital nomad offers the opportunity to find more balance in your daily life. The essence of work–life balance is deciding how much time to dedicate to different aspects of your personal and professional life.

Following the previous tips in this chapter help you plan your workday, stay organized, and know when to unplug. But there are a few additional things you can do to maintain balance while living nomadically:

>> When arriving in a new country, test your daily routine. Keep track of what's working for you and what's not. See how things go and adjust your schedule as needed. Remember that it will take time to adjust to your new surroundings and settle into a routine every time you change locations.

>> Travel slowly. The slower you travel, the less time you spend in transit and the more time you have for daily life.

>> Set a bottom line. Create a work schedule for yourself with a designated start and end time. Don't let work bleed into all areas of your life.

>> Take time off. Sometimes digital nomads forget to take vacations because their lives often look like a vacation. Although it can be hard to break away from your business if you're self-employed, it's important to do so on occasion. At the beginning of each year (or right now), block off a couple weeks in your calendar when you can take a holiday — paid or not.

Some productivity experts claim that the concept of having work–life balance isn't realistic or doesn't exist. I interpret this to mean that there will always be trade-offs when choosing which aspects of life to focus on at any given time. Knowing that "perfect" work–life balance doesn't exist can help take the pressure off when things feel unbalanced.

REMEMBER

Work–life balance is personal. You may need more rest or play time compared to other people. Don't compare your journey to others. Always do what's best for you.

Avoiding and recovering from remote work burnout

Remote work burnout is more common among remote workers than you might think.

Rather than a medical condition, the World Health Organization (WHO) describes burnout as an "occupational phenomenon" or "syndrome" stemming from chronic, unaddressed work stress.

If you ever feel exhausted, negative, or stressed about your remote job, you may be burned out. But you're not alone.

A Monster.com survey found that 69 percent of respondents reported experiencing burnout since they began working from home during the Coronavirus pandemic, up from 52 percent previously.

Meanwhile, NordVPN found that workers across the United States, Canada, and Europe added two to three extra hours to their workdays during the same time period.

Although remote work can offer more flexibility and better work–life balance, it's also easy to replace your commute with more time at your desk.

The top three warning signs of burnout include:

>> Feelings of energy depletion or exhaustion

>> Increased mental distance from your job (also associated with absenteeism and turnover), according to the World Health Organization.

>> Reduced professional efficacy

How much work is too much?

That's for you to decide. But you may be overdoing it when:

>> You feel guilty about not being productive enough.

>> You work more than eight hours per day.

>> You have work-related insomnia.

>> You skip lunch breaks and exercise.

>> You're tired all the time.

>> You've been calling in sick to work.

>> You're struggling with procrastination.

Some tendency to procrastinate is normal. But the WHO cites "increased feelings of negativism or cynicism" as a primary indicator of burnout syndrome.

There could be such a thing as being *too* productive when working remotely, if you focus all your energy on work, and not much else.

Humans aren't robots. We need time to reboot and recharge. Don't sacrifice your health and well-being in the name of productivity.

The first step in overcoming burnout is recognizing that it's a problem. The WHO has taken the first step by classifying the syndrome as an occupational hazard. But there's more you can do.

Reducing your workload is the most important way to cure or prevent burnout.

Christine Sinsky, MD, a Vice President at the American Medical Association says that "burnout is primarily related to [your] environment," when there's a "mis-match" between your workload, time, and resources.

Make sure that you're working for a company whose culture doesn't reward long hours or encourage overwork. If you're self-employed, be a compassionate boss to yourself.

"Burnout takes many forms," Jason Fried, the CEO of Basecamp, once told me. Make sure you have "plenty of time to [yourself], lots of autonomy to make decisions, ample time off, sabbaticals every three years, [and] outlets to discuss stress."

In my personal experience, when it comes to reversing burnout, it's best to take a less is more approach.

Rather than adding "fix burnout" to your to-do list, ask yourself what you can eliminate. Which activities (and people) drain your energy the most? Which tasks can you outsource, delegate, or eliminate?

Once you've determined what you want to *stop* doing, here are some tips to help regain control of your well-being.

>> **Sleep more.** Sleep is the foundation of health and wellness. Allowing your body and mind sufficient time to rest and recover will help you cope better with work stress. Set a cut-off time for work at least a few hours before bed.

» **Limit your communication.** You don't need to be available on every platform all day, every day. Check email once or twice per day and close communication apps when you're in deep work mode.

» **Adopt the idea of "slow mornings."** Start your day with a morning routine that supports your physical and mental health. Read, journal, exercise, eat breakfast, listen to a podcast, and reflect before jumping into your inbox.

» **Prioritize.** If you constantly find yourself "too busy" to function, track your time for a few days to see where it goes. Delegate or eliminate unnecessary tasks.

» **Get outside.** Immersing yourself in sunshine, fresh air, and nature will boost your mood and well-being.

» **Move more.** Make time for daily exercise. If you're on the phone a lot, take calls while walking or join meetings from your standing desk or kitchen counter rather than an office chair.

» **Hydrate and eat well.** If you're putting in long hours at the virtual office, fuel your body with plenty of water and clean food. It's harder to concentrate when you subsist on coffee, carbs, and takeout. If you don't have time to cook, sign up for a healthy food delivery service.

» **Practice mindfulness.** You've heard it before (earlier in this book!), but meditation decreases stress and increases feelings of well-being.

» **Ask for help.** Find support or someone to talk to on Talkspace.com or Betterhelp.com.

» **Take a vacation.** Whether you unplug for the weekend, plan a staycation, or go on a quick road trip, time away from work is necessary.

» **Get a new job.** If all else fails, change employers. See Chapters 5 and 6 for how to find a remote job and or create one of your own.

Combining work sprints with sabbaticals

One way some digital nomads find balance and get things done is with work sprints.

Work sprinting is working full time on a single project for one to three months. It's like a 24-hour "hackathon," but for a longer time.

After your work sprint is over, you take a one-week vacation or a one-month sabbatical to decompress and recharge before starting the process again.

Work sprints are good for projects that have a distinct start and end date or a measurable outcome. You could set a one-month sprint to build a website or a three-month sprint to write a book or launch a podcast.

Work sprints are a good way to focus on one clear goal to achieve, and then accomplish it without managing multiple projects or burning out at the same time.

What makes work sprints successful is having a clear start and end date, plus time to rejuvenate afterward. Combine work sprints with the tips in the previous sections of this chapter to help you maintain a healthy schedule, get things done, have fun, rest, *and* avoid burnout.

Chapter **14**

Meeting People and Making Friends

One of the concerns you might have as you embark on your nomadic journey is how you'll meet people in foreign lands. You might be wondering how you'll make new friends, keep up with old ones, avoid feeling lonely, and perhaps meet a special someone along the way.

In this chapter, I offer ideas for how you can date, network, and find community as a digital nomad. Because life sure is sweeter when it's shared with other people.

Whether you're solo traveling, traveling with a significant other, or as a family, this chapter helps you maintain a healthy social life while on the road or abroad.

Meeting People In Real Life

Meeting people while traveling or living in different places as a digital nomad isn't much different than meeting people in your regular life. Being a digital nomad can even enhance your social life. Instead of the same hum-drum happy hour routine, your workdays and weekends could be filled with plenty of new friends and adventures.

Throughout your travels, you'll surely meet many different types of people, from fellow remote workers to locals, expats, business travelers, and tourists.

This section provides examples of how you can meet people in person, the old-fashioned way.

Daily life abroad

To meet people in your day-to-day life, it's important to look up from your screen sometimes and get out and about. Find events and activities that interest you and go for it!

If you're a runner, join a running club. If you're into working out, join a gym. If you love to cook, sign up for a cooking class.

Your new friend circle starts with one person. I once connected with an expat from the Dominican Republic who was living in Amsterdam. We had a mutual friend on social media and she was kind enough to give me a tour of the city the first day I arrived (in the rain, mind you). She showed me a around, taking me to famous sites such as the Albert Cuyp market and Museumplein, where the Amsterdam sign used to be. Over the following months, through spending time with Julia and her friends from around the world, I began to feel like I fit in. My social network grew organically and before I knew it, I was being invited to weddings, girls' trips, concerts, and Halloween parties, as if I had lived in the Netherlands all my life!

As a nomad, you will often meet people through serendipity and chance. I once became friends with a girl from Germany because I asked her to take a photo of me at the Hong Kong harbor. We ended up chatting for hours along the waterfront, exploring the night markets together, and have stayed in touch ever since.

Finding local events and things to do

While traveling is great for helping you expand your mind and worldview, local events can give you a real taste of a place's culture and flavors.

I've attended many memorable events in my years as a digital nomad. I'll always remember going to the Medellín Food & Wine Festival, the Cannes Film Festival, the Bulgarian Rose Festival, and a soccer match at Camp Nou in Barcelona against Real Madrid. But small events and meetups are just as special.

Large events, such as Spain's Running of the Bulls, recur annually. But you can find unique things to do almost every day of the week through Eventbrite, Ticketmaster, Facebook Events, Meetup.com, Tourism Boards, newspapers, expat websites, and even through searching Instagram hashtags.

Meetup.com has been especially useful to me in my travels. Thousands of events are shared each day on Meetup. There's bound to be something you're interested in! To find things to do and people to meet, search by topic, keyword, or category, such as Dancing, Games, Technology, or Identity & Language.

One of the best Meetup events I've ever attended was an intimate dinner party in Berlin with guests from Germany and around the world. I ended up running into one of the people I met there at a beach club in Spain a few months later, and then again in an airport security line. It's a small world, as the saying goes.

Not only can you have a good time and meet people, but you can learn new skills! Through Eventbrite, I've taken creative writing and screenwriting classes, learned how to bake bread, and painted pottery while sipping wine with strangers.

I also have Airbnb Experiences to thank for introducing me to the art of DJing, which has become a new side hustle and passion project for me.

TIP

Follow local bloggers and newspapers to uncover even more events. When I lived in Amsterdam, I used WhatsupwithAmsterdam.com and DutchReview.com to find out about local goings-on in the Netherlands. When you find a site you like, sign up for email updates to stay in the loop.

TIP

Keep an eye out for free local guidebooks, coupon books, and magazines at hotels and coffeeshops, which are always filled with the most current local events. In picking up free magazines in Miami, I found out about full moon yoga sessions, local tours of historic places, and read an article about sustainable travel that inspired me to invite the author on my podcast.

Joining expat organizations

Connecting with other people who are traveling or living overseas can help you feel more at home in a foreign country. It's also a great way to expand your network if you're living in your home country and want to meet new people from around the world.

Expat organizations have been around for many years, founded with the purpose of helping people find information and make connections in their new cities. The most popular communities include Expat.com, Expatica, and InterNations.

Each community offers an annual membership, but you can also register to attend events á la carte. For example, you don't have to be an InterNations member to register to attend their events.

InterNations (Internations.org) is one of the oldest expat communities on the planet, with chapters in 420 cities worldwide. Through InterNations, you can meet people, get information and tips about your destination, and even find housing and expat support groups. More than 6,000 InterNations events happen worldwide every month, such as picknicking at the Eiffel Tower in Paris or swimming with manatees in Florida. I once ate giant pretzels and drank (probably too much) beer at an InterNations event at Oktoberfest in Munich. I also learned how to roll sushi with InterNations members in San José, Costa Rica.

Beyond expat websites, local English-language newspapers are a great resource to learn about local and current events.

The Tico Times in Costa Rica publishes a list of clubs and organizations for every interest under the sun. There's even a "Coffee-Pickin' Square Dance Club!" Sounds good to me!

Finally, check with your home country's embassy or consulate for even more ways to meet people. They can provide information on local expat or interest-based organizations and may even host events of their own. For example, U.S. Embassies around the world hold 4th of July celebrations each year. Your country's embassy abroad may hold an annual Independence Day celebration or throw a New Year's party.

Meeting fellow travelers

One of my favorite things to do when I arrive in a new place is join a free walking tour. Walking tours give you an overview of your new area and provide the opportunity to connect with fellow tourists. Find tours on TripAdvisor or Freetoursbyfoot.com.

Couchsurfing or staying at hostels are also classic ways to meet travelers. Hostelworld.com has a platform that lets you connect with people before you arrive in your destination. Couchsurfing.com offers a groups feature and an events calendar.

ASMALLWORLD (ASW; www.asmallworld.com) is a website, app, and global community for people who share a passion for travel. As a member of ASW since 2007, I've attended Dîner en Blanc in Vancouver, happy hour events in London, and a Christmas party in Tampa, Florida.

Through ASW, you can connect with people for socializing, business, or romance. Membership costs €79 per year.

Volunteering

Want to meet people, feel fulfilled, and give back at the same time? Try volunteering! Through volunteering, you can meet locals and foreigners alike — all of whom are united for a good cause.

Some volunteer opportunities are paid, while others are free. Contact local charities and non-profit organizations in your destination to find ways to help. Some international sites to try are GlobalVolunteers.org, Goabroad.com, Volunteerhq.org, Wwoof.net.

Nomads Giving Back (https://nomadsgivingback.com) is an organization founded to help digital nomads give back to local communities. It offers a service to match your skills with organizations in need. Services you can offer include website design, bookkeeping, legal consulting, animal care, and more.

WARNING

Voluntourism, combining tourism with volunteering or aid work, is a controversial practice. Critics say it can cause more harm than good. Read about the issues facing the destinations you visit and contemplate how you can get involved in a way that benefits the local community. Research organizations before getting involved.

Meeting the locals

One of the questions people ask me most often is how to meet locals in their new destinations. No one wants to stick out as a tourist, I suppose (even if you are one).

Fitting in with the locals takes time and trust. It won't happen overnight, but it can happen organically if you stay in a country for an extended period.

For better or worse, I have often left a country as soon as I started to feel comfortable and like I was fitting in. It's exciting to plan where you'll go next, but the longer you stay in one place, the more people you'll meet and the more you'll understand the language and culture.

Speaking of which, learning the language makes it easier to make friends with local people (See Chapter 16 for more about language schools.)

As mentioned previously, volunteering is a great way to meet locals and foreigners alike. Through volunteering, you get to meet people helping people. Plus, you'll gain insights into the culture of the people you're working alongside.

THE BUTTERFLY EFFECT OF MEETING PEOPLE WHILE TRAVELING

In 2007, I bumped into a woman I knew from New York on a flight from Nosara to San Jose, Costa Rica.

She invited me to dinner at her apartment that night, where I met her friend, María Jose (MJ) Flaqué. Little did I know at the time, MJ would become my best friend and digital nomad travel partner for the next ten years.

Before I went nomadic, however, I decided to relocate from Nosara to the Central Valley. When looking for a place to stay, MJ introduced me to her friend Natalie, from Columbia, who had a room to rent. Shortly thereafter, Natalie advertised the third bedroom of our house for rent on Craigslist and a girl named Andrea answered the ad.

Ten years later, I gave a toast at Andrea's wedding in Iceland. But the story doesn't end there. At the reception, I met Marysia Do, a location-independent yoga teacher who had just moved back to the United States from Singapore, with her husband, John.

The following year, while living in Bulgaria, I flew to nearby Cyprus to attend one of Marysia's yoga retreats. She mentioned she was headed to Novi Sad, Serbia, next, to attend the EXIT music festival with Serbian friends she had met while living as an expat in Singapore. Being nomadic, I decided to join them, and it was one of the best weeks of my life. I learned a lot about the Serbian culture, met incredible people, danced to electronic music, and vlogged about the experience for my YouTube channel.

In 2020, I invited Marysia to be a guest on my podcast, Badass Digital Nomads, where she shared business, travel, and living abroad advice with thousands of listeners in my audience.

A year later, her husband, John (a former DJ in Los Angeles), helped me prepare for my first DJ gig in Miami.

In 2022, MJ, now a four-time author and digital nomad living between Bali, Costa Rica, Spain, and Portugal, gave me tips for writing the book that you're holding in your hands.

And today, as I write these words, I RSVP'd to Marysia and John's baby shower in Chicago, where I will reunite with my former Costa Rican roommate, Andrea, and her family.

When you step outside your comfort zone and travel or live abroad as a digital nomad, your life will change in ways you can't imagine at first. The magic of the digital nomad lifestyle is truly found in the people you meet, perhaps more than the places you go.

Meeting People on the Job

Becoming a digital nomad provides new opportunities for networking and professional development, whether you're a remote employee, independent contractor, or online business owner.

In this section, you find out how to expand your remote business network and meet potential partners, customers, and mentors, regardless of which industry you work in.

Networking abroad

Networking in other countries is very similar to what you might experience at home. You'll find general business meetups online and offline, as well as industry events.

Eventbrite, Facebook Events, ASW, and Meetup.com are great resources to find in-person business meetups.

I once attended a networking event in Amsterdam that I found through Eventbrite. I met local Dutch businesspeople, expats, nomads, and business travelers. Not only did I make new friends, but I met a fellow relocation consultant to partner with and a content creator to collaborate with. I also got to hang out on a historic boat in Amsterdam's famous canal district, sipping wine and tasting hors d'oeuvres. Even if cold herring isn't your cup of tea, trying new foods while chatting with nice people is a good way to spend the day.

Co-working spaces are another way to get involved in the local business community. Startdock (https://startdock.nl), a co-working space in Amsterdam and Rotterdam, holds weekly networking events and happy hour get togethers that you can join online or in person. Coworking Bansko (https://coworkingbansko.com) in Bulgaria coordinates game nights, barbeques, and outdoor activities for members. Work Central (https://workcentral.ng) in Lagos, Nigeria hosts monthly events focused on business-centric topics such as marketing, coding, and fundraising. And WeWork (www.wework.com) in Buenos Aires, Argentina, often held rooftop parties with live music.

TIP

Being a digital nomad also allows you to travel to international events in your industry without taking time off from work. I've leveraged my location independence to attend podcasting, YouTube, entrepreneurship, and affiliate marketing conferences in Orlando, Los Angeles, London, Montreal, and Barcelona.

Also consider attending virtual summits in your industry and connecting with people on social media platforms. Networking online is easier than ever before. After all, one of the biggest business networks in the world — whether you're a digital nomad or not — is LinkedIn.

Finding a mentor

Beyond connecting with people through conferences, events, and Facebook groups, seeking an online mentor can help you grow your business network and career. You can find a mentor through a local chamber of commerce, LinkedIn, or inquiring with friends and colleagues.

Websites for finding a remote mentor include:

>> SCORE for small businesses (www.score.org)

>> iMentor (https://imentor.org)

>> MentorCity (www.mentorcity.com)

>> Mogul for women (https://onmogul.com)

Cold contacting people

Another effective way to network is to reach out to people that you admire. If you read or consume someone's online content that inspires you, reach out and tell them why. Sometimes people will respond, sometimes they won't. But you never know unless you try!

I once got a job offer ghostwriting for a popular blog because I sent an email to one of my writer heroes. And I've accepted plenty of people as guests on my podcast because they reached out to me in a cold email.

Joining a mastermind

A mastermind is a group of three or more people who come together to give each other advice and support. A mastermind can meet online or in person and strategize about any topic, business problem, or industry.

You can join a pre-existing mastermind such as Dropship Lifestyle, Tropical MBA, or Growth Masters. You can also search online for a mastermind in your niche. Or you can start your own with a group of friends or strangers on Reddit.

The benefit of joining a mastermind is that you get to meet new people, brainstorm ideas, share successes and wins, and find solutions to problems.

You can join a mastermind with digital nomads or traditional, location-based workers around the world. Many conferences, events, and retreats function as masterminds or have mastermind groups that split off from the main event. I was in a weekly mastermind for three years with two Dutch digital nomads who I met at a co-working space.

Growing your own network

Organizing your own meetups, events, or masterminds is also a way to get to know fellow remote workers and digital nomads. The Nomad Summit conference started as a meetup at a coffee shop in Chiang Mai. It's since welcomed thousands of attendees over the years who come to learn, network, and connect with like-minded people.

German digital nomad, Johannes Voelkner, got the idea for Nomad Cruise after a Facebook post about going on a cruise together went viral. A few years later, thousands of people can call themselves "Nomad Cruisers," and Johannes started a second community (on land this time) called Nomadbase (https://nomadbase.com). Figure 14-1 shows what's included in a Nomadbase membership.

Source: NOMADBASE

FIGURE 14-1: What's included in Nomadbase membership.

By starting your own online community or organizing a meetup offline, you have nothing to lose and everything to gain!

Meeting people through content creation

Rather than searching for new friends and potential colleagues, why not attract them to you by publishing content online? With a smartphone and an Internet connection, anyone can be a writer, podcaster, or YouTuber.

When you share helpful information in your area of expertise, you begin to create a reputation and personal brand as an expert in your field. This strategy takes time to bear fruit, but it's worth the investment.

Publishing valuable content attracts like-minded people with shared interests. It also gives you a legitimate reason to reach out to other people in your industry.

I frequently invite people I've met online to come on my weekly podcast, Badass Digital Nomads, for a chat. My list of people to interview next is longer than the number of episodes I've published (150), and it's growing every day!

After connecting with your readers, subscribers, or followers through email or social media, you can then meet in person or collaborate on projects together. Chances are, they might work remotely, too!

You never know what will happen when you put yourself out there, create content, and start conversations online. It's worth a try and could change your life.

Becoming a Part of the Digital Nomad Community

In my years of travel, I've met many people — locals, tourists, backpackers, business travelers, and expats alike. But as recently as January of 2018, I had yet to meet another digital nomad. So, I vowed to change that by setting out to meet as many digital nomads as I could in one year.

My mission was a success. By December 31, I had met over 1,000 digital nomads!

The digital nomad community is borderless and highly connected. After you start meeting people, you're bound to run into familiar faces in the farthest corners of the globe (especially if you're frequenting digital nomad hubs, which you can read about in Chapters 19 and 20).

Although you may feel shy at first, you'll soon find out how open, inclusive, diverse, and friendly the digital nomad community is. It doesn't matter where you're from or what you do, everyone is welcome in the digital nomad lifestyle.

This section offers ways you can meet digital nomads online or offline, wherever you are.

Once you meet people in person, it's easy to keep in touch with them online. And the more remote working friends you meet, the more mutual connections you'll have when you arrive to a new place.

Digital nomad conferences and events

One of the fastest ways to meet nomads in-person is at digital nomad events. You can meet hundreds of people at a single event — all in less than a week.

The first digital nomads I ever met were on a cruise ship headed from Spain to Greece during the spring of 2018. I had solo-traveled my way from Japan to Barcelona to embark on the Nomad Cruise (www.nomadcruise.com), a floating conference and co-living experience for digital nomad enthusiasts. I was nervous at first to be on a boat for ten days with 250 strangers. But we soon became friends. When the cruise ended, many of us continued traveling together or have remained in touch ever since.

The same year, I reconnected with people I met on Nomad Cruise in Greece, France, Lithuania, Bulgaria, and Brazil. I've since reunited with more of them in Miami, Las Vegas, and beyond.

Nomad Summit (thedigitalnomadsummit.com), founded by digital nomad Johnny Jen (also known as Johnny FD), was one of the first digital nomad conferences. It's held in a different location every year, although it was on hiatus for two years during the coronavirus pandemic. It started in Chiang Mai, Thailand, before moving to Las Vegas, Nevada, Playa del Carmen, Mexico, and Tbilisi, Georgia.

The all-female-led 7in7 conference aims to hold a digital nomad event on all seven continents (including Antarctica!) within seven years. Previous events have taken place in New Zealand, Spain, and Colombia. Between conference dates, you can stay in touch with fellow attendees as a member of the private 7in7 society (https://7in7.co/society) for $15/month.

Nomad City (www.nomadcity.org) is a popular event held annually in Gran Canaria Island, off the coast of Spain. With good infrastructure, mild weather year-round, and plenty of things to see and do, the Canary Islands have quickly become a popular digital nomad hub with an events calendar that's bursting at the seams.

The Nomad Train (`NomadTrain.co`) is an "epic train experience with amazing people." While traveling on the trans-Siberian railroad, you can make friends, co-work with 4G Internet, and eat bowls of borscht at the same time! Sounds like a win-win to me.

Freedom X Fest (`https://freedomxfest.com`) is a three-day live and online event based in the Spanish countryside. It's for anyone (nomad or not) who wants to be part of a community, learn new skills, and explore remote job opportunities.

REMEMBER

Many nomads and remote workers describe themselves as introverts. If you feel the same way, know that you're in good company. Don't be afraid to strike up a conversation with a stranger or walk up to a group of people who are talking or eating together. They are likely to welcome you in with open arms. Likewise, if you're not feeling social, you can still benefit from attending events and workshops as more of an observer than a participant, listening to speakers while absorbing information and the atmosphere around you.

Digital nomad Facebook groups

Many digital nomads congregate in Facebook groups, which are organized primarily by destination. There's a Facebook group for almost every country in the world. So, no matter where you are, you can connect with digital nomads in the same place.

I'm in almost every digital nomad group there is on Facebook — there's no limit to how many you can join.

To find a Facebook group in your current area, simply search on Facebook for "*your location* digital nomads" and see what you find. "Lisbon Digital Nomads" and "Digital Nomads Croatia" are two regional examples. There are also international groups such as the Global Digital Nomad Network, founded by Johannes at Nomadbase.

Beyond digital nomad groups, there are groups for every interest under the sun. There are groups created especially for women, solo travelers, or software engineers. There are groups for expats, entrepreneurs, or small business owners in each city as well. Want to join a group for guitar players in Geneva or a book club in Brazil? There are groups for that!

TIP

Can't find a group you like? Try starting one of your own! I opened a Facebook group for digital nomads in 2018. Four years later, we have more than 5,500 members. You can join us at `facebook.com/groups/digitalnomadsuccess`.

Digital nomad membership sites and forums

Slack is a place that many digital nomads like to hang out online. It seems like there are new free and paid Slack channels starting every day for nomads.

One of the biggest ones in the world is Nomad List's Slack Community (`www.nomadlist.com/chat`), with more than 38,000 members. It's $200 for a lifetime membership.

Job boards Remotive.io, WeWorkRemotely, and Pangian also offer paid membership communities for remote workers.

Virtual summits

With so many conferences and events moving online these days, virtual summits have become a widespread way to meet people remotely.

The Digital Nomad Summit (`https://thedigitalnomadsummit.com`) in 2022 brought together thousands of experienced and aspiring digital nomads from around the world for a week of speakers, networking events, and live question and answer panels.

The Virtual Working Summit (`https://virtualworkingsummit.com`), in its 12th year, boasts participants from more than 70 countries.

Running Remote (`https://runningremote.com`) is the largest remote work conference in the world, which takes place live in person and online each year.

You can meet all types of people at virtual summits (not just digital nomads and remote workers). Search online for remote summits in your industry for additional networking opportunities.

Co-living arrangements

Living with someone is the fastest way to get to know them, and co-living is no exception. People who choose co-living typically *want* to meet other people. If that sounds like you, co-living could be right down your alley!

Some co-living providers, such as Noma Collective and work-travel retreat groups, such as WiFi Tribe, cater to digital nomads. At other co-living establishments, such as the Outpost Club in New York and Philadelphia, or Hive Coliv in Dubai, the resident population may be more diverse and less transient.

When I lived at a co-living space in Japan, I befriended locals who didn't speak English, as well as digital nomads, retirees, and backpackers from around the world. One of my housemates worked remotely in IT, one was a university professor on sabbatical, and one was a cryptocurrency investor from South Africa (just to name a few). I'll never forget cooking "family" dinners with them, exploring the streets of Tokyo together, and eating sushi for breakfast at the Tsukiji fish market.

See Chapter 10 for a list of co-living providers and resources.

Dating as a Digital Nomad

Dating as a digital nomad — your results may vary. As with other aspects of a location-independent lifestyle, dating as a digital nomad offers you more choices than you probably had before. You can keep things casual and date while traveling. But you can also use your location freedom to relocate to a city or country where you feel that the people and culture align more with your values, beliefs, and lifestyle. This section explains some of the pros and cons of dating in a location-independent lifestyle.

Dating as a "settler"

A digital nomad settler is someone who's location independent but moves somewhere long term. You may decide to relocate to a different part of your home country or apply for a long-term visa or residency permit to live abroad (which you can find out more about in Chapter 9).

The upside to dating as a settler is that you have flexibility and stability. Going nomadic can expand your potential dating pool to the farthest corners of the globe. If you're from a small town, island, or country with a low population, you could move to an urban area with more opportunities to date and meet people. For instance, Iceland, Estonia, and Lapland, Finland are a few sparsely populated countries in Europe. Iceland has a population of 345,000 people in 2022 and a population density of three people per square kilometer (nine people per square mile). That's quite a difference compared to living in Macau, which had a population density of 19,373 people per square kilometer in 2020.

You could also relocate to a country where you identify more with the culture and people compared to where you were born. While in your adopted home and going about your daily life, you'll have opportunities to date locals, travelers, or other foreigners who are living there or passing through.

As a settler, meeting potential romantic partners while working remotely is probably quite similar to what you've experienced in the past.

Most people today meet through dating apps, websites such as eHarmony, Match, or OKCupid, or through mutual friends, regardless of where they live. Rather than meeting a future significant other at a physical workplace, you could meet them at a local event, bar, restaurant, the supermarket, co-working or co-living space, or perhaps while on a retreat or vacation. You could also enroll in a matchmaking service, such as Tawkify or Pacific Match Global, a company which aims to help you find a lifelong partner anywhere in the world.

If you're using dating apps, search online for local platforms. Dating apps vary by country. Some are international, such as Bumble and Tinder, whereas Badoo and Happn are more popular in Europe and South America. Also investigate which messaging apps people use in the region. WeChat is a leading app in China, LINE is popular in Japan, Viber is the go-to in Eastern Europe, and WhatsApp is common throughout Latin America.

REMEMBER

When dating anywhere in the world, be safe. Use protection. Always get consent. Set personal boundaries. Meet in public places. Research cultural norms and dating etiquette. Get to know local laws and emergency numbers. Find a list of safety apps and tips in Chapter 15.

Dating as a perpetual traveler

The experience you have dating while traveling full time depends on whether you're looking for a long-term or short-term relationship and if you plan to date locals, tourists, or other digital nomads.

Dating fellow travelers and nomads can be a whirlwind, typically characterized by a short but intense romance with an exotic backdrop.

It can be a bit like starting off a relationship on your honeymoon. Imagine falling in love with a stranger in Rome, strolling along cobblestone streets on your way to drink wine and eat pasta al fresco.

Or imagine meeting the love of your life on a beach in Bali, paddling out for a surf session before riding off into the sunset together on a moped without a care in the world.

Dating while traveling can be dreamy, to say the least. But, like anything in life, it has pros and cons.

On the upside, travel gives you more opportunities to meet people than you would living at home following the same everyday routine. The people you meet might also be more open, easy-going, and sociable, too (especially if they're travelers).

Plus, if things don't work out, getting over your ex is a lot easier if you live in another country.

On the other hand, moving around often means that you spend more time making acquaintances rather than forming deep relationships. You might also cross paths with your soulmate while (literally) going in different directions.

I once met a special someone on a bus to Bosnia. Unfortunately, he was on his way home to England, and I was headed for Montenegro.

As "ships passing in the night," you may feel pressure to get to know people faster than normal. In many cases, the only option to stay together and see where the relationship goes is to decide to travel together (something that doesn't typically happen in the early stages of a relationship).

At the very least, living, traveling, and remote working together helps you learn pretty quickly if you're compatible with someone!

Things get even more complicated if you're a traveling nomad dating a local resident who leads a traditional lifestyle. They might not understand or agree with your nomadic ways. Plus, it's hard to envision a long-term relationship if you're leaving when your tourist visa expires. A long-distance relationship is also an option, however.

When you travel full time compared to leading a traditional lifestyle, there are also fewer opportunities to let a platonic friendship progress into a romance. Friendship can often turn into love, but you won't typically know that right away. Some couples only start a romantic relationship after a year or more of getting to know each other.

Finally, the digital nomad community is small compared to the global population. Dipping into the digital nomad dating pool can get awkward if things don't work out. There are some dating apps specifically for digital nomads and travelers, however. Options include:

>> Fairytrail (www.fairytrail.app), is an app that helps you find friends and dates anywhere and go on fun adventures together.

>> Flip the Trip (https://flipthetrip.com) helps you find a travel mate or companion.

>> Nomad List has a dating and friend finder feature (https://nomadlist.com/friend-finder).

» Nomad Soulmates is a Facebook community with more than 16,000 location-independent people looking for love.

» Grindr (www.grindr.com) and HER (https://weareher.com) are go-to apps for the LGBTQIA community.

Despite the challenges of dating as a digital nomad, I still recommend giving it a try.

After meeting a former boyfriend abroad, we lived, worked, and traveled the world together for five years — throughout the United States, Canada, Costa Rica, Mexico, Europe, and the Bahamas.

Either way, communication is important when dating as a nomad. Be forthcoming about what you're looking for and what your plans are.

Wherever you call home, relationships take work. Dating as a digital nomad isn't better or worse than dating in the traditional sense. It's just different.

Staying Connected with Friends and Family

Although you'll naturally meet many new people as a digital nomad, remember to stay in touch with your friends and family back home. Texting, video calls, and keeping up on social media are three ways to stay connected.

With a Wi-Fi connection, you can send messages or talk to people for free using apps such as WhatsApp, Viber, Telegram, and Facebook Messenger. Skype, Zoom, Discord, and Google Meet are other options.

TIP

The Teleparty app (www.teleparty.com) is a way to watch TV shows together with friends, family, or a significant other.

See Chapter 11 for more tips on setting up an international phone plan and finding Wi-Fi on the move.

Other ways to share your experience with loved ones include:

» Create a shared photo album using iPhoto, Google Photos, or Flickr.

» Send a postcard or letter: A handwritten note tells people you're thinking about them.

>> Track your travels. The Polarsteps app (`www.polarsteps.com`) lets you plan, track, and share your travels privately or publicly. You can create a travel map, share itineraries, and upload photos along the way.

>> Go public. Start a blog about your experiences, vlog on YouTube, or publish stories on Medium.com.

>> Be real. Share the lows as well as the highs (even if your Instagram feed tells a different story).

TIP

The Marco Polo app (`www.marcopolo.me`) lets you send a video to someone to watch later. Perfect for when you're in different time zones!

FINDING FRIENDS ON FACEBOOK

Here's a little-known but very useful search feature on Facebook that you can use to connect with friends anywhere in the world.

Type in the search bar: "my friends who live in _____," and insert the name of any city or country. A list of people you know will show up who currently live there.

If you don't get any results, try expanding your search radius. Instead of putting, "my friends who live in Chiang Mai," try "Bangkok" or "Thailand".

Then, reach out to whoever comes up and tell them that you are moving or traveling there. Maybe they can meet up or give you some travel tips!

You can also type "my friends who have been to _____," and put the destination you're looking for.

Now, a list of people will come up of your friends and possibly people you know who have traveled to that destination.

This is a great way to get travel tips from people you know and see whether they can introduce you to anyone they met while there.

If all else fails, post your travel dates and location as a status update on the Facebook feed and see who responds. Or post in a Facebook group that you are looking to meet people when you arrive.

» Adapting to a new culture and language

» Overcoming loneliness and culture shock

» Staying safe in a foreign place

» Preparing for the unexpected

Chapter **15**

Adapting to Life in a Foreign Country

When you step off the plane in a new place, it takes some time to adjust (even if you're excited about living there). Culture shock, communication, and language barriers are a few of the most common hurdles you'll face when moving to a new country. This chapter gives you tips for adjusting to the rhythm of daily life in your temporary or adopted home. It helps you anticipate and overcome challenges, stay safe, and adjust to the culture and lifestyle of a foreign country, faster.

Getting Settled In-Country

The first days and weeks of your arrival in a new place are critical for your adjustment abroad. In this section, I offer ideas for how to get settled fast in a new place, including finding good Wi-Fi and which cell phone providers to use to stay connected.

First things, first

One of the first things I like to do when I arrive in a new city is get to know the local area. First, I do a walk-through of my apartment or house and make sure everything is in good shape. I look for any obvious damages, missing items, cleanliness issues, or inconsistencies from the property listing and alert the owner or host in writing, if applicable. I read the property guide, if there is one, and I look up local emergency numbers and nearby hospitals or doctors.

Then it's time to hit the pavement. I look up local restaurants in my maps app or TripAdvisor. (I usually look for a coffee shop first.) I also walk around, go grocery shopping, and pick up any essentials that may be missing from the rental property. After that, I unpack, sign up for exercise classes or a gym membership, and start planning my week and continuing my daily digital nomad lifestyle.

Scoping out the neighborhood

A good way to get to know your neighborhood fast is with a free walking tour. You can find one on www.freetoursbyfoot.com. Your guide will point out points of interest (especially places to eat) and interesting facts about the history of the area. You can also meet fellow new arrivals this way.

In the first days and weeks of my arrival, I make it a point to walk or bike everywhere or use public transportation. I also connect with people on apps or social media to see who's in town, sign up at a local co-working space, and scope out the local events calendar online or in a local tourist magazine or newspaper.

Once I get into a daily routine, I start to explore farther afield. I look for workshops, classes, tours, events, and experiences on Eventbrite or Airbnb Experiences. I also bookmark museums and cultural sites to visit. Learning about the history, art, culture, and people of your location helps you feel a kinship with your new community and surroundings. Some of my favorite museums in the world include the Museum of the Revolution in Havana, Cuba, the Budapest History Museum, and the Vasa Museum in Stockholm.

TIP

When you arrive, search online for free things to do. There are 26 free museums in London, for example.

Another thing I like to do is try to find somewhere with a view of the area. In some cases, you can get a good view from a public park, such as Regent's Park in London, Olympiapark in Munich, or the Belgrade Fortress in Serbia. You can also get a different perspective of a city from the top floor of a hotel or skyscraper, such as the Sky Garden in London or the Radisson Blu hotel in Vilnius, Lithuania. Bangkok is known for its many sky bars and the view from the Eiffel Tower is pretty good, too.

In the first week of my arrival, I also try to get out and meet people.

Chapter 7 helps you find co-working spaces, Chapter 13 helps you build a daily routine, and Chapter 14 has tips on how to make friends, fast.

Getting around

As mentioned, walking is my preferred way of getting around, but it's also the slowest way. Wherever you go, however, there are likely plenty of ways to get around. A maps app, such as Google Maps or Waze, gives you travel times and options for different forms of transportation. Maps.me and many running apps, such as Strava or Map My Run, have offline maps, too.

If you're in an urban area, buy a reusable metro card that you can top up during your stay with per-ride credits or daily, weekly, and monthly passes.

Look for bike, moped, or scooter rentals. Some cities have public bikes you can unlock with a credit or debit card. Also check out local rental agencies and consider buying a used bike or vehicle if you will be there long term.

Renting a car can be a surprisingly affordable option. When I lived in Lofoten, Norway, I rented a car for $500 per month from a guy that I met through the owners of a local co-living space. In Bulgaria, I rented a car from an airport vendor for the same monthly rate. You can also find private rentals through classified ads or Facebook Marketplace. (Of course, always make sure you get car insurance, as well.)

Ride sharing apps, such as Uber and Lyft, are plentiful. Many countries have local ride sharing and taxi apps, such as GrabTaxi in Malaysia and eCabs in Malta.

Trains can also be faster and more comfortable than taking a car. It's also a good opportunity to get some work done.

Flying is another way to get around. Costa Rica has two private domestic airlines called Sansa Air and Nature Air, that also fly to Nicaragua and Panama. European airlines, such as Vueling and Ryan Air, often have good deals. You can fly Peruvian Airlines in Peru, Nok Air in Thailand, and ANA in Japan.

Most countries also have their own unique forms of transportation. Medellín, Colombia is known for its gondola system, Peru for its overnight buses, Southeast Asia for their Tuk Tuks and ferries, and Japan for its high-speed train system (to name a few).

WARNING

Be careful on local transportation (Tuk Tuks don't have seatbelts and I had a near-death experience on a scooter in Paris once). Search safety records online and never drive under the influence of drugs or alcohol.

Receiving mail

Receiving mail can be complicated if you don't have an address. Ask your host or landlord if you can receive mail there. If not, try a local co-working space or business center, which can provide a physical address.

Many countries also have private couriers. You can have a package shipped to the courier's address — either in your home country or abroad — and pay a fee for the company to deliver it to you.

Another option is to receive mail and packages at an office supply store such as FedEx, UPS Store, or Mailboxes, Etc. (or local equivalent).

Finding Internet anywhere

Ideally, you'll be working from a reliable Internet connection at your rental property, a library, or a co-working space most days. (See Chapter 7 for how to find a co-working space and best practices for working remotely.) But when you're on the move, you need to improvise. Fortunately, Wi-Fi finder apps exist to help you connect to millions of Wi-Fi networks around the globe.

REMEMBER

Use a VPN for security when navigating the web, especially when on public Wi-Fi networks.

>> Wi-Fi Finder is one of the most well-known apps for finding Wi-Fi on the go. It's available in the Apple and Android stores.

>> Wiman (www.wiman.me) shares the passwords to millions of Wi-Fi networks worldwide.

>> WiFiMap.io has a network of over 120 million Wi-Fi hotspots.

TIP

Also travel with a Wi-Fi hotspot, which Chapter 11 tells you about.

DRIVING IN DIFFERENT COUNTRIES

Did you know you can save money on rental cars if you drive a car with a manual versus automatic transmission? Automatic cars are in short supply in some places. Learning how to drive with a stick shift can save you money and increase your car selection.

Riding the Cultural Adaptation Curve

Progress doesn't go in a straight line, and neither does the process of adapting to life in a new place.

Living in a new country is like riding a roller coaster. Each time you move, you inevitably experience some highs and lows. Some days you might see everything through rose-colored glasses, while other days, you might feel like there's a rain cloud following you around.

Things that used to be second nature to you, such as checking your mail, getting around town, or ordering pizza delivery can suddenly become a challenge. As you exert more energy on everyday tasks that used to be on autopilot — for example, figuring out how to buy a metro pass or where the closest grocery store is — you may feel tired or frustrated sometimes.

Daily activities get even more complex when you don't speak the language. But don't worry — there's a science to cultural adjustment. The following sections help you know what to expect when you move abroad so you can navigate the ups and downs like a pro.

Coping with culture shock

Culture shock is something that everyone inevitably experiences to some degree when moving abroad. It's a feeling of discomfort prompted by a sudden change in your life or environment. Foreign foods, customs, and values each contribute to culture shock in different ways.

Culture shock can be something that seems (quite literally) shocking to you in the moment, such as being offered a plate of worms for dinner. Or, it can be more subtle — a gradual feeling of being out of place or alone in your new home.

Each person experiences a different degree of culture shock on a unique timeline. Like a tide, your feelings of culture shock may come and go.

Fortunately, research can explain what you're experiencing. The Curve of Cultural Adaptation, shown in Figure 15-1, shows the phases of adapting to a new country. The longer you're in one place, the farther through these stages you'll progress.

Source: Sverre Lysgaard, 1955.

FIGURE 15-1: The four stages of culture shock.

The four phases of culture shock include:

» **Honeymoon:** The honeymoon phase is the most fun part of moving to a new place, when everything appears interesting and new. The food tastes better, the people are nicer, the rent is cheaper, and so on. Everything is great and better than it was at home. At least, it is at first. This period typically lasts from a few weeks to a few months, but eventually wears off once you realize that nowhere is perfect and every country has problems. Cultural norms that seemed endearing at the beginning — such as "island time" — can become irritating later.

» **Frustration:** Speaking of frustration, the next stage of adaptation is the frustration phase. This is a time where everything seems more difficult than it needs to be, whether it's working out the local bus schedule, booking a doctor's appointment, or tiny things that go wrong but add up. Your laptop gets stolen, your power goes out, your rental car breaks down in a river — any number of things could happen. You may feel sadness, loneliness, anger, or even depression. You might question your decision to become a digital nomad altogether. Fortunately, these feelings (and your bad mood) usually pass with time.

WARNING

If you're traveling quickly, you may not be in a country long enough to move through all the phases of cultural adaptation. In that case, you may never get out of the honeymoon or frustration phase of each country. That's okay, just be aware.

» **Adaptation:** At this point, you begin to feel more comfortable and at home in your surroundings. You start to understand more of the language, get in a daily routine, and generally start adapting to life in a new society. It's not all sunshine and roses, but you've also moved beyond the frustration stage. You feel more stable and adjusted now. You know your way around without being glued to a map, and things that used to take time and energy are now effortless. You begin to feel a sense of autonomy, independence, and competence in your life as an expat.

» **Acceptance:** In the last stage of the process, you begin to feel like a local. You adopt a country as your home and begin to identify with its cultural norms and values. You may use local slang when you talk, pick up a slight accent, and feel more and more detached from your home country. You may adapt so well to your new country, that you experience *reverse culture* shock when you go back home for a visit. (Read about how to cope with reverse culture shock in Chapter 16.)

What comes next? I'd like to introduce a fifth, unofficial phase of culture shock, which comes *after* the acceptance phase. After adapting to a new culture, digital nomads are faced with a choice. You can either stay where you are, re-integrate into your home country, or move to a different country. If you stay where you are, you may remain in the acceptance phase. If you move back home, you may experience some reverse culture shock. And if you change countries, you start the process of cultural adaptation over from the beginning.

REMEMBER

The longer you travel, the faster and easier it is to integrate with foreign countries. The confusing part of this is that you can start to feel at home everywhere and nowhere at the same time. You become like a chameleon!

Tips for coping with culture shock:

» Know before you go. The website, Hofstede Insights (www.hofstede-insights.com/product/compare-countries), has a tool where you can compare your home and destination countries on six cultural dimensions, allowing you to anticipate challenges and differences before you arrive.

» Remember that you are not alone. Everyone experiences culture shock.

» Don't take things personally if locals don't completely accept you as one of their own. Accept your status as an outsider and do your best to fit in.

>> Hang out with other digital nomads who can empathize with what you're going through. Reach out to other foreigners through Facebook groups and Meetup gatherings.

>> Seek out events from your home country. For example, U.S. embassies around the world are known to host annual 4th of July celebrations.

>> Confess your struggles to local friends. See whether they have any advice or can lend a sympathetic ear.

>> Learn as much as you can about the country you're in. Buy books, visit museums, and watch videos and documentaries.

>> Sign up for cultural adaptation classes online or in person.

>> Find, buy, or do something that reminds you of home. When my sister and I lived in Nicaragua together, we drove three hours to watch Sex and The City at a Managua movie theater. It transported us (mentally) to New York City for a few hours.

>> Be patient. Adapting to a new place takes time. You will be onto the next phase of the curve soon!

>> Keep an open mind. Realize that there's no one way or "right" way to do anything. Be open to changing your opinion about how things "should" be done.

>> Journal, blog, or vlog about your thoughts and feelings. Writing about or sharing what's going on in your life can help you process situations and find solutions to problems. Your journal can be a place for you to vent about injustices and discomforts you're experiencing while expressing gratitude for the blessings in your life. Going public with a blog, podcast, YouTube channel, or other form of content helps you connect with people who can relate.

Learning a new language

To accelerate your cultural adjustment process, it helps to learn some of the local language or dialect. Being able to communicate with people helps you feel more confident, comfortable, and less like an outsider. It also helps you better understand a society's culture and make friends with locals more easily. And at an advanced level, you can begin to perceive more of the slang, idioms, topics, and sense of humor that contribute to a society's shared cultural identity.

Learning the language makes life easier. Speaking Spanish has helped me navigate throughout Central and South America and Spain. It's also helped me understand other romance languages such as French, Italian, and Portuguese.

If you don't have time to achieve fluency in another language, however, don't despair. You can absorb a lot through daily life. Immersion is the best way to learn a language. And by being abroad, you've taken the first step.

Once you're there, sign up for a few in-person classes, begin talking to locals, and you're on your way.

REMEMBER

You can survive and even thrive abroad *without* learning the language. Don't let a language barrier hold you back from traveling. I've been to 60 countries, but I only know two languages.

Tips that can take you far when learning a new language:

>> Focus on learning how to conjugate verbs rather than memorizing vocabulary words. You'll pick up common nouns naturally in conversation.

>> Download a dictionary or translation app on your phone so you can look up words you don't know. Google Translate (https://translate.google.com) and iTranslate (https://itranslate.com) can also translate voice recordings and images.

>> Talk to people! Strike up conversations with locals to practice your skills. (Although they might want to practice their English or your language with you.)

>> Watch TV or movies with subtitles, especially your favorite shows and movies that you know by heart.

>> Read signs and restaurant menus in the local language and order food in that language.

>> Listen to the local radio and try to understand what they're saying.

>> Read the local newspaper and highlight or circle words you don't know (better for retention than reading digital media).

>> Practice at home with apps and websites and label items around your house with sticky notes.

>> Be patient, consistent, and don't give up! You never know when your language breakthrough will happen.

Try these online language-learning resources:

>> Babel (www.babbel.com): A combination of classes, podcasts, and more

>> Duolingo (www.duolingo.com): Fun, free, and effective language-learning

>> iTalkie (www.italki.com): Practice conversing with locals

» Lingopie (https://lingopie.com): Learn a language with TV

» Pimsleur (www.pimsleur.com): Access to 51 languages for one price

» Tim Ferriss on "How to Learn Any Language in an Hour" (https://tim.blog/2007/11/07/how-to-learn-but-not-master-any-language-in-1-hour-plus-a-favor)

» YouTube: Search online for free language classes and tutorials that interest you.

TIP

Look for language schools or classes that teach in the local language rather than in English.

Handling homesickness and loneliness

Loneliness is one of the most oft-cited downsides of the digital nomad lifestyle. The paradox of loneliness is that it can hit you anytime, anywhere — whether you're nomadic or not. Loneliness isn't an emotion exclusively experienced by world travelers. You can feel lonely if you're single or in a relationship. You can feel lonely at home or abroad. You can feel lonely in your family. Loneliness doesn't discriminate. You just have to accept that you will feel lonely sometimes because you're human.

Working online somewhere far from home can be particularly isolating, however. And as easy as it can be to meet people while traveling, it's also hard to say good-bye.

Here are a few of my tips for overcoming loneliness and homesickness:

» Allow yourself to feel homesick. It's normal and natural to feel that way sometimes. Acknowledge your feelings. Sit with them or meditate on them. Notice how your emotions pass through you and remember that you are not your emotional state. Feelings are temporary and tomorrow is a new day.

» Travel with something comforting that reminds you of home. (I bring a feather pillow that my grandma bought me.)

» Take care of yourself. Eat well, get enough exercise and sleep, and take time off to recharge.

» Get outside. Sunlight, fresh air, and nature boost your endorphin levels.

» Phone a friend, relative, or therapist. Sometimes you just need someone to talk to.

>> Get out and about. Attend events and meetups. Do things you like to do. Go on a date. Connect with other nomads who can relate to what you're going through.

>> Avoid social media sites. They can contribute to feelings of anxiety and depression.

>> Get involved in your local community. Nomads Giving Back (https://nomadsgivingback.com) helps you volunteer and get involved in your home away from home.

>> Do something that makes you happy. Watch a funny movie or motivational video, read a book, dance in your living room, or peruse the Good News Network (www.goodnewsnetwork.org).

>> Challenge yourself. Learning a new skill, going on an adventure, or doing something you've never done can give you a feeling of accomplishment and boost your mood.

>> Go home for a visit. You might realize you miss it (or remember why you left in the first place)!

>> Make a change. If your feelings of loneliness or homesickness become stronger or more frequent, it could be time to move somewhere you feel more at home.

If you find yourself feeling particularly lonely or homesick on the road, see Chapter 12 for help on maintaining your health, Chapter 14 on how to meet people, and Chapter 16 on how to succeed long term as a digital nomad.

Ensuring Your Personal Safety and Security

Safety is an extremely important aspect of living nomadically, as your environment will change frequently. You'll want to be prepared for anything ranging from health issues to crimes, accidents, food poisoning, and the threat of terrorism or war.

When I lived in Costa Rica, I had my house and car broken into multiple times. I once saw a girl get mugged outside my apartment, and some of my friends were the victims of home invasions. Crime is a big reason why people change countries.

Although the risks involved with travel are real, the upsides of seeing the world outweigh the downsides (in my opinion). Regardless, there's no such thing as being "too" prepared. Do what you can, prepare for the worst, and hope for the best.

REMEMBER

Becoming a digital nomad can also make you *safer*, especially if working remotely allows you to escape a dangerous situation in your home, neighborhood, or country.

Taking precautions

Staying safe has a lot to do with planning ahead. In this section, I give tips on how you can protect your personal safety while on the road (or in the air).

Health precautions

General health precautions you can take are:

>> Get travel/medical insurance that covers you in case of medical emergencies, natural disasters, and theft of valuables and luggage. See Chapter 12 for more on travel and health insurance.

>> If traveling internationally, make sure you bring your prescriptions with your doctor's info and enough medications to cover you while away. If you can't have a refill mailed to you, check with local doctors or pharmacists in your destination to see whether you can get what you need locally.

>> Wear a medical bracelet or set emergency contacts on your phone and carry an emergency card in your wallet. If something were to happen to you, how could an innocent bystander or medical worker reach your loved ones? Invisawear (www.invisawear.com) makes jewelry and accessories that double as safety devices.

>> Follow health and safety protocols in each country. See Chapter 9 for more on travel logistics and entry requirements.

>> Get required and recommended vaccinations. You can find out what you need by going to your country's state department or embassy website or by checking with the public health department in your destination.

>> Be careful with what you eat and drink to avoid food poisoning or bacteria in water. I ended up in the emergency room after contracting diphtheria at an all-inclusive resort in the Dominican Republic.

Safety precautions

General safety precautions you can take are:

>> Check travel advisories and register with your country's government agencies abroad. If you're a U.S. citizen, you can enroll in the Smart Traveler Enrollment Program (STEP; `https://step.state.gov/step`), which helps the embassy or consulate reach you in case of an emergency or natural disaster.

>> Get acquainted with local laws. Ignorance is not an excuse for breaking laws. Research common crime threats and scams in the country you're traveling to. You can do a few searches, check with Interpol (`www.interpol.int/en/What-you-can-do/Stay-safe`), or contact your country's embassy. Some countries require you to carry your passport with you.

>> Look up the local emergency numbers and authorities in each country you go to. You want to know what each country's emergency line is. Look for TripWhistle Global SOS in the Apple Store (it's available only for Apple users), with 70+ international emergency numbers.

TIP

Interpol is the International Criminal Police Organization among 195 member countries. Check its website for tips on staying safe, preventing crimes, and avoiding scams abroad (`www.interpol.int/en/What-you-can-do/Stay-safe`).

>> Protect yourself online by using a virtual private network (VPN) when surfing the web or on your phone. Surfshark and NordVPN are two options.

>> Leave your valuables at home. If you need to bring valuables with you while traveling, try not to carry them around on the street.

TIP

>> When out and about, bring one credit or debit card and leave a backup in a safe or hidden at your hotel or rental property. Make a copy of your passport to carry with you and keep your original document secure.

>> Remain aware of your surroundings. Don't look down at your phone while on the street. Stay alert on public transportation. Keep an eye on your stuff, especially if traveling by bus or train.

>> Be wary of pick pocketers (including children). My mom and I were once pickpocketed in broad daylight while accepting change for pizza slices in Prague.

TIP

Many companies make theft-proof bags, such as TravelOn and the Valcen personal pocket bag.

>> Only take official taxis or book transportation through trusted apps.

>> Put your safety first over material things. If you get held at gunpoint on the street, hand over your phone or wallet rather than risking your personal safety.

>> Avoid public protests and riots. I once got stuck in a political uprising in Managua, Nicaragua. Through this experience, I learned to keep my distance whenever possible.

>> Stay in safe places. Opt for secure buildings rather than single family homes, which can be vulnerable to break-ins.

>> Travel in groups when possible. If you meet fellow trusted travelers or locals on your journey, join forces if desired. Ask to go along with them on side trips or excursions. Solo travel is fine but traveling in groups can be safer. You can find a travel companion through Tourlina (https://tourlina.com), Fairytrail (www.fairytrail.app), or TravelBuddy (www.beatravelbuddy.com).

>> Travel to tolerant countries, especially if you have concerns about racism, sexual freedom, or equal rights. Research the countries you want to travel to before booking your ticket. The Hofstede Index (www.hofstede-insights.com/product/compare-countries) and Nomad List (https://nomadlist.com) are two places to begin.

>> Use common sense. Don't walk around alone at night. Don't invite strangers into your house. Don't leave your drink unattended. You know the drill!

>> Trust your intuition. If something seems too good to be true, it probably is. If something seems off or someone you meet seems shady, exit the situation. If someone is acting aggressively, distance yourself immediately. Ask others for a second opinion if you're unsure about something.

WARNING

If you are the victim of a crime, report it with the local authorities, alert your country's embassy, and hire a legal professional for help if needed.

Planning for emergencies

I say it many times in Chapter 12, but it's worth saying again here: Get insurance before becoming a digital nomad. (Chapter 12 includes insurance plans and providers.)

Draft a contingency or emergency plan if something were to happen to you. Create a living will or set up a trust with a power of attorney. Store important documents in a secure place, such as a lawyer's office or a safe deposit box.

Before leaving home, share your itinerary and international contact info with friends or family members.

Register with your embassy or state department before traveling abroad and enroll in emergency alerts on your phone.

Check the weather and seasonality of the destination you're traveling to. Follow local protocols for preparing for extreme weather events like a tornado or tsunami.

And always give yourself more time than needed when heading to the airport or train station.

TripWhistle Global SOS for iPhones and Travel Safe for Android phones help you call emergency numbers in countries worldwide, quickly and easily.

APPS FOR SAFETY WHILE TRAVELING

Your phone can be an ally to help keep you safe and loved ones informed while traveling.

- Bsafe (www.getbsafe.com): A voice-activated SOS button in your pocket.

- Cairn (www.cairnme.com): Safety location tracking and alerts for hikers and travelers. Includes offline maps.

- Centers for Disease Control and Prevention (wwwnc.cdc.gov/travel): The official CDC app gives you access to travel health information plus tips on how to protect yourself and what to do if you get sick. You can download the app in the Apple or Google Play stores.

- Geosure (https://geosureglobal.com): Gauge personal safety in more than 65,000 cities worldwide with the color-coded "GeoSafeScores" index.

- GreenPass (https://ec.europa.eu/info/live-work-travel-eu/coronavirus-response/safe-covid-19-vaccines-europeans/eu-digital-covid-certificate_en): Store digital COVID certificates for EU countries.

- Noonlight (www.noonlight.com): Emergency response services. Whenever you're feeling unsafe, press the hold button. When released, the app sends help to your exact location.

- Red Cross (www.redcross.org/get-help/how-to-prepare-for-emergencies/mobile-apps.html): Apps to help you prepare for accidents and emergencies.

- Sitata (www.sitata.com): This app aims to provide you with "worry-free travel," offering travel insurance and solutions to help you understand international travel restrictions, disruptions, and changing country entry requirements.

(continued)

(continued)

- Smart Traveler (`https://2009-2017.state.gov/r/pa/ei/rls/dos/165020.htm`): The U.S. State Department's official app provides a wealth of information for U.S. travelers abroad. You can use it to enroll in the Smart Traveler Enrollment Program (STEP), which helps authorities contact you in case of emergency. The app is updated regularly with country information and travel advisories.

- Tourlina (`https://tourlina.com`): Traveling alone? This app helps you find female travel companions in a trusted women-only network.

- TripLingo (`http://triplingo.com`): An app to help travelers stay "safe, productive, and savvy during trips abroad." Offers communication and safety tools, a culture guide, and access to a live translator.

- TripWhistle Global SOS (`https://apps.apple.com/us/app/tripwhistle-global-sos-international-emergency-phone/id839654331`): Through this app, you can dial more than 70 different emergency numbers in 196 countries. Reach police, fire, or ambulance phone numbers worldwide with a single tap. (Available only for Apple iPhone.)

- World Health Organization (`www.who.int/news-room/apps`): Keep up to date with the latest global health information and news.

Chapter **16**

Succeeding Long Term in the Digital Nomad Lifestyle

B ecoming a digital nomad is one thing, but *staying* a digital nomad is another. In this chapter, I provide tips for sustaining a nomadic lifestyle long term. I help prepare you for some of the ups and downs you might encounter after months, years, or decades of perpetual travel. I also present three examples for designing a digital nomad "exit strategy." That is, what do you do *after* becoming a digital nomad? Should you keep traveling, settle in one place, or return home? Read on to find out.

Improving Your Odds of Success

One of the things I love about the digital nomad lifestyle is that it's open to everyone. You don't have to go to college, get a certain SAT score, or snag a fancy job to become a digital nomad. Being location independent is a decision you make.

You can be of any age, race, nationality, or industry. As long as you have an income stream, you can work remotely and travel.

What does it mean to *succeed* at being a digital nomad, though?

If success is accomplishing a goal and that goal is to become a digital nomad, then you've already won. After that, it's up to you to define what *continued* success means for you.

Your goals and priorities will change over time, but your desire to keep your freedom and location independence probably won't. Research indicates that people who go remote, stay remote.

According to Buffer's 2022 State of Remote Work Report, 97 percent of respondents said they'd like to work remotely "at least some of the time" for the rest of their careers.

A 2018 Fiverr study on Anywhere Workers found a similar result, suggesting that "the longer you work remotely, the more you love it."

Chances are, you could adopt the mindset of "once a nomad, always a nomad." How you define being nomadic might change, however.

Measuring what success means to you

If you ask a mindset coach or business guru how to become successful, they'll probably ask you to define success, first. That was my problem when I first became a digital nomad. I didn't know how to define the life I was leading. I felt alone and uncertain at times, mostly because I didn't know anyone having a similar experience. Fortunately, there's now a collective understanding of the lifestyle. Millions of people can relate to having the ability to live and work remotely, choosing their degree of "nomad-ness."

Whether you consider yourself a location-independent professional, perpetual traveler, remote worker, expat, freelancer, or anything in between, it's *your* choice. For instance, only 24 percent of remote workers in the Anywhere Workers study would call themselves "nomadic."

Identifying with a label (or none) is a choice. You may want to live like a nomad for a few months per year. You may want to travel until you find somewhere to settle down. Or you may want to be nomadic *forever*!

Likewise, figuring out when to "quit" is also a form of success. Living as a digital nomad can be a phase of life. It doesn't have to be your *whole* life.

Matt Bowles, host of The Maverick Show podcast, has traveled to 65 countries in his nine years as a digital nomad. While he hopes to keep his freedom of mobility "forever," he admits that it's hard to predict how he'll choose to exercise that freedom in the future. After an 18-month stint working from his parents' home in North Carolina, he went nomadic again. "I just do what feels right, fun, or exciting at the time," he told me. "And right now, that's traveling."

Your definition of success in this lifestyle is personal. You can change your mind whenever, wherever. Regardless, in the next sections, I share a few of the commonalities between digital nomads who *stop* versus *sustain* the lifestyle long term.

Understanding why some digital nomads fail

There's not much data on why digital nomads "fail." (After all, failure is subjective, and all failure is a learning experience.) But in my experience, failure can stem from a combination of challenges. Financial strain, culture shock, loneliness, burnout, and exhaustion can all contribute to people giving up on the lifestyle. Lack of clarity over why you wanted to become a digital nomad to begin with can also be a source of confusion. (Chapter 2 can help you sort out your "why.")

The Anywhere Workers study cited the following struggles among remote workers, many of which also apply to nomads:

>> 30 percent loneliness and lack of community

>> 28 percent overwork and inability to "shut down" [technology]

>> 24 percent lack of opportunities for career advancement

>> 13 percent lack of motivation

>> 5 percent other reasons

Your brain craves safety, stability, human connection, and a plan. But living as a digital nomad often comes with uncertainty, loneliness, and constantly changing plans.

On top of that, many digital nomads fail to fully adapt to their new locations. Chapter 15 helps you cope with and overcome culture shock, however.

Overall, the ability to balance work and travel while adapting to different places requires extra energy, effort, and organization that you may not have needed before. Figure 16-1 is a humorous look at the reality of balancing work, life, and travel.

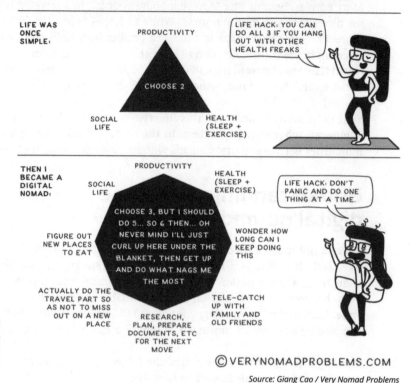

FIGURE 16-1:
Struggles
that a digital
nomad can face.

Source: Giang Cao / Very Nomad Problems

When things get difficult, it can be tempting to call it quits and move home. Don't give up so soon, though! Try to remain calm and diagnose the cause of the problem(s), first:

» **Cultural:** If you feel out of place, remember that there's a curve to cultural adaptation. You might just need more time to move through the four phases of cultural adjustment. (Chapter 15 walks you through each step in the process.)

» **Financial:** If money is an issue, try moving to a more affordable place, applying for a higher-paying job, starting a side hustle, or increasing your freelancing rates. (See Part 2 for tips on how to do that.)

» **Logistical:** If you're overwhelmed with the details of planning travel, consider hiring a virtual assistant or travel agent to help. You could also join a remote work retreat group that does all the planning for you or enroll in a housing subscription plan, such as the Blueground Pass, which makes finding digital nomad-friendly accommodation easier. You can find out how to manage your travel logistics in Chapter 11.

>> **Relational:** If loneliness is a factor, set a goal to meet more people or get involved in the local community. Chapter 14 is full of tips for how to make friends as a nomad and find a support network, while Chapter 12 helps with mental health and wellness.

Life has ups and downs whether you're a digital nomad or not. There are struggles sometimes, but you *can* overcome them.

However, there could come a time when a nomadic lifestyle is incompatible with your other personal or professional goals. You could change jobs, get married, have kids, or enter a new phase of life where you have other priorities. Or you could just be "over it" and make a change. There are no wrong answers when it comes to how to live your life. You could be a nomad in your 20s and then settle down. Or you could live a full life, have a rewarding career, and go nomadic in retirement.

Rolf Potts, an early nomad, travel writer, and author of *Vagabonding: An Uncommon Guide to the Art of Long-Term World Travel*, happily resides in Kansas with his wife, actress Kristen Bush. He still travels and works remotely, but he also has a home. Tim Ferriss, author of *The 4-Hour Work Week*, has inspired millions of people to pursue online business ventures, travel the world without quitting their jobs, and embrace the concept of lifestyle design. He could, too, live and work anywhere, but he chose to make Austin, Texas his home base.

Brushing up on the secrets to success

Many people assume that succeeding as a digital nomad is about how tech-savvy you are, but I think that soft skills are more important. The following attributes help nomads sustain a location-independent lifestyle long term:

>> **Acceptance:** Accepting cultural differences and things you can't control can help you become more resilient and overcome challenges while living as a digital nomad.

According to the ancient Stoics, acceptance is linked with distinguishing between what you *can* and *can't* control. When challenges arise in your business, travels, or life, ask yourself, "Can I control this?" If the answer is "yes," do something about it. If not, let it go and focus on what you *can* control.

>> **Autonomy and personal responsibility:** The independence you have as a digital nomad is a form of responsibility as much as freedom. Without anyone to report to in person, you become more accountable to yourself. As an adult, you're in control of your environment, your finances, your career, your outlook, and much more. The more you embrace personal responsibility, the more sustainable and manageable your nomadic life will be.

>> **Communication:** Digital nomads need to be able to communicate well from anywhere. Communication is as important for travel as it is for the remote workplace. Always be polite when you're a guest in a foreign country. Use translation apps or take language classes to help you communicate better abroad. Keep in touch with friends, family, and clients. Set clear expectations with the people you work with. Chapter 7 has tips on how to navigate time zones and communicate well remotely, while Chapters 10 and 11 help you stay connected anywhere.

>> **Curiosity and learning:** Whether you're learning a new software, solving a business problem, or finding the right platform at a train station, cultivating the ability to learn and adapt to new experiences helps you thrive as a digital nomad.

We live in a time where the combined knowledge of the world is available at the tap of a screen or a question to Siri or Alexa. Exploit this power and privilege. Follow your natural curiosities. You won't always have all the answers, but when you combine access to technology with human ingenuity, creativity, and resourcefulness, there's nothing you can't do.

>> **Open-mindedness:** No matter how many books you read or videos you watch, moving to a new place gives you a close look at a society's political, cultural, and ideological differences. There are many ways to do everything, but rigidly holding onto the "old" ways of doing things can make the digital nomad lifestyle more difficult.

Instead, try to see the world from new and different perspectives. Start talking with locals, learning the language, and following community leaders. Cultural integration classes help, too. Chapter 15 helps you adapt to life in a foreign country.

REMEMBER

It's okay to disagree with cultural norms you encounter in other places, too. Denounce what you feel is wrong, and report unlawful behavior.

>> **Organization:** Successful digital nomads are fluent in time management and prioritization. Attention is sacred (and limited). Chapter 13 helps you organize your work and play, making time for the things that matter most.

>> **Persistence:** Tenacity serves you well regardless of where you live and what you do for work. But persistence is especially important when you're nomadic or self-employed. Things rarely go as planned when you travel. And — spoiler alert — working for yourself, starting a business, or balancing all the responsibilities that life entails is hard. Successful digital nomads understand that "if at first you don't succeed, try, try again." Look at each obstacle you face as something to go around or through. Never give up.

>> **Proactiveness:** Successful digital nomads know that problems won't solve themselves. To be more proactive, you must *act*. Be action oriented and proactive in anticipating and solving problems, whether it's in the remote office or IRL. Think big picture and long term. When you face problems, solve them rather than running from them.

TIP

When you feel more like procrastinating than being proactive, give Mel Robbins's Five Second Rule a try. Count down out loud from 5 to 1. When you get to 1, say "go," get up, and act on the thing you need to do next, whether it's clearing out your inbox, making a sales call, heading to the gym, or rushing off to the airport.

Finally, successful digital nomads slow down when they need a break from travel. Slowing down gives you time and space to diagnose problems, come up with solutions, and figure out your next step.

Developing Your Digital Nomad Exit Strategy

Every digital nomad should have an exit strategy, which is a contingency plan for what to do when it's time to adjust or depart from the digital nomad lifestyle. The goal of an exit strategy is to try to forecast or anticipate what would prompt you to move somewhere new, stay where you are, or return home.

In forming your exit strategy, ask yourself:

>> **Moving:** Under what conditions will you leave your current location? For example, when your visa is up, when your money runs out, when you want to see a new place, or when you don't like it there anymore.

>> **Staying:** What would prompt you to rent long term, invest in real estate, or apply for permanent residency or citizenship somewhere? For example, falling in love with a country (or person), a business opportunity, political motivations, or tax reasons.

>> **Returning:** Under what conditions would you likely discontinue the digital nomad lifestyle? For example, meeting a life partner who isn't nomadic, losing interest in traveling, focusing on your business, raising a family, or taking care of a loved one.

Your exit strategy will change over time. At first, you may want to maximize your newfound freedom by seeing the world as fast as possible. Later on, you might want to slow down and stay in one place for six months, six years, or forever.

You can combine exit strategies together or create your own.

Some digital nomads hold citizenship in multiple countries or buy residences around the world that they rotate between. You might have other ideas.

Again, there are no right or wrong answers. It's all up to you! Following are three exit strategies you can use as examples.

Remaining nomadic

One possibility for your exit strategy is to remain nomadic. Select this option if you're happy in the lifestyle and you can afford to keep going. There's no limit on how long you can be a digital nomad for as long as you can support yourself and you have permission to stay in the country you're in. If you choose this route, your biggest decision is where to go next and when. Have fun with it! And circle back to this chapter when you feel it's time for a change of pace.

"Forever nomads" that you can follow include Kevin Martin from the 30 and A Wake Up YouTube channel (www.youtube.com/c/30AndAWakeUp) and travel bloggers, Brent and Michael are Going Places (www.brentandmichaelaregoing places.com).

Settling abroad

After some time as a digital nomad, you may arrive in a city or country that you identify with more than others. If you encounter a place where you want to stay, explore possible long-term residency or citizenship options. Chapter 9 has more details on visas, permits, and citizenship alternatives.

Returning home and experiencing reverse culture shock

Eventually, you may decide that you're done traveling or that you want to take a break for a while. Perhaps you miss your family and friends or you need to take care of something in your business or personal life. In that case, your exit strategy could be to go home.

In my case, I lived abroad for almost 20 years before the coronavirus pandemic prompted me to return to my home state of Florida, where I've now been for more than two years. *Am I still a nomad?* I like to think so, as I still work remotely and plan to travel again in the future.

You may find over time that your home country no longer feels like home, but neither does your current location. Although, you might also start to feel at home *anywhere* in the world.

Likewise, when returning to your home country or hometown, you may experience reverse culture shock. That is, you may feel like an outsider in the place you once considered home. That's a normal occurrence that usually passes with time as you adjust back to life where you're from. Don't be surprised if your friends and family think you've changed, however (you probably have). Embrace the freedom to become a new version of you, especially if that means bringing back some beliefs, ideas, and habits from your travels with you.

Tips for coping with reverse culture shock:

>> **Be patient.** The longer you've been gone, the more culture shock you may experience and the harder it could be to re-adjust. Culture shock and reverse culture shock follow the same phases of cultural adjustment, which you can find out about in Chapter 15.

>> **Stay in touch.** Keep in contact with friends you met in your travels. You can also start a blog (or a TikTok channel) to share your experiences and reflections from your time nomading (especially useful for when family and friends get tired of hearing your travel stories!).

>> **Maintain perspective.** You might feel nostalgia for your travel lifestyle without remembering many of the hard times. But there are also benefits to being home.

>> **Find a hobby.** Learning a skill, building a side business, or picking up a new interest can present a new mountain to climb.

>> **Keep traveling.** Keep your love of travel alive by taking short trips or exploring closer to home.

NOMAD EXIT STRATEGIES

Take a look at some case studies for creating your digital nomad exit strategy. These are six examples of the unlimited combinations of nomad itineraries you can dream up.

Exhibit 1: You're a non-EU citizen who's been hanging out in France for 2.5 months, but your 90-day European Schengen visa is expiring soon. You want to stay in the region, however, so your exit strategy is to move to a non-Schengen European country, such as Bulgaria, Croatia, Ireland, or Romania. You could also apply for a digital nomad visa in Europe to stay on the continent longer.

Exhibit 2: You've been traveling full time for a year and feel like slowing down. You apply for a one-year digital nomad visa in the Caribbean to take a pause. And perhaps learn how to sail.

Exhibit 3: You've been living nomadically for a while but you're not sure what to do or where to go next. You decide to move back to your hometown and re-assess your long-term plan.

Exhibit 4: You've been traveling for two years but keep thinking about how much you miss Vietnam. You decide to apply for an investor visa and move back to start a business.

Exhibit 5: You've been traveling for a year and things are going great, but you want more stability. You decide to buy properties in two places, so you have a winter and a summer home. You rent your houses out when you're not there.

Exhibit 6: You've been abroad for 5+ years and you're certain you don't want to move back to your home country. You buy a "golden visa" somewhere, which gives you permanent residency or citizenship by investment, and never look back.

Predicting Digital Nomad Migration Patterns and the Future of Work

Millions of people already call themselves digital nomads. *What's next?*

The remote working, traveling lifestyle that used to be considered "alternative" is now becoming mainstream. Countless studies support the consensus that remote work is here to stay. According to Gallup, 45 percent of the U.S. workforce reported working at home "all" or "part" of the time in 2021. Among white collar knowledge workers, the number is even higher — up to 67 percent. Although some workers will return to a physical workplace, it could be a temporary return. Researchers at the career site, Ladders, estimate that the number of remote job opportunities in North America will have increased from 4 percent before the COVID-19 pandemic to 25 percent by 2023.

If the millions of people who quit their jobs during the 2020–2022 period of "great resignation" are any indication, flexible work has become more than an employee perk. It's a requirement in many cases. While not everyone who works from home or works remotely will want to become digital nomads, many will travel more often or relocate to a new town.

As the number of anywhere workers grows, so will the variety in companies, services, and government policies catering to the location-independent population.

Digital nomad visas, insurance plans, housing subscriptions, and co-working vacation retreats are already a reality, as well as digital nomad communities and islands. The first digital country on the Internet is also on the way.

In the future, there will be products, services, and policies that haven't been invented yet. We may see digital nomad "time shares," a global tax category for remote workers, and a digital nomad passport. More companies will have a Head of Remote and an official company policy for nomadic employees.

NORA DUNN, THE PROFESSIONAL HOBO, ON RETURNING HOME

On the cusp of turning thirty years old, Nora Dunn had achieved what she thought she wanted — a successful financial practice in Toronto, Canada that allowed her to vacation throughout the United States, Europe, Mexico, South Africa, and the Caribbean. But it wasn't enough. She longed to spend more time abroad, immersing herself in different cultures. So, in 2006, she sold everything she owned and set off to travel the world. Selling her business gave her a buffer of savings while she began her new career as a freelance writer.

After twelve years of full-time travel in 65 countries, Nora decided to return to Toronto to be near family and set up a home base. She still travels for about half the year and says that, while she doesn't identify with one specific country anymore, being part of the digital nomad community helps her feel at home everywhere in the world. Her advice for aspiring "anywhereists" to remember is that "there are no rules! You get to call the shots. You can travel and work anywhere, with anybody, in any way that you choose."

The consumption habits of remote workers tend to change as well, with people spending more money on experiences over material goods. More people will move to rural areas or different countries. We'll continue to witness the globalization of business and an intermingling of cultures. Borders could all but disappear some-day. And hopefully, more and more people will have an opportunity to travel and support themselves with a remote income.

Embrace your nomadic future with confidence, as you're in good company.

5

The Part of Tens

IN THIS PART . . .

Learn top tips for succeeding as a digital nomad (and common mistakes to avoid).

Discover ten of the most popular destinations for digital nomads.

Consider countries with digital nomad visas.

Chapter **17**

Ten Tips for Success as a Digital Nomad

As with starting any new venture in life, you may kick off your digital nomad lifestyle with plenty of excitement. However, if you've ever tried to form or break a habit, you know that change is hard and initial enthusiasm wears off. Transitioning from a traditional to a location-independent lifestyle is no different. Your energy and motivation can wane over time. You'll soon realize that *becoming* a nomad is much simpler than *staying* a nomad. Buying a plane ticket is one thing. But staying nomadic for years is more of a challenge. So, in this chapter, I share with you ten tips for sustaining the digital nomad lifestyle long term. These tips have been gathered through more than 15 years of living nomadically. They also reflect feedback shared by thousands of other digital nomads.

Getting Clarity on Why You Want to Become a Digital Nomad

There's a lot of talk about finding your "why" in the world of business, personal development, and self-help. That's because it's important! Your "why" is your motivation for acting. It gives you a sense of purpose when the going gets tough.

Many people enter the digital nomad lifestyle under the guise of wanting more freedom or to travel more. But what comes next?

Why do you want to become a digital nomad? Journal or think deeply about why becoming a digital nomad is important to you before you "take the leap." Spending a few minutes reflecting now can give you a sense of clarity and meaning that serves you in the future. Chapter 2 has an exercise to help you find your why.

Having a Reliable Source of Income

Whether you earn money through a paycheck, an online business, freelancing, or investments, having a reliable income stream while traveling is important. Sure, some nomads figure out their finances on the fly. But it's much easier to sort out your job *before* adding travel to your to-do list.

I've been helping people relocate to different countries since 2005. My clients have different jobs, but the one thing they all have in common is a source of recurring income. Lack of money is one of the challenges to entering and staying in a nomadic lifestyle. You can't go very far without a source of income.

If you don't have a remote job yet, check out Chapters 5 and 6 for ideas on how to find or design one of your own.

Taking Action on Your Career and Personal Goals

Although working remotely is the foundation for a digital nomad lifestyle, travel can sometimes overshadow other aspects of life. Collecting passport stamps, making new friends, and otherwise living your best life may take priority over working at times. That's okay, as long as it's a conscious decision. But successful nomads dedicate time to their career and personal goals, despite traveling the world. Throughout your digital nomad journey, remember to make space for learning new skills and staying current in your field.

Achieving Work-Life Balance

Remote workers tend to work more hours per day than traditional office employees. Despite the freedom that digital nomads have, they could be at a higher risk of burnout than other sectors of the workforce.

To succeed long term in a nomadic lifestyle, strike a balance between how much you work, rest, and travel. The modern-day lifestyle is exhausting as is. But, when you add travel and logistics to a full-time workload, it can become untenable. Your energy ebbs and flows throughout life. Don't be afraid to slow down sometimes to reassess your focus and rest.

For more on how to maintain health, wellness, and balance as a digital nomad, see Chapter 12.

Traveling at a Sustainable Pace

Becoming a digital nomad can feel like indulging in a smorgasbord of food at Thanksgiving. You know you should use moderation, but there are so many temptations to choose from!

The truth is, it's not realistic to travel to a new place every day, week, or month forever. Especially if you're working at the same time. Be thoughtful about where you're traveling next and why. When you travel too fast for too long, something has to give. You may end up working while everyone else is at the beach or a waterfall without you. Likewise, in an effort to see and do everything fast, you could fall behind on projects or feel guilty for not working enough.

When it comes to succeeding as a digital nomad, the journey is the destination. Travel at a pace that feels sustainable for you. Savor every moment. Slow down if you feel like you're burning out.

Creating a Daily Routine

Having structure to your day is important for automating recurring tasks and conserving energy for what matters. But all too often, the concept of consistency disappears when you enter a nomadic lifestyle. Formerly fixed aspects of your daily routine, such as where you sleep, when you work, and what you eat can suddenly become variables. You could find yourself jet-lagged on a Monday, hungover on a Tuesday, and taking work calls at 4am on a Sunday if you don't set a schedule or boundaries.

REMEMBER

Living nomadically without any structure inevitably results in lost productivity or burnout. Meanwhile, healthy habits are shown to increase creativity, focus, energy, and motivation while decreasing stress and anxiety.

Creating a daily routine is indispensable to succeeding long term in a nomadic lifestyle, even if it changes from place to place. See Chapter 13 for tips on designing a morning routine and workday ritual that works for you.

Staying Open-Minded and Maintaining a Flexible and Resilient Attitude

Part of the beauty of travel is that it exposes you to different people, cultures, and ways of thinking. But experiencing a lot of change at once can be jarring. That's why it's so important to keep a flexible attitude while on your digital nomad journey. The thought of moving to a new city or country seems romantic and exciting. That is, until you experience your first hardship. Keeping a positive mindset can help you stay calm when facing challenges.

Flexibility defines the nomadic lifestyle. You'll have more choices in your career, work schedule, location, and more. Things won't always work out the way you planned. But if you expect the unexpected and stay agile, you'll be in a good position to succeed in this lifestyle for the long run.

Integrating with New Cultures

Becoming a part of the local community as an outsider is easier said than done (especially if you don't speak the language). But spending extra time in in one place will help you learn more about a country's culture and people while feeling more at home.

See Chapters 14 and 15 for more ways to make friends abroad and adapt to life in foreign countries. And remember, when it comes to integrating with a new culture, there's no such thing as perfection. You might never feel like you fit in 100 percent, but something is better than nothing.

Finding a Community and Relying on Your Support System

Humans weren't designed to survive in isolation. Before the world's first organized cities and countries, people evolved in tribal communities. As a nomad, make it a point to find a community wherever you go. Having a support group can be the difference between thriving in a nomadic lifestyle or cutting your adventure short. Expanding your social circle is also a good way to network, land a new job, or find solutions to problems. See Chapter 14 for guidance on how to meet people and make friends even as a solo traveler.

Being Honest with Yourself and Reflecting Regularly

Have you ever set a New Year's resolution, only to forget about it a short time after? As you travel around as a digital nomad, your goals and priorities will change. You'll change as well! That's why it's important to check in with yourself on occasion to reassess your goals and level of happiness.

Going location independent is an opportunity to design the life you've always dreamed about. So, set a reminder to check in with yourself once per month, quarter, or year, to ensure you still feel aligned with your travel, lifestyle, and career goals. Ask yourself questions such as, Are you happy? How's business? What do you need right now? What would you like to change? What should you do next?

Sometimes that means you're ready to stop being a digital nomad. If that's the case, see Chapter 16 to create an exit strategy.

Chapter **18**

Avoiding Ten Common Mistakes New Digital Nomads Make

When starting your digital nomad journey, you might worry about handling travel and remote work logistics, such as finding fast Wi-Fi or knowing what to pack. While those aspects are important, many common missteps are more related to soft skills. Persistence, resilience, and maintaining a positive mindset are some of the biggest challenges facing digital nomads.

The digital nomad lifestyle is ideal in many ways, with writers Brent Hartinger and Michael Jensen calling it "a secret of the universe." But few people point out the potential pitfalls. In this chapter, I expound on ten common challenges that can cause you to struggle or abandon the lifestyle too soon.

Lacking Clarity on Goals and Your Why

Having goals and ambitions give your life a sense of purpose. Without them, it's hard to know where you're headed and when you're off track. Reaching your destination when navigating a car, boat, or plane requires minor adjustments and course corrections along the way. It's the same in life, especially if you're traveling the world.

Whenever you feel lost in your journey, think back to why you wanted to become a digital nomad. *What did you want to achieve? How does being nomadic change your life for the better?* Knowing why you started something helps you stay motivated when the going gets tough. See Chapter 2 for how to get clarity on your "why" for becoming a digital nomad.

Planning Too Much or Not Enough

New digital nomads tend to plan too much or not at all. Knowing how far in advance to plan comes with experience. But when you're getting started, aim to strike a balance somewhere in the middle. You want to have an outline of a plan while leaving room for flexibility and spontaneity.

The problem with planning too far ahead is that you don't know what you don't know (yet). You might want to stay somewhere longer or leave sooner once you get there. Changing your itinerary gets expensive when you have a rigid plan in place. I once met a nomadic couple who planned their first year of travel in advance. Although they weren't happy in the first few destinations they had booked, they couldn't cancel their plans without losing thousands of dollars in pre-paid rent.

Not planning *at all* is also costly. If you travel without a plan, prepare to pay more for last-minute airfare and housing. Sometimes, going where the wind takes you is a good thing. But it doesn't bode well for anyone who wants to sustain a nomadic lifestyle long term.

REMEMBER

The average person makes a whopping 35,000 decisions per day, according to researchers Barbara Sahakian and Jamie Nicole Labuzetta. There's no need to add more questions or uncertainty to your daily decision matrix.

TIP

A good rule is to plan one to three months ahead. This amount of time gives you space to adapt to a new place before deciding whether to move on or extend your stay.

Failing to Budget Accurately

Financial problems could be the main reason people "fail" in the digital nomad lifestyle. Without money, it's hard to keep your location-independent lifestyle going. People run out of money for various reasons. It could be losing a job, over-spending, or allowing travel and other activities to creep into your billable hours.

So, before you go nomadic, make sure that you've budgeted realistically. I once had a client run out of money within one month of relocating to Costa Rica because he didn't have a steady job.

REMEMBER

Don't leave home without a reliable income stream. Save at least three to six months of living expenses before departing. Then, add a cushion of 10 percent or more to cover unanticipated expenses. Check out Chapter 3 for how to create a digital nomad budget and Chapter 8 for help estimating the cost of living in different destinations.

Spending Too Much Time SightSeeing and Socializing

This one's a doozy. Few digital nomads like to admit that their work quality is suffering because of their lifestyle. But it *can* happen. Seeing the world and meeting new people are a blast. No one would blame you for wanting to enjoy yourself and take advantage of the freedom that a location-independent lifestyle offers. (That's probably why you want to become a digital nomad to begin with!) But there is such a thing as *too much of a good thing*. When traveling through foreign lands, you'll naturally want to connect with people so you don't feel alone. But this desire for connection can take priority over other aspects of your personal and professional life.

If you live in a co-living space or near a digital nomad community, there will always be opportunities for things to do. Activities, excursions, meetups, and networking events can replace time that you used to spend working or relaxing. But when you consider your traditional lifestyle and a 40-hour work week, there's a limit to how much free time you have.

To prevent extracurricular activities and social engagements from creeping into your work or personal time, set a remote work schedule and stick to it. Be cognizant of how fast your calendar fills up and don't be afraid to decline invitations. Remember to leave time to relax and do nothing sometimes.

Traveling Too Fast

Another common mistake that new digital nomads make is traveling too fast. Have you ever felt like you needed a vacation from your vacation? Adding work, networking, cultural adjustment, and learning a language on top of a packed travel schedule becomes unsustainable. You may want to see the world and fill up your passport as fast as possible. But remember, the journey is the destination.

How do you know if you're traveling too fast? Travel should inspire you, not tire you. If your health, work, mood, or bank account suffer, those are all big signs. If you begin to feel weary of travel, that's a sign of travel burnout. I always know I'm traveling too fast when I lose the desire to go out and about.

So, if you find yourself feeling indifferent to exploring or connecting with other people, slowing down or going home for a while can make space for your wanderlust to return. Settling down isn't "failing" as a digital nomad; it's a change of priorities.

Fast-paced, perpetual travel can negatively impact your health, mood, and earnings and relationships. It's also expensive. (See the earlier section, "Failing to Budget Accurately.")

See Chapter 13 for how to develop a digital nomad routine that promotes work-life balance.

Struggling to Adjust to Different Cultures

Adapting to a new culture is easier said than done. Often, the very differences that intrigue you about a place may be the hardest things to adjust to. Traveling as a tourist only gives you enough time to experience the honeymoon phase of the culture shock curve.

But as a digital nomad, you'll most likely move through the frustration, adjustment, and adaption phases. The initial discomfort you experience eventually passes. You start to understand the language, culture, and people better. You get into a routine, learn your way around, and find your rhythm. The problem is there's no guarantee of how long each phase will last. Completing the cycle of cultural adjustment could take one year (or ten). But knowing what to expect helps you cope with this confusing and uncertain time. (See Chapter 15 to find out about the phases of culture shock.)

Remaining Close-Minded and Inflexible

The longer and farther you travel, the more you'll be exposed to different ways of doing things. If you hold onto one way as the "right" way, it's difficult to adjust to a new place. Instead, remain open-minded and curious about what you see and experience. Adopt a beginner's mindset, as if you were learning something new for the first time.

When embarking on a nomadic lifestyle, you'll retain certain preconceived ideas from your past. The more open you are to changing long-held beliefs, the better you'll adapt as a global citizen. Think resilience; not rigidity!

Likewise, you may also witness universal injustices, such as violence, war, racism, corruption, theft, poverty, slavery, and environmental destruction. It's okay to denounce or disagree with anything that's flat out wrong.

Being Unable to Cope with Occasional Loneliness

Everyone feels lonely sometimes. But it's a mistake to give up on the digital nomad lifestyle at the first hint of home sickness. I would encourage you to give yourself some time to adjust.

Loneliness can creep up at any time. Yes, you will feel lonely sometimes — regardless of the lifestyle you lead. But, like any emotion, the feeling of loneliness will pass or transform.

A nomadic lifestyle is transient by nature. Sometimes, you might have more new friends than you can count, while at other times, you might feel alone in the world. Whatever you experience, know that it's normal. Rather than trying to avoid ever feeling lonely (which is impossible), welcome it, explore it, and strive to learn from it. Let loneliness be a map to point you in a new direction or suggest something you might need.

REMEMBER

One thing that puts me at ease when an unpleasant emotion strikes is remembering that we have feelings for a reason. Emotions are timeless, universal, and central to the human experience. Life wouldn't be the same without them.

Inconsistent Daily Habits and Routines

Although location independence is the pinnacle of freedom, that doesn't mean every day should be an adventure. Having some structure to your day is helpful.

Having a routine allows your brain to automate recurring behaviors and reinvest energy in more important things. Routines have also been linked to reducing stress while promoting better sleep and mental health. Thinking you can make daily decisions on the fly without a routine is one of the biggest mistakes new digital nomads make.

I once heard a nomad on a podcast mention that he never stays in the same place for more than a week. He also said he takes business calls at all hours of the day and from anywhere — even when on a boat to go scuba diving. But there's more than one reason why you wouldn't wear a wetsuit to the office.

Life is messy and sometimes responsibilities overlap. But creating separation between work and play helps you stay focused when in the remote office and unplug during your time off. See Chapter 13 for tips on creating a daily routine.

Putting Others' Opinions Ahead of Your Own

Becoming a digital nomad is an opportunity to hit the reset button in life. You can change where you live, what you do for work, and who you surround yourself with. But humans become a product of their environments to some degree. After meeting many people in different places, you could feel like a ship without an anchor and begin to adopt other people's dreams and ideas as your own.

There are many opinions about the "best" digital nomad hubs, new technology you should buy, and the "next big thing" in business or social media. But you don't have to listen to what society or other digital nomads have to say. Being location independent is a chance to design your life how you see fit. Do what makes you happy, regardless of what others say or think!

Chapter **19**

More Than Ten Popular Destinations for Work and Play

The beauty of being a digital nomad is that you can live almost anywhere in the world. But over the years, a few destinations have stood out among the rest.

Remote workers tend to flock to safe places with good Internet, mild weather, a low to moderate cost of living, and a community of fellow remote workers. In this chapter, I introduce you to ten (or so) popular destinations for you to consider.

REMEMBER

Nowhere in the world is "perfect." Everywhere has its pros and cons. The best place for you might not rank on someone else's Top Ten list.

REMEMBER

There aren't any hard statistics on how many digital nomads there are in the world or where they live (or for how long), so this list is based on the consensus online among nomads.

Argentina

Argentina has long attracted remote workers for its low cost of living, affordable housing, delicious food, and international population. (Did I mention, wine?) In 2020, the Argentine government made an effort to welcome digital nomads to Buenos Aires through a program called Nómades Digitales. Besides boasting a diverse entrepreneurial and tech scene, Buenos Aires has also been ranked the number one place to study in Latin America.

But Buenos Aires isn't the only place for digital nomads in Argentina. Other hotspots include Mendoza, Salta, Cordoba, Ushuaia, and the beaches of Mar de Plata. You can also hop a ferry to visit Uruguay or explore Patagonia while you're there.

WARNING

Argentina's currency is notoriously unstable. The Argentine peso's inflation rate usually works to the advantage of foreigners, but make sure to check the exchange rate before traveling there.

Bulgaria

Bulgaria might not be the first place you think of when considering digital nomad destinations, but it checks all the proverbial boxes. Bulgaria is safe, affordable, has lightning-fast Internet, plenty of co-working spaces, and has become a hub for digital nomads. The winter months bring cold weather but also some of the best skiing in the region. Spring and summer are perfect for hiking in the mountains. Citizens of most countries can travel to Bulgaria for 90 days with a passport. It's also a popular destination for acquiring permanent residency due to its low, flat tax rate of 10 percent.

Popular digital nomad cities in Bulgaria include Bansko, Plovdiv, and the capital of Sofia. Bansko has a core community of nomads year round, thanks to the many co-working spaces there. Nomads tend to stay for months at a time versus days or weeks, so it's less transient than other nomad hotspots. Also check out the seaside towns of Varna and Burgas in the summer months.

TIP

Bulgaria is central to other popular digital nomad destinations, such as Turkey, Greece, Cyprus, Serbia, and Romania — perfect for a weekend getaway. From Sofia, you can find direct flights on low-cost carriers to many destinations in Europe and the Middle East.

Canary Islands, Spain

If you're looking for an island paradise close to Europe, look no further than Spain's Canary Islands. Nomad City calls it a "remote work paradise" for its sunny weather (360 days per year!), high-quality healthcare, and growing digital nomad community. The Canary Islands ranks in the top 5 percent worldwide for its combination of a low cost of living with a high quality of life.

Popular outposts for digital nomads in the Canary Islands include Las Palmas de Gran Canaria and Santa Cruz de Tenerife.

REMEMBER

Don't forget about the mainland! There are plenty of digital nomads in Barcelona, Madrid, Malaga, Valencia, and beyond. I'm partial to towns in Basque Country, such as San Sebastian and Zarautz. The islands of Ibiza, Mallorca, and Menorca are also popular.

Croatia

Croatia has some of the bluest water I've ever seen. It's also an ideal destination for location-independent professionals due to its warm climate, moderate cost of living, stable infrastructure, and growing digital nomad community. English is also widely spoken there.

In 2021, Croatia launched a digital nomad visa program, which allows remote workers to stay in the country for a period of up to one year.

Popular cities for nomads you can check out in Croatia include Dubrovnik, Split, Zadar, and Zagreb.

Indonesia

Indonesia is home to one of the most popular digital nomad destinations in the world — the island of Bali, which has attracted remote workers for its low cost of living, friendly locals, and laid-back lifestyle. When you're not out surfing, shopping, watching the sunset, or practicing yoga, you can co-work from Hubud in Ubud or Dojo Bali in Canggu.

If you want to live with other nomads, you have plenty of opportunities in Bali. Co-living groups such as WiFi Tribe pass through there a couple times per year. There's also plenty of shared nomad accommodation available.

The most popular places for digital nomads in Indonesia include Bali and Jakarta. Within Bali, check out Canggu, Kuta/Seminyak, Ubud, and the Bukit Peninsula. For a quieter lifestyle, consider Sanur, Nusa Lembongan, Lombok, and Gili Trawangan.

WARNING

There are more than 17,500 islands in Indonesia (the government isn't quite sure of the exact number). Unfortunately, not all of them have the connectivity that digital nomads need to work effectively online. For the best Internet, stay close to urban areas or stock up on pre-paid SIM cards.

Mexico

Mexico is one of the best entry-level destinations for new digital nomads due to its low cost of living, large international population, and location in the North American time zone. Citizens of most countries can travel to Mexico for up to 180 days at time with a tourist visa, although that doesn't guarantee you'll receive the maximum number of days in your passport.

In Mexico, you have the choice of living in the city, mountains, or along the country's nearly 6,000 miles of coastline. The most popular destinations for digital nomads include Cabo San Lucas, Guadalajara, Mexico City, Mérida, Oaxaca, Playa del Carmen, Puerto Vallarta, Rosarito, and Tulum. Retirees particularly like San Miguel de Allende.

TIP

Although the cost of living in Mexico is generally affordable, touristy areas (ahem: Tulum) are more expensive. You can save money and live more like a local by choosing to reside in smaller towns off the beaten path. On Nomad List, the average cost of living in Tulum is $2,500 per month, compared to $1,000 in Querétaro.

Portugal

Portugal is one of the highest ranked countries in the world for foreigners and digital nomads alike due to its mild climate, friendly people, good infrastructure, and beautiful countryside. Portugal is the fourth most peaceful country in the world according to the Global Peace Index. It was ranked as the fifth best country in the world for expats in Internation's 2021 Expat Insider Survey and the best place to retire in 2020 according to International Living.

The accolades don't end there, though! In 2021, the Government of the Madeira islands with Startup Madeira created the world's first Digital Nomad Village. Like much of Portugal, Madeira offers ideal conditions for remote workers, such as an attractive climate, fast connectivity, and plenty of opportunities to make nomadic friends.

Other top places for digital nomads in Portugal include the Algarve, Azores islands, Ericeira, Lisbon, and Porto.

TIP

If you're interested in living in Portugal long term, search online for the Portugal D7 visa.

Taiwan

Taiwan was voted as the best place to live in the world three years in a row on the InterNations Expat Insider survey. The country ranks highly on safety, healthcare, walkability, weather, and cost of living. Said one expat, "I feel safe wherever I go, and everything is convenient." 95 percent of nomads on Nomad List also approve. Digital nomads consider Taiwan a great destination for females, foreigners, and the LGBTQIA community. If you go to Taiwan, you can expect swift Internet speeds and a cost of living around $2,000 per month.

Places to check out in Taiwan include Taipei, Kaohsiung, Tainan, Kinmen, and Taichung.

TIP

Digital nomads love the Taiwan Gold Card, a 4-in-1 work permit and long-stay visa valid for three years. You can use the Gold Card to work remotely or apply for local jobs.

Thailand

Thailand has been attracting digital nomads since the dawn of the Internet age. Digital nomads flock to Thailand for the low cost of living, high quality of life, friendly people, and unlimited pad thai. And did I mention the postcard-esque beaches and islands? At the time this book was written, the island of Ko Pha Ngan was the highest-ranked digital nomad destination in the world on Nomad List.

More top digital nomad hangouts in Thailand include Bangkok, Chiang Mai, Koh Phi Phi, Koh Samui, and Phuket.

Chiang Mai is widely regarded as one of the digital nomad "capitals" of the world. There are at least 27 co-working spaces there, in an area of 15.53 square miles.

Van Life

Sometimes, the best destination for digital nomads is a mobile one! Why choose one place to live when your house can be on wheels? Living and working from a van or RV is a popular choice for the wandering nomad attracted to the freedom of the open road. It's not for everyone, though. When living in a van, you may face challenges such as flat tires, inclement weather, and Internet outages (among other surprises). Consider van life if you want the flexibility of a nomadic lifestyle without leaving home.

Popular places to experience van life include national parks around the United States, Canada, Europe, Australia, New Zealand, and Iceland.

TIP

To learn more about van life, check out r/VanLife on Reddit. Find people to follow under the #VanLife hashtag on Instagram and YouTube.

Vietnam

Da Nang, Vietnam is one of the Top Five destinations on Nomad List, standing out with a nomad cost of living of $1,013 per month. Vietnam is a safe, affordable place to live, with fast Internet, friendly locals, and a wide selection of places to work from. When you're not behind your laptop, you can explore the many beaches, islands, temples, and cultural sites around this peaceful, Buddhist country.

For city living, look up Da Nang, Ho Chi Minh City, and Hanoi. If the coast is calling your time, check out Hoi An, Phu Quoc, and Da Lat. For a mountain escape, consider Sa Pa.

TIP

You can apply for a 90-day multiple entry visa to visit Vietnam for around $50.

United Arab Emirates

The UAE has long attracted foreigners from around the world for its plentiful job opportunities. In 2021, expats made up 89 percent of the country's total population (equivalent to 8.84 million people).

In 2020, the capital of Dubai attracted international attention when it announced a one-year virtual working permit for entrepreneurs, freelancers, and remote employees. Dubai has ranked highly for expats, remote work, safety, and beaches. It's also known for being a trade and financial hub situated between the East and West.

Dubai is especially attractive to UK digital nomads, with between 120,000–240,000 British expats residing there.

United States of America

American digital nomads frequently look outside of the United States to find more exotic places to live, but stateside cities and rural areas have much to offer to remote workers. Since the coronavirus pandemic, workers across the country have been exploring beyond the confines of expensive cities such as New York and San Francisco. Some workers have opted for less expensive tech hubs such as Austin, Texas, Atlanta, Georgia, and Baltimore, Maryland. Others have traded city living for a more rural existence, putting down roots in Colorado, Wyoming, Idaho, Montana, and Tennesee. Still others have changed states for tax reasons, with Nevada and Florida absorbing an influx of remote workers in recent years. Whether you choose a state based on cost of living, climate, or proximity to family members or your head office, the United States has plenty of options to choose.

If you're from outside the United States, you can apply to travel to the States through the ESTA website. However, if your country is not part of the Visa Waiver Program, check with your local U.S. Embassy for entry requirements.

Chapter **20**

Ten (or So) Digital Nomad Visas

n 2020, Barbados became the first country to offer a visa program for digital nomads and remote workers. Previously, most digital nomads traveled exclusively on tourist visas, working online in an unregulated "gray area." Times have changed, however. Digital nomad and remote work visas offer you the opportunity to get official status to work abroad from your laptop.

Applying for a digital nomad visa is optional, but doing so allows you to stay longer in a country compared to traveling as a tourist with a passport. This chapter tells you about ten digital nomad visas you can apply for and what the basic requirements are. For more about travel visas and paperwork, see Chapter 9.

TIP

New digital nomad and remote work visa programs are announced often. Countries with visas in development at the time of writing this book include Brazil, Colombia, Costa Rica, Italy, Latvia, Montenegro, South Africa, Spain, and Serbia. Before traveling, search online to see whether the country you want to visit has a digital nomad visa.

WARNING

A digital nomad visa is a temporary stay visa for people who work remotely for themselves (as freelancers or online business owners), or for a company registered outside of the country you're applying in. It's not a work permit to work for a local company, nor is it a path to permanent residency or citizenship.

Bahamas BEATS

Fancy working from a white sand beach? The Bahamas Extended Access Travel Stay program (bahamasbeats.com) gives you permission to work remotely from the Bahamian islands for up to one year. The cost is $1,000 to apply, with an additional $500 for each dependent traveling with you.

Requirements include a completed application form, a passport valid for at least twelve months after arrival, a medical insurance policy, and proof of self-employment or a job letter from your remote employer. There's also a remote study option for students.

Belize Work Where You Vacation

The Belize Work Where You Vacation program (travelbelize.org) is your ticket to spending six months living and working in tropical Central America. The program includes special discounts on activities, entertainment, and accommodation. Remote working parents are also able to enroll their children under 18 in the public school system.

To apply for this program, you must have a valid passport, clean criminal record, travel insurance policy, and notarized banking reference. You must also prove a minimum annual income of $75,000 as an individual or $100,000 for couples and families.

Croatia Digital Nomad Visa

The highly anticipated Croatia temporary stay permit (https://mup.gov.hr/aliens-281621/stay-and-work/temporary-stay-of-digital-nomads/286833) allows non-EU/EEA/Swiss remote workers who earn at least HRK 7,822.50 per month (around $2,500) to live in the sunny, Adriatic nation for up to one year.

It's $187 to apply. You also need a passport valid for three months longer than your expected length of stay, health insurance coverage, a work contract or proof of self-employment, and an address in Croatia.

Cyprus Digital Nomad Visa

The Mediterranean Island of Cyprus, located between Greece and Lebanon, is known for its turquoise water and 340 days of sunshine per year. In October of 2021, the country's ministers approved a Digital Nomad Visa Scheme (https://www.e-resident.gov.ee) giving select remote workers the option to live in Cyprus for up to three years. The cost is €70 to apply, and you must prove a monthly net income of at least €3,500, among other requirements.

To snag one of the 500 visas available, you should enter Cyprus on a tourist visa first and apply at the Civil Registry and Migration Department within three months of arrival.

WARNING

Visa holders will be considered tax residents after 183 days (unless you're a tax resident in a different country).

Estonia Digital Nomad Visa

Estonia — one of the most digitized countries in the world — is a Baltic nation rich in history, culture, nature, and fast Internet. Since August 1, 2020, you can stay in Estonia for one year with the Estonia Digital Nomad Visa (e-resident.gov.ee).

To be eligible, you must earn at least €3,504 (pre-tax income) as a freelancer, online business owner, or remote employee for a company outside of Estonia. The cost is €80-100 to apply, depending on the visa type.

TIP

Estonia also offers an e-Residency program for entrepreneurs who want to open an EU-based company remotely (not a travel visa).

Greece Digital Nomad Visa

If you're interested in diving into Greek culture, history, food, or working from a Greek island, consider the Greece Digital Nomad Visa (https://workfromgreece.gr), valid for stays of twelve months. There are four requirements specific to the Digital Nomad Visa: a declaration letter detailing your plan to work remotely from Greece, proof of independent or remote employment for a company outside of Greece, income of at least €3,500 per month, and a €75 application fee.

Applications can be made by mail, email, or in person through a Greek consular authority before you travel. Find a consulate near you at mfa.gr.

Hungary White Card

Hungary's capital of Budapest has become a popular digital nomad destination for its low to moderate cost of living, high quality of life, fast Internet, and plethora of coffee shops and co-working spaces. Qualifying for the Hungarian White Card (mbmah.hu) allows you to stay in the country for one year with an option to extend.

You must apply in person at a Hungarian consulate outside of the country at least one month before arrival. The list of requirements is long, including health insurance, proof of accommodation, and proof of income of at least €2,000 per month for the six months prior to your application.

Iceland Remote Work Visa

Iceland is a northern European destination where you can explore glaciers, ice caves, waterfalls, and hot springs during your free time. Iceland is also the most peaceful country in the world, according to the Global Peace Index.

The Iceland Remote Work Visa (https://work.iceland.is) allows you to stay in Iceland for up to six months. Requirements for this visa are steep, however. Applicants must show proof of income of at least ISK 1,000,000 or $7,618 per month, among other requirements.

Malta Nomad Residence Permit

Malta is a small archipelago of islands located just south of Sicily in the Mediterranean Sea. If you earn at least €2,700 per month as a remote worker or freelancer, you could live in Malta for a year under the country's Nomad Residence Permit (https://nomad.residencymalta.gov.mt). You need to provide a health insurance policy, rental agreement, and pass a background check to qualify.

Mauritius Premium Visa

Mauritius is a small island in the Indian Ocean off the coast of Madagascar. It's also one of the first African nations to offer a digital nomad visa program (www.edbmauritius.org/premium-visa). The one-year Mauritius Premium Visa is available to tourists, retirees, and online professionals alike. Unlike many other digital nomad visas, you can apply for the Mauritius visa online. Requirements include a valid passport, flight reservation, health insurance, and proof of income of $1,500 per month.

Other African countries offering digital nomad visas include Cape Verde and the Seychelles. South Africa also has a visa in development.

Romania Digital Nomad Visa

Romania is a popular Eastern European country for digital nomads, due to its low cost of living, fast Internet speeds, and plethora of coffee shops. Under the Romania Digital Nomad Visa (https://evisa.mae.ro), you can stay in the country for six to twelve months with an option to renew. To qualify, you must earn "at least three times the average gross monthly salary in Romania," which works out to about $4,000 per month.

As with other digital nomad visa programs, you'll also need a valid passport, health insurance, proof of remote or self-employment, accommodation, and a letter of intention explaining your purpose of traveling to Romania.

You can begin your application online, but you must also appear in person at a Romanian embassy or consulate in your country of residence.

Index

H

hand washing, 216

happiness, 22

health

benefits of digital nomadism, 22

blue zones, 218

checking before relocating, 161

cons of digital nomadism, 22

costs related to, 42

good hygiene, practicing, 216

jet lag, minimizing, 218–219

maintaining mental, 223–225

maintaining physical, 219–223

overview, 215–216

precautions, taking, 276

protection, using, 217

remote work in, 82

requirements at destination, checking, 201

switching costs, 47

water, drinking, 217

health insurance

emergency travel medical, 162, 216, 226–228

home country, 231–232

international, 162, 216, 226, 228–230

local, 216, 226, 228, 230–231

purchasing, 200, 232–233

for seniors, 232

healthcare systems, 233–234

high season for tourism, 135

hive mind mentality, 117–118

Holiday, Ryan, 208

holidays, taking, 241, 244

home, work from. *See* remote work

home country health insurance, 231–232

home stays, 184

homesickness, 274–275

honesty, 299

honeymoon phase, 270

house, deciding what to do with, 160

house-sitting, 183

house-swapping, 182–183

housing

alternative, 181–182

co-living, 116, 179–181, 259–260

home stays, 184

house-sitting, 183

house-swapping, 182–183

ideas for finding perfect, 198

inspecting upon arrival, 266

long-term, 177–178, 190–191, 196, 198

overview, 175

pet-sitting, 183–184

planning search for, 184–188

private, 178

reserving and booking, 195–197

searching for

Facebook groups and forums, 191–192

in-person searching, 195

local classifieds listings, 193

long-term housing, 190–191

overview, 188

property management companies, 194–195

real estate offices, 195

search engine strategies, 193–194

short-term vacation rentals websites, 188–190

shared, 178–179

short-term, 176–177, 188–190, 196, 198

travel retreats, 180–181

workspaces in, 113

housing subscription plans, 46, 189

human connection, embracing, 224

Hungarian White Card, 318

hygiene, practicing good, 216

hygiene items, packing list for, 207

hyperactive hive mind, 117–118

I

Iceland Remote Work Visa, 318

icons, explained, 3

incentive programs, remote work, 146–147

income. *See also* work

as benefit of digital nomadism, 22

of digital nomads, 14

importance for long-term success, 296

multiple streams of, combining, 64, 72–73, 104

needs as digital nomad, 41–42

passive, 64, 71–72

pre-departure budgeting, 48

independent contractors, sourcing, 124–126. *See also* freelancing

Indonesia, 309–310

Industrial Revolutions, 16

industries, digital nomads across, 13

inflexibility, as common mistake, 305

influencers, 10, 78–79

information technology (IT) jobs, 76

innovation, 21

insurance

costs related to, 42

health, 162, 200, 216, 226–232

overview, 162, 226

purchasing, 200, 232–233

for seniors, 232

travel, 162, 200, 226, 227

International Driver's Permit, 165

batching, 150–151
as benefit of digital nomadism, 22
common mistakes, 304
costs of, 42, 49–50
dating and, 261–263
deciding on frequency of, 150–153
by digital nomads, myths about, 20
expediting, 34
as full-time digital nomad, 28
group, 30–31, 278
with kids, 31–33
pace of, relation to setup costs, 45
with pets, 208–209
planning in advance, 152–153
productivity mistakes related to, 240
slow
  defined, 150
  housing options for, 198
  jet lag, minimizing through, 218
  strategies for, 152
  switching costs and, 45, 47
solo, 30–31
at sustainable pace, 297
switching costs, 45–47
tips for departure and arrival, 209–210
traditional jobs involving, 91
types of, 33–34
travel bloggers, 20
travel budgeting apps, 50
travel insurance, 162, 200, 226, 227
travel medical insurance, 162, 216, 226–228
travel retreats, 180–181
travel rewards cards, 156, 201
travel rewards programs, 200–201
travel tribes, 180–181

U

uncertainty, as con of digital nomadism, 23
United Arab Emirates, 313
United States
  digital nomads in, 12, 15, 313
  remote work incentive programs, 146–147
  taxation in, 157, 158

V

vacation rentals websites, 188–190
vacations, taking, 241, 244
vaccinations, 161, 276
valuables, deciding what to do with, 160–161
van life, 181, 312
Vietnam, 312
virtual assistants (VAs), 80, 124–126, 187
virtual job fairs, 87–88
virtual mailboxes, 162–163
virtual remote work tools, 126
virtual summits, 259
visa runs, 171–172
visas
  applying for, 169
  in Asia, 140
  in Caribbean and North Atlantic, 140–141
  digital nomad, 173–174, 315–319
  in Europe, 144
  golden, 171, 172–173
  knowing if needed, 166–168
  long-term, 170–172
  in North America, 143
  in Oceania, 145
  role in destination choice, 134
  tourist, 166–169, 171–172, 315
visibility, in remote teams, 122–124

vitamin D, getting, 222
volunteering, meeting people through, 251

W

walking tours, 250, 266
Warning icon, explained, 3
washing hands, 216
water, drinking, 217
water cooler, remote, 124
weather, role in destination choice, 135
wellness. See health
Wi-Fi, finding anywhere, 268
Wi-Fi hotspot devices, 164
Wilson, Kristin, 24
women digital nomads, 13, 33
word-of-mouth marketing, 108
work. See also remote work
  deciding whether to keep or quit job, 52–55
  determining quantity of, 236
  digital nomads, defining, 9
  industries for digital nomads, 13
  meeting people at, 253–256
  networking to find, 89–90
  non-tech jobs, 19
  overview, 51, 63
  peak hours, planning around, 110–112, 237, 238
  popular digital nomad jobs
    accounting and finance, 72
    affiliate marketing, 73
    blogging and writing, 73
    coaching, consulting, and teaching, 75
    computer and information technology, 76
    creative and design work, 78
    customer service and virtual assistance, 79
    digital marketing, 80

work *(continued)*
  dropshipping and ecommerce, 80
  influencers, 78–79
  medical and health, 81
  project management, 81
  sales, 82
  social media management, 82
  routes to becoming digital nomad
  freelancing, 64, 67–69
  multiple income streams, combining, 64, 71
  online business, 64, 69–70
  overview, 64
  passive income, earning, 64, 71–72
  remote employees, 64, 65–67
  side hustles, 54, 101
  traditional jobs involving travel, 91
  workday and daily routine, planning, 237–238
  workspace, designating, 238–239
  work environment, 112–113, 133, 138
  work sprints, combining with sabbaticals, 244–245
  work visas, 171
  workday, planning, 237–238
  work-from-home plan, creating, 110–113
  working holiday visas, 171
work-life balance
  burnout, avoiding and recovering from, 242–244
  combining work sprints with sabbaticals, 244–245
  importance for long-term success, 297
  overview, 241
workspaces
  alternate, 114–116
  co-working, 114–116, 239, 253
  designating, 238–239
  mixing up, 112–113
writing jobs, 74–76

About the Author

Kristin Wilson is a long-term digital nomad and relocation consultant who has traveled to 60 countries in 20 years. After a successful career in real estate abroad, she founded an international relocation company in 2011. She has since helped over 1,000 people move to different countries while working remotely with her fully distributed, global team.

Today, Kristin shares her expertise on travel, remote work, and living abroad through writing, audio, and video. She's the creator of two YouTube channels, YouTube.com/TravelingwithKristin (www.youtube.com/travelingwithkristin) and YouTube.com/DigitalNomad (www.youtube.com/digitalnomad). She's also the host of the top-rated, Badass Digital Nomads podcast (www.badassdigitalnomads.com), with listeners in 170+ countries.

Kristin has been a Top Writer on Medium and Quora on topics such as Business, Life, Technology, Travel, Productivity, Digital Nomads, and Location Independence.

She has appeared in mainstream media outlets, including *Atlas Obscura*, *Bloomberg Businessweek*, *Business Insider*, *HuffPost*, HGTV's House Hunters International, *The Independent*, *The New York Times*, The Today Show, *Wall Street Journal*, and more.

When she's not traipsing the globe making videos or helping people move overseas, you can find her spinning music behind the DJ decks. Learn more at www.travelingwithkristin.com.

Dedication

For my grandmother, Josephine, who inspired my love of travel and always encouraged and supported my unconventional life.

I also dedicate this book to you, dear reader. To everyone who is exploring the possibility of living life differently. To everyone pursuing their dreams of freedom and location independence. And to the diverse, international community of anywhere workers leading the way into the future of work.

And to my first YouTube subscriber, Teklordz, this book is for you, too. Rest in peace.

Author's Acknowledgments

Writing a book about a topic I'm so passionate about has been a lifelong dream come true. But it certainly wasn't easy! So many people behind the scenes over the years have helped make this book possible.

First and foremost, credit is due to the original digital nomads, Tsugio Makimoto and David Manners. Thank you for writing the book that gave us a glimpse into the future and for inspiring the new generation of global citizens.

Thank you so much to my incredible family, who has always believed in me. Mom, Dad, Jimmy, Shannon, Aunt Melissa, and the cousins were always there to lend an ear or word of support, while Koura and Chloe supplied the smiles and hugs. And to my dear, late grandmother who asked when the book was coming out every time I saw her!

I would like to express my deepest gratitude to all the digital nomads who contributed their stories to this book. Also, to my friends worldwide for your ongoing encouragement and support. Thank you for your kind messages to check in with me, helpful ideas and words of advice, and for being there when I needed a boost — especially Anita Flaque, Camila di Marzo, Chase Warrington, John Gorman, Liam Martin, Dave Mastronardi, Matt Bowles, Michelle Farina, Mike Vardy, Nora Dunn, and Brent and Michael. Thank you, Marco, for prying me away from my computer screen to see the big picture.

Special thanks to MJ Flaque for always being there for me (even when we're on opposite sides of the world!), to Izzy Braly, my lifelong travel partner-in-crime, and to Vanya Drumchiiska for her patience and support.

I'm also thankful for Erick Prince, The Minority Nomad, for contributing his extensive wisdom and expertise as the technical editor of this book, Giang Cao for contributing her art and perspective on the digital nomad lifestyle, and Joe Kraynak, for his generosity, help, and guidance along the way.

My heartfelt thanks to my subscribers, patrons, Facebook group, podcast listeners, and moderators for creating the most amazing community *ever* at Traveling with Kristin and Badass Digital Nomads. You are family to me. Thank you for including me in your journeys.

To my team at Traveling with Kristin: Thank you for filling in for me when I was out of the [remote] office.

To my mentor and coach, Liz Germain — I am forever grateful for your guidance, encouragement, friendship, and support. It's been an incredible ride so far! To my manager, Val, who has been an integral part of the process throughout — thank you for your positive vibes and strategic eye.

I would also like to express my sincerest gratitude to the entire team at Wiley for making this book possible in every way: Steve Hayes, Rebecca Senninger, Kristie Pyles, Vicki Adang, and everyone behind the scenes. Thank you for your trust, confidence, and support. Thank you for publishing this book and making the digital nomad lifestyle more accessible to people everywhere.

Special thanks to Rolf Potts for inspiring all the vagabonds out there and helping me find my voice as a travel writer. And to Tucker Max and the team at Scribe Media for the helpful content, motivation, and tips for each phase of the writing process. Thank you for encouraging first-time authors everywhere to write (and finish!) their books.

Publisher's Acknowledgments

Development Editor: Rebecca Senninger
Executive Editor: Steven Hayes
Technical Editor: Erick Prince

Production Editor: Tamilmani Varadharaj
Cover Image: © Kaspars Grinvalds/Shutterstock